Fourth Test Match

AT Bourda, Georgetown, Guyana
ON April 6, 7, 8, 9, 11, 1972.
UMPIRES Messrs H. B. D. Jordan, C. P. Kippins

West Indies v New Zealand

First INNINGS OF New Zealand
ON April 8, 9, 11, 1972
SCORERS G. G. A. Sauley, K. Sookram

| MINUTES FOR 50 / 150 | MINUTES FOR 100 / 200 | IN / OUT | Minutes | Balls Rec'd | BATSMEN | RUNS | 4's / 6's | HOW OUT | BOWLERS | SCORE |
|---|---|---|---|---|---|---|---|---|---|---|
| 162 / 428 | 321 / 552 | 12.10 (8) / 12.24 (11) | 704 | 759 | Turner G. M. (250 in 682 minutes) | 2112132121421112141111414221144311112111111441111112111412 / 111132221232111411441114112111141111421141114211112111424111 / 121124111111221121212111114241 — | 22 | l. b. w. | Howard | 259 |
| 181 / 486 | 363 | 12.40 (8) / 4.40 (9) | 540 | 555 | Jarvis T. W. | 213114141111121144121111124111121112111241134141111141424 / 1222211411112111114125144111242144141221 — | 19 | c. Greenidge | Holford | 182 |
| 204 | | 4.45 / (2.20) | 235 | 215 | Congdon B. E. | 11112111122211111212212213111411411421111 | 3 | not out | | 61 |
| | | 12.25 / 1.32 | 27 | 27 | Burgess M. G. | 1421 — | 1 | bowled | Howard | 8 |
| | | 1.33 / (2.20) | 47 | 57 | Hastings B. F. | 44411211 | 3 | not out | | 18 |
| | | | | | | R. W. Morgan, G. E. Vivian, B. R. Taylor, K. J. Wadsworth, R. S. Cunis, H. J. Howarth — did not bat | | | | |

| | |
|---|---|
| BYES | |
| LEG BYES | 2 1 12 31 1 |
| WIDES | |
| NO BALLS | 1 1 11 |
| I. D. C. at 2.20 p.m. on 11.4.72 | TOTAL for 3 wickets |

| FALL OF WICKETS | 1 — 387 | 2 — 482 | 3 — 496 | 4 — | 5 — | 6 — | 7 — | 8 — | 9 — | 10 — |
|---|---|---|---|---|---|---|---|---|---|---|
| TIME | 4.40 9.4.72 | 12.24 11.4.72 | 1.32 11.4.72 | | | | | | | |
| BATSMEN OUT | Jarvis 182 | Turner 259 | Burgess 8 | | | | | | | |
| BATSMEN NOT OUT | Turner 195 | Congdon 27 | Congdon 33 | | | | | | | |
| PARTNERSHIPS RUNS | 387 | 95 | 14 | | | | | | | |
| PARTNERSHIPS MINUTES | 540 | 159 | 27 | | | | | | | |

RATE OF SCORING

| RUNS | 50 | 100 | 150 | 200 | 250 | 300 | 350 | 400 | 450 | 500 | 550 | 600 |
|---|---|---|---|---|---|---|---|---|---|---|---|---|
| MINUTES | 103 | 166 | 242 | 328 | 390 | 457 | 504 | 557 | 665 | 738 | | |
| FOR LAST 50 | 103 | 63 | 76 | 86 | 62 | 67 | 47 | 53 | 108 | 73 | | |

| PARTNERSHIPS | MINUTES FOR 50 | 100 | 150 | 200 | 250 | 300 / 350 |
|---|---|---|---|---|---|---|
| Turner - Jarvis | 103 | 166 | 242 | 328 | 390 | 457 / 504 |
| Turner - Congdon | 96 | | | | | |

| | |
|---|---|
| TIME FOR INNINGS — MINUTES | |
| RUNS SCORED PER HOUR | |
| OVERS BOWLED IN INNINGS | |
| OVERS BOWLED PER HOUR | |
| RUNS SCORED PER OVER | |

TOSS WON BY West Indies

NEW BALL

| DATE | TIME | SCORE | OVER | BALL |
|---|---|---|---|---|
| 9.4.72 | 11.08 | 171 | 99 | 1 |
| 11.4.72 | 10.34 | 410 | 211 | 3 |

INTERVALS — NOT-OUT BATSMEN AND SCORES

| DATE | LUNCH | TEA | CLOSE |
|---|---|---|---|
| 8.4.72 | 11-0 Turner 7 Jarvis 3 | 104-0 T 59 J 42 | 163-0 T 87 J 71 |
| 9.4.72 | 246-0 T 132 J 104 | 345-0 T 179 J 156 | 410-1 T 210 Congdon 4 |
| 11.4.72 | 483-2 Congdon 28 Burgess 0 | | |

NOTES — Weather, Wicket, etc. Fine. Pitch slow.
New Zealand's highest total in test cricket.
Turner 259 - best individual score for N.Z in tests.
N.Z. record for first wicket in all first-class matches and for any wicket in test matches

RESULT Match drawn

STOPPAGES OF PLAY
none

The scorecard for the fourth test at Bourda, showing the epic 387-run stand by Glenn Turner and Terry Jarvis for the first wicket, the stand that broke all kinds of records, and almost the West Indies bowlers' hearts. The scorecard was also specially prepared by Dr H. J. A. Colvin, of Auckland.

# CARIBBEAN CRUSADE

# CARIBBEAN CRUSADE

The New Zealand Cricketers
in the West Indies
1972

by

D. J. CAMERON

HODDER AND STOUGHTON
Auckland, Sydney, London

First printed 1972

ISBN 0 340 16609 6

Printed and bound in New Zealand for
Hodder and Stoughton Ltd
52 Cook Street, Auckland
by Wright and Carman Ltd, Trentham

# Contents

# *Foreword*

by GARY SOBERS, West Indies cricket captain

I toured New Zealand twice, in 1956 and 1969, and what I saw during that last series did not make me surprised when New Zealand did so well in the West Indies in 1972.

When I saw their technique on the New Zealand pitches, which are not really top class, I knew the New Zealanders would perform well in the West Indies. Their technique, application and concentration is something to be seen, to admire and respect.

Although the New Zealanders played their own way I don't think it for us to criticise. They set out to do a job and they did it adequately.

It has been a thrill and a pleasure to play against the New Zealanders in the West Indies. I have made many friends among them, and it was a privilege and a joy to see them in the West Indies.

New Zealand have got a tremendous number of good players. When they start playing strokes—and they have got the players to do this—New Zealand will be a cricket nation to be reckoned with. Until they start doing this I don't think New Zealand cricket will improve in the way it should.

The New Zealand tour had helped West Indies. Our younger bowlers have blossomed. They have been given experience against a tough team, against players not prepared to give their wickets away. This has been good grounding for our young bowlers.

West Indies young batsmen have done well against New Zealand. The New Zealand bowling, I know, had its limitations and they bowled within them. I would still like to see our young players experience real pace bowling.

By saying that I am not taking anything away from the New Zealand bowling. Bruce Taylor bowled extremely well. Hedley Howarth is a tremendous bowler—control, guile, flight, no-one could ask for more.

West Indies soon face three test series. The proof of West Indies future is in the hands of our young players.

I would like to thank New Zealand for coming to West Indies. Congratulations on the excellent way they played. I wish them all the luck in the future.

I am sure readers will enjoy this book. I have met and talked with Don Cameron many times in New Zealand and here. He is a keen student of the game, and I know anything he puts in this book will be worthwhile. I wish him all the luck with it.

West Indies 1972.

# 1

# "Not to Yield"

"The boys have fought like hell for 90 days, and yet if they had not survived those last 90 minutes they would have fought for nothing."

These were the words of Murray Chapple, manager of the New Zealand cricket team, as the New Zealanders flew out of Trinidad, the memories of the epic fight to save the fifth test against West Indies the day before still etched vividly in their minds.

For 90 days the New Zealanders had battled through the heat and turmoil of what must be physically the hardest cricket tour in the world. They had started as nervously as any tyro putting his first tentative foot on to a tight-rope.

There were several times when they teetered on the brink of collapse and fewer times when they marched sure-footedly onward. Yet they did not fall, they did not fail and the mere fact that they reached the end of the tour unbeaten was more a triumph than the record books can ever indicate.

Twelve matches, twelve draws—these are hardly figures which suggest triumph, let alone moderate success. Yet those last 90 minutes, and the 90 days of the tour, represented for the New Zealanders the kind of triumph that cannot be measured in runs and wickets, even in matches saved and a test rubber tied.

It was a triumph for the New Zealanders—victory over their own failings, over hard and often harsh conditions, over the excruciatingly bad luck of losing all five test tosses, over all the ingredients that make a tour of West Indies a physical and mental ordeal. A triumph gained simply because they, perhaps more than West Indies, but that one priceless thing that will never find a place in Wisden's records. Guts, spirit, morale, esprit de corps—call it what you will. The New Zealanders had it in ample measure. They refused to yield even when the odds seemed impossible. By refusing to yield they survived, sometimes bloodied, but never bowed. A triumph, yes. Modest by the standards of the harsh, hard world of international cricket, but still a victory that must hold a place of pride in a New Zealand cricket history that has not always been a saga of success in terms of tests won.

Since the end of the tour many people have asked me whether the no-wins no-losses tour of West Indies (leaving out the tail-end win over Bermuda) represents a step upward for New Zealand cricket. Can we now play Australia or England, or perhaps even South Africa on more level terms than in the past?

The answer is a qualified yes. The West Indies tour helped New Zealand develop a core of test-hardened, tough-minded cricketers. Yet I find it difficult to relate the lessons learned in West Indies to the future struggles against England next year or the Australians in the season of 1973-74.

A tour of the West Indies is something apart. The conditions there are unlike those anywhere else in the world. The name of the game is the same, but so much else is different. The heat, the pitches, the crowd, the insularity among the territories, the unashamed bias of the news media—all these things mixed together present a peculiar tour situation which, in my limited experience, defies comparison with tours of other countries.

The New Zealanders' tour of West Indies must, then, be placed in a special category which cannot bear comparison either with tours past or future. The New Zealanders, through their own wish and through the unusual circumstances of the tour, developed a tight-fisted style of cricket which would be less successful in either England or Australia. It would not be popular in those places, and I am sure that the New Zealanders would not be happy trying to maintain their West Indies methods in other lands.

The New Zealanders' economical style of cricket was a product of the circumstances of their own strengths and weaknesses and of the conditions in West Indies. They almost forced West Indies into a similar pattern, which was some kind of victory on its own.

In technical terms the brilliant fielding and the successes of Glenn Turner, Bevan Congdon, Bruce Taylor and Hedley Howarth, the improvement of Terry Jarvis, Graham Vivian and Ken Wadsworth and the obvious ability of Mark Burgess and Brian Hastings were most reassuring in view of the tough battles ahead.

Yet, under different conditions which offer a better balance between batsman and bowler the priority list developed in West Indies might be adjusted or even reversed. The New Zealanders who succeeded most in West Indies were those who adapted more readily to the conditions and to the style of play which these forced upon the New Zealanders. So it might be that on the greener fields of England or on the bouncier pitches of Australia Bob Cunis or Murray Webb or Richard Collinge might rank with Taylor, or that Burgess and Hastings might challenge the high scores of Turner and Congdon.

Thus the value, in terms of technical ability or improvement, of the West Indies tour can only be related to that tour and its peculiar conditions.

And peculiar they were. It did not take the New Zealanders long to find out that much of their pre-tour homework—based on exhaustive study of recent tour accounts—was not always directed along the right lines. Much of this preliminary reasoning suggested that the pitches would be rather quicker than those in New Zealand. This extra speed, so the reasoning went, would help make Webb and Collinge the spearhead of the attack, and would assist the strokemakers such as Hastings, Burgess and Vivian who play best when the ball is coming through quickly.

Yet there was also the evidence that the Indian spinners had succeeded in the previous season, so Howarth and Jack Alabaster seemed to round off the attack nicely.

In the days before the first big match, against Jamaica, the New Zealanders listened with interest to the talk that the Sabina Park pitch would be at its fastest and liveliest on the first morning, and would probably be the quickest pitch the New Zealanders struck in the major games.

Imagine, then, the shudders that went through the New Zealand camp when the opening overs by Collinge and Cunis against the Jamaicans showed none of these things. The pace was slow, the bounce low and in the dozen or so overs that the shine remained on the ball it moved only a fraction. There was compensation in some fine spin bowling from Alabaster and Howarth, but as Lawrence Rowe went implacably on to the first of his big scores there was also the excruciating feeling that Webb and company would be like infantrymen trying to stop a tank with rifle-fire, rather than with armour-piercing artillery. As later matches showed, Sabina was in fact one of the fastest pitches of the tour, even if the bounce was modest.

On the other hand Jamaica brought big scores for Turner, Dowling, Hastings and Burgess, a promising start by Congdon and the first signs of Wadsworth's gritty defence.

So the New Zealanders had to change their ideas, and to form a new pattern built round the hard-headed batting of Turner and Congdon and round a semi-defensive bowling system based on Taylor, Congdon and Howarth.

They also had to adapt to the leisurely pace of the West Indian game. The heat and the indifferent light of late afternoon insisted on a five and a half hour playing day. The heat was worst, often in the 80s or 90s in mid-afternoon. There were two drink breaks in the post-lunch session, 40 minutes apart, and these often became four- or five-minute rituals.

These things produced a type of cricket far removed from the high-pressure, three-day bonus points style of the Plunket Shield competition, but the New Zealanders adapted quickly. Perhaps too quickly, for in the last half of the tour—with their thin resources further strained by Jack Alabaster's injuries—the New Zealanders' deliberate methods came under fire.

They were indeed slow. West Indies, with their multitude of spinners, got through their overs very quickly while New Zealand, especially when Cunis was bowling, were slow. On average, New Zealand scored a fraction under two runs an over during the tests. West Indies scored at 2.6.

The New Zealanders were chided for these things, and perhaps rightly so. Gary Sobers had a cut at them at tour's end, and said that these methods would not be as readily accepted in other countries as they were in West Indies where, I might add, the crowds were remarkably patient in the duller parts of the tests.

In the New Zealanders' defence—or at least in explanation of an over and scoring rate that would have had Plunket Shield crowds hollering for blood—two things should be mentioned.

One was that Sobers could have added to his criticism that playing conditions in other countries would not have allowed the New Zealanders to adopt their economical style of cricket. On the faster, bouncier pitches of, say, Australia (or even New Zealand) Turner would not have scored 259 in 704 minutes, as he did in the first innings on the gruesome Bourda pitch. If he had batted so long, say, at Sydney he would have scored many, many more runs simply because he could have played many, many more strokes. The same would apply to Congdon or Hastings or Burgess or Vivian, for the last three were severely affected by the slow, low bounce of West Indies pitches.

The second point was that as the tour developed the whole atmosphere tended to bring out a stubborn spirit among the New Zealanders. They withdrew into their shell, and let the groans about slow bowling and batting bounce off.

By the time of the second and third tests the New Zealanders had, as the slang goes, got the message. They realised that the whole atmosphere of the tour was geared toward the home players. The newspaper and radio commentaries, with a few exceptions, were aimed at the West Indies players. Among the exceptions was Tony Cozier, the Barbadian writer and commentator who treated the New Zealanders well, although with a few cuts toward the end of the tour.

It soon became obvious that the crowds, and many of the officials, went to the games to see their own players do well. Sometimes the fact that the New Zealanders were in opposition seemed almost incidental, that they were there merely as the backdrop to some dramatic West Indies action in centre stage.

Chapple, for example, was rarely interviewed by the local newspapers so that there could be some balance between the West Indian and New Zealand viewpoints. Amid the hallelujahs accompanying the feats of Rowe and Sobers, Charlie Davis and Inshan Ali, the wonderful deeds of Taylor (who was certainly the great bowler of the series) or Turner were virtually overlooked.

I am not offering this as criticism of West Indian methods for they are only as partial as, I would suggest, New Zealand may seem to a visiting Rugby side. But at least a touring Rugby side such as the Lions or Springboks tends to hold centre-stage quite a lot, and is not shuffled off to the wings as the New Zealand cricketers seemed to be in West Indies.

So, for good or ill, the New Zealanders got the impression that they were being put down in the playing sense. In other ways they were treated extremely well, the hospitality was lavish and warm-hearted and they reacted well to the friendliness.

But once into action on the field they adopted their hard-nosed, damn-their-eyes attitude. They were less sensitive to criticism of their deliberate style of cricket than they would have been in Australian or England, or even New Zealand.

One reason why the New Zealand scoring rate was inferior to that of West Indies in the tests was that the New Zealanders did not take the risk of changing their batting style. The New Zealanders, or most of them, had been brought up in the method which insists that the batsmen get into the line of the ball before playing shots, especially on the drive. The front foot goes toward the ball, and bat and pad are closely together lest the ball nip back and go through the "gate".

On their own pitches West Indies batsmen have a different method. Knowing that the ball, especially from the faster bowlers, will not deviate once it has hit the pitch they play through the line of the ball. The feet need not be in the correct places, all it needs is a quick eye and a full stroke—and the result is usually an exciting looking shot backward (especially when Charlie Davis was batting) or forward of point.

Chapple fielded at slip for some time when Alvin Kallicharran was batting for Guyana. He found the experience harrowing and not only because of vast expenditure in sweat.

"To just about every ball I felt Kallicharran was going to give a chance near me," said Chapple afterward, "for he played away from his pads so often—yet never got an edge."

The New Zealanders eschewed such batting methods, at some cost to their run rate, for it would have been dangerous and risky to change methods in mid-tour.

The problem was that the New Zealanders' batting style of playing up the line, rather than through or across it, made defensive field-setting against them the more simple. Deepish mid-on and mid-off, and widish extra cover and mid-wicket closed off many of the New Zealanders scoring strokes. By contrast New Zealand had to post a thicker off-side field, sometimes with a point on the boundary, to block the West Indians' favourite strokes through the line. With the bounce both low and slow there was little chance to cut or hook, or to force the shortish ball through mid-wicket, which Burgess and Congdon can do on better pitches.

Only Turner, with his wonderful technique, produced a diversion—what he calls a "flat-batter"—as he forced away, with the wrists rolling over the stroke, left-arm spinners' balls outside the off stump.

Otherwise the New Zealanders kept to their own up-the-line style, reinforced with massive bat-and-pad defence against Lance Gibbs, still a superb off-spinner. The results were unglamorous, but effective. Gibbs, the spinner the New Zealanders feared most, took three wickets for 267 in the first two tests from 130 overs. He pleaded to the heavens for justice as Turner and Congdon padded ball after ball away. Gibbs was dropped after the second test, virtually kicked out of the test series by the obdurate New Zealanders.

The heartless, drab pitches in West Indies place tremendous influence on winning the toss—and Sobers won them all in the tests. Only once did he guess wrong, when he misjudged the amount of moisture remaining in the third test strip at Bridgetown and Taylor cut the West Indians up simply because he bowled superbly and the West Indians' technique against the lifting, moving ball was inefficient.

Otherwise Sobers and West Indies started the tests with a

tremendous psychological advantage. To win the toss and bat first in West Indies makes it essential to bat at least until tea on the second day. By that time the score should be 400 plus and the opposition weary after eight or nine hours in the sun. From that position it is hard to lose, and with a good chance of winning as the pitch becomes worn during the fourth innings.

With the exception of the third the New Zealanders thus started the tests on the back foot, knowing that they had first to contain the West Indies first innings with their limited bowling attack. This did not matter greatly at Sabina, where the New Zealanders were still feeling their way. It did not matter greatly at Bourda, where everyone had decided days before the match that the fourth test would be drawn.

But it did matter at Port of Spain for the fifth test. If New Zealand had won the toss and batted first there they had an excellent chance of winning the test and the series. This is not only hindsight.

The long, slow stand of 387 by Turner and Jarvis in the fourth test, following the 348 and 288 for three in the second test and the 422 in the third, showed the dominance the New Zealand batsmen were gaining over the West Indian bowlers. By the end of the Bourda test the West Indies bowlers' morale was low, so much so that with the pitch playing easily New Zealand should have scored 300-plus, or perhaps even 400-plus, if they had batted first in the final test. They knew they had the West Indies bowlers on the back foot and relished the chance of keeping them under pressure in the vital fifth test.

They also knew that if they again lost the toss they would face another one or two days in the field with their champion bowler, Taylor, severely weakened with influenza.

The toss was lost, and so was a real chance of winning the test. In the end New Zealand had some luck in holding out for a draw. Had not David Holford, the leg-spinner, been taken out of the West Indian attack by a hamstring injury the West Indian spinners might have ripped right through the New Zealand second innings, instead of being thwarted by Taylor and Ken Wadsworth.

While the pitches remain the same test cricket in West Indies will continue to be a battle of attrition. They are so heavily loaded in favour of the batsmen, and of the team winning the toss, that it seems impossible to get a balanced match out of them.

Some West Indians are concerned about their frustrating pitches, others scoff and say they are ideal.

Keith Walcott, the Barbadian who is a test selector and who has seen much cricket overseas, gave me an interview in Guyana during which he pleaded for grassier, faster pitches that gave some balance between batsmen and bowlers. Walcott knows his West Indians, for he asked for a copy of the article before I filed it. "I had better have it," said Walcott, "in case there is any reaction."

There was. Several officials were critical of Walcott's comments and said that the number of drawn tests in West Indies was caused more by the low standard of the players rather than the state of the pitches. They did not remark that the reverse could apply.

After the fifth test Sobers maintained that grassier pitches would make life so difficult for batsmen that matches would be over in two or three days.

At Guaracara Park, after New Zealand had played Trinidad on yet another feather-bed completely shaved of grass, I pointed out to a Trinidad official that the pitch-area alongside had enough grass to provide a first-rate all-round pitch.

"Oh, no," he said. "If we left grass on the pitch the ball would fly. Someone would get killed."

It seemed a passing strange comment in a country that used to relish the sight of Wes Hall and Charlie Griffith scaring the wits out of visiting players a decade or so before.

But until West Indies produce pitches that give bowlers some hope, from first day to last, they will continue to frustrate both their own and visiting players.

And West Indians will continue to be frustrated by teams that have the fighting, do-or-die spirit of the 1972 New Zealanders.

This spirit never shone more brightly than when the New Zealanders were embattled and apparently at the end of their limited physical resources.

In the midst of the worries about the injuries to Collinge, Dowling and Alabaster several West Indies officials, players and newspapermen wondered aloud why New Zealand had only 15 players. Their wonder increased when they found that West Indies had invited New Zealand to send only 15 players and a manager—and that New Zealand might well lose several thousand dollars on the tour.

"What are you, poor relations?" asked a Barbados newspaperman.

In effect the New Zealanders were, and one lesson to be learned from this tour is that the New Zealand Cricket Council must never accept similar conditions for such an arduous tour.

In fairness to the NZCC its board members were as much in the dark about West Indies conditions as were the players. The tour was arranged in mid-1971 at a time when there was considerable doubt that the South African team would be able to tour both Australia and New Zealand in the 1971-72 summer. The Springboks were not allowed to tour Australia, and were unwilling to tour New Zealand, simply because at least four of their leading players would not have been available for the New Zealand section of the tour.

Thus the invitation to tour West Indies came at precisely the right moment. The only hitch was that West Indies agreed to pay only for a manager and 15 players, and offered players' allowances rather below those normally paid by the NZCC to its players. Rather than jeopardise the tour the NZCC agreed to a 15-man team and to subsidise the players' allowances, at a total cost of about $NZ5,000, to bring them up to the normal level.

The players, entranced by the novelty of being the first New Zealand side to tour West Indies, hardly complained, although one of these days the NZCC will have to scale up their allowances to cover the increased cost of living.

They could hardly complain, either, at the standard of the hotel accommodation which the West Indies board provided and paid for, as this ranged from good to excellent. Likewise the New Zealanders were treated well, and sometimes royally, in countries which react to touring cricketers as New Zealanders are inclined to offer hospitality to visiting Rugby teams.

Yet the financial structure of the tour tended to be overbalanced in favour of the West Indies board and its players. I am not criticising West Indies for this, for their financial methods are their own business and have been adopted to meet the high costs of running an international tour among such widely scattered centres.

But I wonder whether the NZCC had been right to risk the loss of some $5,000 on the tour, which could be increased by the need to replace Collinge.

They tended to accentuate the "poor relation" status of the New Zealanders. Apart from Turner, who as a fulltime professional is entitled to special treatment—and how he earned it—all the New Zealanders were paid on the same scale and, while I am not at liberty to quote in dollars and cents, their allowances were modest.

Yet the New Zealand players were soon aware of the disparate treatment of the West Indies test players. The senior members of the home side received a test fee plus $5 East Caribbean currency (about $2.40 NZ) for every test they had played. So a home player in his 30th test would receive at least $EC150 for that game, and $EC155 for the next, and so on.

There can be no quibbling at this type of incentive payment, for more and more of the leading West Indies players are county professionals who have little income other than from cricket.

But it did tend to reinforce the "poor relation" argument. There were other cases. In some matches there would be monetary prizes for the best batsmen and bowlers of each side. In addition various local firms might weigh in with cash prizes. But these inevitably were for the highest-scoring West Indian batsman or the most successful West Indian bowler, and so forth. The sponsors got some advertising mileage, the home players got the cash and the New Zealanders were left in the cold.

Indirectly, this poor relation feeling tended to arouse still further the dogged, we'll-show-'em feeling among the New Zealanders, and so was of some use to the New Zealand cause.

But it is impossible to dismiss the feeling that the New Zealand players were sold a little short on this tour. The NZCC board accepted the terms of the tour, and could hardly have done otherwise without knowing its full cost-structure. There would, too, have been the risk of snubbing West Indies, who had treated New Zealand well with three tours of this country in 16 years.

Still, the lessons were plain. New Zealand can never accept such future tours with less than 16 players. They are sufficiently strong in the international cricketing family to insist that they are not poor relations. One of these days, too, the two national bodies concerned must agree that any sponsorship money be shared as equitably as possible. The NZCC has not been inclined, in the past, to throw its weight around, but the ins and outs of the West Indies tour showed that the time has come for the NZCC to show a little muscle when negotiating for tours.

If the material gains, in terms of dollars and cents, will be small for New Zealand the less tangible assets of international standing and the development of players of international ability will still make the West Indies tour most valuable.

To draw two series against West Indies, at home in 1969 and abroad in 1972, is a staggering effort even if West Indies occupy a comparatively modest place in test cricket these days.

The feats of Turner, Congdon and Taylor during the series entitled them to the highest international ranking, with Howarth, Burgess, Hastings, Jarvis and Wadsworth not far below that mark.

Turner's feats were quite staggering—four double centuries, 1,284 runs in 17 tour innings (average 85.6), 672 test runs (average 96) and first-rate slip fielding—he must now be among the foremost opening batsmen in the world.

Tony Cozier remarked during Turner's 259 in the fourth test slow march that he doubted whether New Zealand would ever win a test while Turner was playing. This judgment was harsh. Turner on tour showed he could bat completely in tune with the conditions and the state of the match. Unfortunately for the West Indian crowds, and Turner, the situation never arose when Turner could abandon his dedication and play the shots he possesses. The pitches hardly helped in this either, but I am sure that if New Zealand had ever faced a run-chase on the last afternoon of a match Turner would again have batted completely in rhythm with the needs of the team.

Congdon ranked with Turner as the main pillar of the New Zealand batting. His four centuries in consecutive matches in mid-tour were masterly efforts, for at that stage Turner was in a comparatively thin period and Congdon had to bear a heavy load.

Cozier also remarked, very early in the tour, that Congdon would have to bowl a lot—a remarkably clever piece of judgment, for at that time the New Zealanders were regarding Alabaster and Howarth as the key bowlers. Congdon bowled 296 overs of what he calls his "dribbly stuff" and with his clever command of length and movement and angle of delivery he turned almost into New Zealand's secret weapon. From the sideline it seemed the same old mixture that Congdon used to bowl, and seldom with quick success, in home Plunket Shield matches.

In the middle, however, he became adept at breaking a stand, or of suddenly producing a ball which could bowl Rowe or have Sobers caught or pin Holford once again leg-before. They were not accidents.

Batting, bowling, fielding and captaincy, Congdon had the heaviest load of all. In each phase of the game his performance improved immensely. The toll on his physical and mental resources must have been immense. Yet he never complained and never looked as if he would not contribute a 100 percent effort.

Figures sometimes lie, but in the case of Turner and Congdon they did not. There were 14 century partnerships during the tour, ranging from 387 to 100. Turner or Congdon figured in all of them.

Taylor was a complete puzzle to the West Indians, for they could never estimate when, from the most barren pitch, he might suddenly get a ball to jump or move a little. There were suspicions that the amiable Taylor was never quite sure, either, when something unusual would happen. But, like a good punter, he played the percentages. By the time he was fully fit—he had rather a large shadow in Jamaica—Taylor had almost complete control of length and direction. He seldom offered the drive, unless the ball was new, and with the lowish bounce he was difficult to pull or cut. He bowled straight and when the ball or the pitch helped him the trimmings of swing or seam or cut would be added.

Yet, for all his tightness of length Taylor was not a "dry" bowler in the accepted sense, and as Congdon sometimes became. Taylor continued to attack and when he got a pitch to help him, as in the third test, he was positively lethal.

Time will tell whether Turner, Congdon and Taylor, as the big three, will be able to maintain this form in future matches for New Zealand, or whether the Jarvises and Burgesses and Howarths will move up to challenge them.

Yet the fact remains that New Zealand produced the three outstanding performers of the test series and the West Indies, with their deeper vein of talent, could not produce three men to compare with their performances.

To add to the two most successful batsmen and the most effective bowler in the series, the New Zealanders could also claim a marked superiority in fielding. Once past the bumpy fields of Jamaica the New Zealanders produced fielding gymnastics that had the crowds roaring, and the officials searching back through the years to find fieldsmen to compare.

Vivian was quite often the best of all, superb with his hands and throwing, and extremely quick in his running. Burgess was not far behind and very soon it became a matter of pride for the rest of the side that they maintain the standards that Burgess and Vivian set. For, if the New Zealanders lacked either hostile batting or bowling, they could turn fielding into an attacking art and this was the one priceless advantage they held over the home teams.

So the series developed, on these lamentable pitches, into a long hard struggle with the more flamboyant West Indies stroke-makers and spinners being countered by the determined, spirited New Zealanders with their dedicated batting, crafty tight-fisted bowling and their superb fielding.

Personally I would have preferred the series to end one-all, for New Zealand did enough to deserve victory in the third and only ruinous luck with the rain, and Holford's injury, held back West Indies in the fifth.

New Zealand, I feel, were not quite strong enough to win the series under such difficult conditions. But it will be an everlasting tribute to their courage and their spirit that they were strong enough not to lose it. If the New Zealanders deserved a tribute, Tennyson probably had the words for it—"to strive, to seek, to find and not to yield".

# 2

# *The New Zealanders*

One of the New Zealanders' great strengths—and perhaps the subtle amalgam which welded them into such a hardy unit on the field—was that they enjoyed one another's company.

Cricket teams sometimes do not lend themselves readily to the fellowship and camaraderie which develop among the better Rugby sides for cricket can be, especially among batsmen, a self-centred sport. A run out in the middle, or stealing the strike, can result in bitchiness afterwards. A dropped catch or two can breed resentment between bowlers and fieldsmen.

Yet the 1972 New Zealanders survived and bypassed these minor traumas simply because they had, in a good, typical and earthy New Zealand way, a capacity to enjoy themselves, and sometimes to laugh at themselves.

The spirit was cleverly initiated by Chapple and Graham Dowling early in the tour, and through thick and thin, it grew and blossomed as the tour went on.

By various foresighted means Chapple, who knows touring and tourists, managed to arrange adequate amounts of beer at various places on the tour. In some cases this was offered freely by the local brewers. In other cases it was the result of an exceedingly generous response from the Dominion, New Zealand and Leopard breweries of New Zealand, who sent numerous dozens to strategic points of the West Indies.

Such manna was warmly received by the New Zealanders for drinking in the West Indies can be rather expensive and their allowances were not expansive. Not that the New Zealanders spent most of their waking hours punching holes in beer cans. Rather they contrived that at the end of play and on returning to the hotel they would gather in some room or another for a natter, a laugh and a can or two. Yachtsmen call this the "happy hour" and it was a regular habit of the British Lions Rugby team in New Zealand last year.

It served the New Zealanders well. There was nothing like

a quiet beer or a joke to break down the tensions or the disappointments of the day's play—or a wisecrack or two to bring down to earth whoever had been the day's hero.

I shall treasure for many years the look of quiet pride on Murray Webb's face when he arrived at one of these impromptu sessions. After labouring hard and long Webb had taken very few wickets on tour. That day he had picked up three. Webb entered the room. "Have a beer, 'wickets'," was the call. "Wickets" Webb had his beer, and judging by the look on his face it must have tasted like ambrosia.

Another feature of the New Zealanders' ability to relax and let down their hair was the weekly Sunday night meeting. These things are not new. The All Blacks have had their "courts" where fines were imposed. The veterans of the 1969 cricket tour seemed to have some reservations about continuing with the Sunday meetings, for sometimes these had been less than satisfactory and had contained a certain amount of back-biting.

The rules were quite simple. Attendance was compulsory, the chairman dictated the dress and conduct of the meeting, fines were imposed, duly recorded and—if you were game—could be appealed against. Sometimes such meetings can become a bore. However, the New Zealanders had the sense to have a different chairman for each meeting, and so ensured that there would be variety, and a never-ending source of fun.

So chairman Webb could call a hippie-style meeting, dress was strictly "doing your own thing", and failing to address Webby as "Superstar" was instantly finable. After putting the fear of the Lord into the troops by stating that "grass" could be smoked, Webb did a quick scamper round the hotel lawn and conducted the meeting with a large bag of "grass" clippings by his elbow.

There were various other forms of meetings, ranging from Communist Chinese to Olde Englishe. It may sound rather undergraduatish nonsense, and perhaps it was. But in a subtle way it helped mould the players together. Someone who might have been getting a little uppity could find all manner of fines being devised against him. He soon got the message. Someone who seemed a bit out of things could suddenly find himself the chairman and the centre of attraction.

I don't think it was coincidence, for example, that Keith Campbell's emergence as one of the personalities of the team came when—after being inactive for almost four weeks—he was installed as chairman, and a right fine one too, of the Sunday meeting at Antigua.

Unfortunately, the New Zealanders did not have a musician among them, even someone who could knock out a tune on a guitar, and so for a long time they missed the comradeship of a team which can sing together, even if they do not sing very well.

One rest day in Guyana choir-master Bob Cunis took the matter in hand. He knew a song or two, and so did some of the others. After much beating out of time with a big stick on the nearest bed Cunis knocked the "choir" into some sort of shape.

It was hardly Carnegie Hall material and the activities of the girls from Roedean rather put the repertoire outside the realms of public performance. But the players sang, lustily, loudly and sometimes in tune, and were the happier for it. In the last few days of the tour Ross Morgan acquired a small steel drum and patiently tonked away until he could coax out "Yellow Bird"—a tune the players had come to hate. Morgan's musicianship came rather too late to become a part of the team's music. For which many thanks!

Sometimes there was horseplay, but generally the players' humour was in the droll, off-beat manner. Flitting from country to country required an immigration form for each plane trip. One of the questions concerned the visitor's occupation. For a start the team played this with a straight bat. Gradually the humour came in.

The St Vincent immigration officials probably did not realise it, but they welcomed one of the few "Moa farmers" extant. At some other place an assistant bongo-drum tuner suddenly acquired an assistant-assistant, and assistant-assistant-assistant and so on. Cunis, as Guyanese found out, was a choir-boy when not playing cricket. Rather too many players tended to come from "Orkland". Someone was a "yellow bird watcher".

Fortunately none of the immigration officials reacted when they found that one of the players had listed his occupation as a "Ganja farmer". Ganja is the Jamaican word for marijuana, grass, pot or what have you. That little joke could have caused some official to jump up and down.

After breezing through Customs in most islands, Chapple was astonished when Bermuda Customs solemnly ploughed through his suitcase in search of something. Chapple is not a tidy packer and the end result was a fine old mess. Only later did we find that the flight had been from Kingston, Jamaica, and was known to Bermudans as the "Ganja Special". Needless to state, Chapple was clean as a whistle.

The knockabout humour of the players also prevented what might have been a clique-situation in the side. Five of the original

15 were from Auckland, and when Morgan replaced Collinge the Auckland contingent grew to six.

There were often some jocular remarks about the Auckland clique, as there had been, evidently, about the red-and-blacks of Canterbury during the 1969 tour. Alan Richards, the hard-working New Zealand Broadcasting Corporation announcer, and myself, were also from Auckland, and were sometimes identified with the Auckland clique. It was harmless enough, although when en route to England with her husband, Betty Leggat, wife of the chairman of the New Zealand Cricket Council, did get in a tasty dig by suggesting to me that the party did contain players from south of the Tamaki River.

Still, the Auckland clique did have one distinction. If anyone was late, if anyone wore a red tour tie when the black official tie was dress for the day, if anyone said that Banks beer was best when we were in Red Stripe country . . . well, you couldn't get a bet on that it would be an Aucklander.

There were doubts expressed in high places that MURRAY CHAPPLE might not have been the best man as manager of the team. He was youngish, even a few months Alabaster's junior. He had been playing as recently as 1966, and selecting New Zealand sides since then. He might, said the doubtful Joes, be rather too close in age and temperament to the players, and without the detachment a manager needed.

The doubtful Joes could not have been more wrong. Chapple's recent playing career, plus two tours of South Africa, meant that he knew the problems that afflict players on tour. He also, and the players soon found out, knew the tricks that touring players can sometimes get up to.

Chapple has been a schoolteacher for many years, and more recently an inspector of schools. Perhaps this training has given him that priceless asset, an orderly mind. He spent a long time preparing for the tour, sending off letters hither and yon. This background enabled Chapple to keep one step ahead of the field for most of the tour. To ask Chapple a question, on what appeared to be a simple matter, could bring such a thoroughly reasoned, logical and sometimes far-sighted reply that you had the feeling he had been waiting for someone to ask that question.

Almost certainly, he worked harded than anyone. He always put in an hour's work before breakfast, taking phone calls, writing letters, organising things for the players or solving one of his biggest problems—the differing currencies and values of each country the team played in.

There were times when Chapple looked about ready to blow his top, especially early in the tour. He expected that if a home official said something would be done at such and such an hour it would be done. But Jamaica, and some of the other countries, did not have Chapple's orderly instinct about time.

He suffered a good deal for his team, too. On the last day of the fifth test I had arranged to get a statement at lunch from Chapple about allegations of gamesmanship that had been levelled against the New Zealanders. One look at Chapple's strained face as he tussled with the inevitable chicken told me to see this was not the time. Tea? O.K. At tea, with New Zealand wickets falling, the Chapple face had a glazed, plum-coloured look. Words were unnecessary. The interview came later, much later.

Chapple also had the capacity to mix with his players freely and be accused of all manner of peccadilloes at Sunday meetings, and still retain the mana that the managership needed. Many other officials have tried this and failed.

Chapple did not fail simply because the players knew that, first and foremost, he was on their side and that their worries and problems were his. If the players did not like the food at lunch, and sometimes it was hardly grade A protein material, Chapple had it changed, and smartly. These may sound like little things. But there were many such and Chapple faced such problems fairly and squarely.

He also had what seemed an uncanny sense of doing the right thing at the right time or, better still, knowing the right time to do something.

Chapple had decided that the New Zealand team should donate $50 to the Sobers benefit fund at the time of the double-wicket event at Kingston. During the third test, some weeks before, Gordon Leggat, the NZCC chairman who watched the match on his way to England, was sufficiently moved by Sobers' calling back of Turner in the first innings to suggest that the $50 should be presented to Sobers then and there. Not so, said Chapple. That was neither the time nor place for it could put the New Zealanders, and Sobers, in an awkward situation. It takes nerve to over-rule your chairman, but Chapple did it because he knew it was right. And so he was.

When the injuries were coming thick and fast Chapple, probably against his better judgment, agreed to stand by, and then to play against Windwards in a three-day match. He batted extremely well at practice, and then the rains came. By the end of the second day, Chapple, who had neither batted, bowled nor fielded in the preceding two damp days, agreed to the local request for a one-day 45-over match, and gracefully withdrew from the exertions of such a quick-fire piece of action.

A pity, for the players had plans for Chapple. But Chapple did not come down in the last shower. As always, he was one jump ahead of the play.

Early in the tour the players, not all of them with similarly orderly minds, showed a sneaking admiration for a manager who got things done. By the end the admiration had turned to total respect, for Chapple had guided a difficult tour through sometimes stormy waters. He had delivered pills and lectures with equal aplomb. He was a cricketer's manager, and he never blew his top. Astonishing.

Perhaps GRAHAM DOWLING, who is a Christchurch accountant, missed his vocation. As soon as the team boarded a plane Dowling could be seen having a quiet word with a hostess; a few minutes later Dowling would disappear through the for'ard door. Later, much later quite often, Dowling would re-appear smiling happily at having passed another stage of his Pilot Officer apprenticeship.

He approached the tour methodically and systematically. On the long Air New Zealand flight from Tahiti to Los Angeles he tucked up his legs (probably not out of choice for the leg-room is limited), pulled out a large file and caught up on his homework. He had plans for everything, from allaying the effects of the celebrated circadan disrhythmia caused by long air travel, to the setting up of various sub-committees among the players so that each had a part to play on the tour.

Sometimes I thought that he was too methodical, especially in the time taken by him, Turner and Congdon, to select the teams for the early matches, for Dowling and deadlines were not on the same wavelength.

Still, the Dowling homework paid off in Jamaica for he shepherded the team undefeated through that critical first stage of the tour. His own form was uncertain. He scored a deliberate century against the President's XI. It was slow by Dowling standards, but he seemed determined to show his team-mates that what Lawrence Rowe had done against them in the previous game for Jamaica could be done by New Zealanders if they were prepared to concentrate and make use of the plumb pitches.

But against Jamaica and West Indies in the first test Dowling struggled for runs, especially against Uton Dowe, a quickish bowler with a low-slung action, simply because Dowling could not adjust his technique quickly enough to play forward nine times out of ten.

Then, quite suddenly, he found at Antigua that his back was playing up, an old injury which he thought had mended completely. Dowling made light of it, but I could see that some of the shine had gone out of his smile.

By the time of the second test at Trinidad there were doubts, even after he had stayed at Port of Spain for treatment while the rest went to Guaracara Park for the territory game, that he would be fit enough to play.

We spoke together on this matter before the test. "I will play," said Dowling, even if the final decision on a player's fitness rested with Chapple and not the captain. So he played, bad back and all, but was plainly below his old form and one day in the field finished him.

It was a cruel blow to such a dedicated man, and to his players for they admired him immensely.

So followed more treatment, and traction, in hospital at Bridgetown. The Dowling upper lip was still stiff, and when released from hospital—with a statement on his future to be made the following day—he was positively chirpy. It could mean only two things . . . that he was fit to play, or that he was relieved that a final decision had been made that his tour was finished. Alas, it was the latter. He felt the departure keenly, even if he spoke coolly and sensibly about it. So did his players.

"When 'Congo' retires from cricket," said one of the players, "he certainly won't get a job in the diplomatic service." "Congo", or BEVAN CONGDON, had evidently just given the players a blunt message or two before they went to field against West Indies.

Congdon is like that. He has worked hard at his cricket over the years, for he is not as naturally gifted as some. Behind his quiet smile and soft drawl is a hard, determined cricket brain. He knows what he wants and sometimes he may tread on someone's toes when trying to get it. It is not a policy designed to make friends everywhere . . . hence the rather terse remark about Congdon's lack of diplomacy.

Taking over from Dowling as captain was not as simple as it appeared. Dowling had gained over the years a rapport with most of his players. Some of them, thinking back to Congdon's captaincy against Sam Trimble's Australians in 1970 (when Dowling was injured) had less than total admiration for Congdon's methods and manner.

So when he took over the leadership by the last third of the second test Congdon probably knew that he did not have the complete grip over his players which a test captain needs. He gained the full admiration and respect of his men by the simplest means possible. He played so well, whether batting, bowling, fielding or in the finer arts of captaincy on the field, that only a churl could have failed to admire him.

He followed his century against Trinidad with a courageous 166 not out in the second test. Then came his almost flawless command of the bowlers as they, including Congdon himself, bundled out West Indies for 133 in the third test. He batted superbly for a century in that match, technically probably the best innings he has ever played. He got another hundred against Guyana. He took wickets, valuable wickets, when they were most needed. He fielded well, and with confidence his field command grew so much in authority that by the end he could trump almost every trick that Sobers played.

For any man such efforts would have been remarkable. For Congdon, who took over the captaincy more or less on the back foot, these achievements established him as a great man, and almost as a great cricketer.

Congdon, who in a sense (and not a nasty one) is a "loner", did not do it all on his own. He had the wit to draw on the deep knowledge of Turner, his new vice-captain. They could be seen talking frequently on the field. Chapple supported him admirably and, through the sheer force of Congdon's own personal example, the players learned to do so, too.

Not that Congdon is a flint-hard, sharp-tongued introvert who retires to his tent to brood. He enjoyed company and clowning as much as anyone. He was a master of the dry-witted crack that, when it sank home suitably, sent Congdon off in a braying laugh that rattled the walls.

Yet he felt keenly about his team and their cricket. At the end of the third test, when Davis and Sobers had rescued West Indies and had been helped on their way by three dropped catches, Congdon sat in his playing gear staring into space while most of the others had changed and were pursuing the handiest beer.

He was almost inconsolable. "We played so well, so very well. But for those three balls out of so many we would have won."

It was a hard time for Congdon in his first full test captaincy. Perhaps then was born, or reborn, the determination that if New

Zealand had not had the luck to win the third test they certainly were not going to lose the fourth and fifth.

Befitting his age (42) and position as mathematics master at Southland Boys' High School, JACK ALABASTER went through the tour with a scholarly aplomb which dreary pitches and two painful injuries could not disturb.

Nothing seemed to faze Alabaster. In the tensest situation, to the most urgent question, the quick Alabaster mind seldom failed to put things precisely in their right perspective.

The skill of his spin-bowling, plus this pleasantly detached approach to the game, promised early in the tour to make Alabaster the key bowler of the series. He got five wickets for 130 from 37 overs against Jamaica. This was fine bowling on such a pitch and a striking rate of a wicket in every seven overs suggested that Alabaster would be invaluable, whether pitches suited him or not.

For, in his quiet way, Alabaster bowled steadily and sensibly, with no visible reaction whether the ball beat the bat or was hammered away for four. Here, I felt, was the man for the crises to come.

Sadly he was struck down during the Barbados game with an inflamed Achilles tendon, caused by too much pounding on the hard ground. Perhaps he compensated too much for his injured ankle, for by Guyana an old back complaint had flared up. He took his treatment, trained as frequently as anyone and was, according to Chapple, considered along with the rest for the fifth test. If such was the case he should have been played, vice Morgan. But I suspect there was the doubt that Alabaster's back might fail again if he tried to play his part in the dynamic fielding that was the New Zealanders' forte.

So, on the one pitch that might have given him help Alabaster did not play. A shame, for fully fit he could have been the perfect foil for the tight, economic bowling of Taylor and the rest at the other end.

So Alabaster was resigned to producing the bulk of the team newsletters, to copious reading (he would rather read in the dressing room than watch the play) and to tying everyone up in knots with his cool, clear logic whenever the conversation developed into an argument about most subjects under the sun. Alabaster had, by his own lights, an indifferent tour. With luck he might have had a splendid one. But indifferent or splendid, Alabaster would not have changed.

By the time that MARK BURGESS had thumped a back-foot drive or two against University of West Indies and then Jamaica people sat up and took notice. Here was a strokeplayer who hit the ball very hard and who seemed to have the technique, either from front or back foot, to attack on these placid pitches. The New Zealanders were happy, too, for if the top men could give a good start Burgess was just the man to chop the bowling to pieces.

By the end of the first test, in which Burgess had scored a blazing three-hour century in the second innings, the West Indian players were beginning to get worried. Unfortunately for himself and the team, Burgess never quite repeated his Jamaica form.

There were several reasons for this. He ran into a bad patch, broken only by two useful scores against Barbados, and never had the time or the innings to work himself back to form. Between the third test at Barbados and the start of the fifth he had only one brief flirt in the fourth test and a hurried trip to Kingston for the world double-wicket tournament.

As sometimes happens, the run of bad form seemed to affect his concentration and he developed the frustrating habit of getting out a minute or so after an adjournment. As the final cruel blow Burgess seemed to lose confidence against Inshan Ali, the gifted little spinner. He tucked away his bat and watched a chinaman zip back and bowl him in the first innings of the fifth test. In more settled times Burgess might just as easily have pasted the ball into the wide open spaces beyond midwicket.

So Burgess' batting fell away, but there were compensations. From the first day against Jamaica, and on a ground bumpy and dangerous for death-or-glory fielding, Burgess set the standard for the New Zealand fielding which was to become so splendid later in the tour.

As Burgess, his long blond hair flying, darted about the covers stopping and fielding and throwing like a rocket the Jamaican crowd sat up and took notice. So did the New Zealanders, for if Burgess could do this so could they. So was born the brilliant fielding which, at least to West Indians, will be the lasting memory of the tour.

Sometimes on tour Burgess played golf, and very well too. Sometimes he bowled, rather better than he himself thought. Sometimes he and Jarvis moved off together, always there was mirth and merriment.

KEITH CAMPBELL was a rather speculative choice as a batsman, spare-time wicketkeeper and occasional bowler. He, like Vivian, had a worrying start to the tour for apart from keeping wickets against University of West Indies in the opening game he was not required until the Leewards game a month later.

It must have been very frustrating for Campbell on his first tour, but in the strong silent manner of men born and bred south of the Waitaki River, Campbell plugged away at practice and if he had woes and worries he kept them to himself.

At Antigua he was promoted to chairmanship of the Sunday meeting. Within a few minutes Campbell showed himself a man of wit and humour. With this start Campbell, or "K.O." or "The Doctor" (for he had charge of the medical kit) was one of the most popular and steadfast members of the side.

He joined the moustache-growing brigade and if there had been a contest Campbell would have won the character section by a mile for at the end of the tour he looked like a cross between Fu Manchu and some Mexican desperado.

Campbell never had much luck. The two times he had a long bowl (and Congdon was remiss in never giving him a chance with a new ball) Campbell twice had chances dropped in his first over. His batting never settled down because he was used as a makeshift opener here and a middle-order man there, and never really had the chance to get his powerful strokes going. He played a useful hand against the Leewards and his two innings on the scenic-railway pitch at St Vincent were, I considered, sufficiently good to give him a place in the fifth test side.

His wicketkeeping improved so remarkably that by the end of the tour he was quick and polished. Campbell was also a first-rate outfield and when he stood in for the injured Dowling in the second test he was frequently in the Burgess-Vivian class.

In terms of facts and figures Campbell did not have a successful tour. But the tour would not have been as successful without him, for he was the Admirable Crichton, a staunch man in any task.

The West Indians were awed by RICHARD COLLINGE's size for they seldom breed 6ft 5in 16-stone-plus giants. Unfortunately they were not quite so awed by Collinge's bowling. He was still hampered by the knee injury which made him a doubtful selection in January—and the lay-off because of the injury had packed some unnecessary pounds on Collinge's huge frame.

This niggling injury, plus the tragedy of the death of his infant daughter, never let Collinge settle down to the accurate hostile bowling he had shown the previous summer. So he went home.

This was a great pity, for a fully-fit Collinge might well have developed into the perfect partner for Taylor. Like the rest he was frustrated by the dead pitches in Jamaica and gave only a glimpse or two of his real form on the bouncy pitch at Antigua. If Collinge had played the whole tour he would have sweated down to his fighting weight. He would have been most useful bowling left-arm over to the hordes of left-hand batsmen the West Indies produced (a feature that worried Cunis more than anyone). Also Collinge, like Taylor, had the height which is essential for a medium-fast bowler to get any help from most West Indies pitches. None of these things happened, more's the pity for Collinge and New Zealand.

No one was treated more scurvily by the abrasive and unsympathetic West Indies pitches than BOB CUNIS, the medium-fast toiler who needs only some grass on the pitch or shine on the ball to beat the stroke and get the edge.

Cunis, then, had to toil and he was especially valuable in the Jamaica matches for he managed to contain the Rowes and Fredericks to something less than two runs an over. Unfortunately, Cunis was seldom able to get out of this containing role. He could not contrive the movement which the taller Taylor obtained, and his bowling came off the bat rather quicker than Congdon's pawky medium-pace.

So Cunis was forced to slog away, hoping for the edge or mis-hit which seldom came. Perhaps in frustration he rather over-did—to the point of tiresomeness—the Freddie Trueman habit of standing, hands on hips, hair flying out like a blond mop, and berating the batsman by word or look for some streaky shot. The batsmen seldom seemed moved by Cunis' histrionics, but they did help to provide one of the more engrossing comments of the tour.

Cunis had been bowling to Rowe for many, many overs at Sabina Park. Rowe was somewhere between one and two hundred, the ball thunking off the middle of his bat stroke after stroke. Somehow Cunis got a shortish ball to move a little. Rowe, surprised, got the ball maybe half-an-inch off the centre of his bat and jabbed it gingerly, but safely in the air near short leg.

Cunis was not amused. "Can't you hit in the middle?" came his jibe as Rowe trotted through for a single. Rowe, in reply, might have gestured toward the scoreboard or the well-used middle of his bat. Instead, with never a twinkle in those impassive eyes of his, he simply remarked: "Well bowled." For perhaps the first and last time on tour Cunis was speechless.

If Cunis had his frustrating times as a bowler, he caused West Indies just as much frustration as a batsman. The 51 he scored in the 136-run stand with Congdon for the eighth wicket in the second test was the vintage Cunis. No matter how Holder and Sobers moved the new ball, or Ali, Gibbs and the rest spun the old one, Cunis kept them all out, and every now and then thumped the ball away for four so that Congdon did not have to carry all the load. He did this again against Barbados, and in the third test, too, even if it was careless of him to get out to a suicide shot when made night-watchman at a critical moment of the fifth test.

Cunis' damaged leg stood up to the rigours of the tour well, and in mid-tour he had to fight back after an annoying back muscle complaint. He fulminated several times on tour after teams had been chosen, but the sight of a green and grassy pitch would have been the best remedy for his complaints.

BRIAN HASTINGS had the distinction of playing in every match on tour, and against Jamaica, and West Indies in the third, fourth and fifth tests he batted extremely well.

It must also be said that Hastings was not rested at any stage of the tour—as were Congdon, Turner and other senior batsmen —because he did not always bat as long or as profitably as the others. He suffered more than anyone from the conditions and the type of bed-rock batting that the tests demanded. No-one strikes the ball more pleasantly than Hastings when he is given the chance to cut or hook, or to clip the medium-fast stuff on the up. But such batting requires a reasonably high and fast bounce and the pitches seldom provided Hastings with these. Gradually, too, the test series developed into a struggle between the West Indies spinners, especially Holford, Ali and Gibbs, and the New Zealand batsmen. Hastings has seldom been the most confident starter against good quality spin and the West Indians were quick to remark that Hastings could not "read" Ali. Maybe, maybe not.

But if he was too often forced to bat in a straitjacket Hastings still did a noble job on tour. His century at Sabina Park when Jamaica were pressing for an innings win was a masterly effort. His other hundred, in the third test at Barbados, showed just how fluent and talented Hastings could be when the pitch gave a reasonable bounce.

And no-one fought harder than Hastings in the vital fifth test, for his scores of 27 and 11 do not even hint at the way he steadied the middle of the innings.

Hastings quickly established himself as the best gully field in a side of first-rate fieldsmen. No matter how hard the shot Hastings woud pick it up with almost casual ease.

There was a casual ease about Hastings the tourist and team-man, too, for it would be difficult to find a more pleasant, even-tempered companion to travel with. He, with Alabaster, compiled the newsletters the New Zealanders sent home. As a leading advertising executive with the Christchurch Press, Hastings studied the local media closely and, knowing some of the problems, frequently provided a friendly and sympathetic ear to the travails that are the lot of a travelling newspaperman.

At a late stage of the tour I had prepared up-to-date and tolerably accurate averages and, in case anyone was interested, took them to the dinner table. Some of the players were interested. HEDLEY HOWARTH was not. "They are only figures, they don't mean anything," said Howarth before returning to his soup.

In his own case, how right Howarth was. In the final facts and figures of the tour—excluding the Bermuda match—Howarth had 22 wickets, average 46.77. In the tests his 14 wickets had cost 50.2. These were inflationary figures for a bowler of Howarth's class and type. But the figures did not always lie. On tour Howarth bowled 495 overs, in the tests 340, and at an average of slightly more than two runs an over.

In conditions which gave him little help Howarth was the bulwark of the attack, simply because he was utterly reliable. From the first test to the last he bowled with that magnificently assertive action of his. From first test to last, apart from one brief flash by Kallicharran, the West Indies batsmen treated Howarth with the respect he deserved and demanded.

After the first test I spoke with two West Indies batsmen. In their typically confident way (at that stage of the tour) they made light of the New Zealand bowling. So-and-so could only do this, such-and-such only did that, what's-his-name was easy to read, and so on. "The only bowler we don't figure," said one of them, Davis, "is Howarth. He is damned awkward, accurate, doing a little bit here and a little bit there—a bloody fine bowler."

And so Howarth was. There was not much turn for him, and in Jamaica this seemed to throw him off his stride, until he knocked over four President's XI batsmen in 11 balls. From then onward Howarth relied mostly on drift and flight, changing his angle slightly from the width of the crease. When there was turn, especially as the Port of Spain pitches became worn, Howarth's fingers were at work.

Howarth bowled best of all to Sobers, and these were private battles that brought out all the arts of cricket. In his second last innings of the series Sobers toiled away against Howarth like a man in chains. Something had to give. Sobers drove, murderously hard but in the air. Fifty yards away Hastings plucked down the catch one-handed. Howarth raised his hands in triumph, for he had won with a superb piece of bowling skill.

When not bowling for hours, Howarth was an admirable companion, conservative in his habits and his euchre-bidding, happy when he spoke of his Louise and Tracy back home.

If TERRY JARVIS ever quit his salesman's job, he could—perhaps unlike Congdon—be a hit in the diplomatic service. En route to Los Angeles, the team stopped for an hour or two, indecently early in the morning, at Tahiti airport. Most of them hastened to the washroom to shave or shower, acquiring from an elderly lady the towels they needed.

Few realised that the concierge expected payment for the towels, and as we lounged about afterward she, airport officials and then the gendarmes started to search about for these errant, free-loading Kiwis.

Jarvis took over. With a touch of blarney, a twinkle in his eye and a couple of decipherable words of the local lingo, Jarvis smoothed over the troubled waters. No-one found out what Jarvis said. Soon there were smiles and laughs all round, and if Jarvis had boarded the plane wearing a policeman's hat or twirling his six-shooter round his finger no-one, least of all Jarvis, would have been surprised.

Some of us, however, were surprised when the team selectors made it clear they wanted Jarvis for the first test, whatever his lack of form or the consequent standing-down of Campbell and Vivian for any first-class action in Jamaica.

Jarvis took time to find his form. Like Dowling he tended to get stranded between back and front foot, something that made him a regular leg-before victim during the tour. Like Hastings, Jarvis' leisurely elegant style of stroke play demanded more speed than the West Indies pitches would provide.

Then Dowling went home, and whether he liked it or not Jarvis had to be Turner's opening partner. He answered the challenge nobly, 60 and 25 against Barbados, 26 in the third test, a second ball duck against Guyana and then his staggering 182 in the 387-run opening stand of the fourth test.

If Jarvis had had the luck to score that 182 early in the tour he might have been pressing Turner and Congdon for the leading batting honours. That long innings gave Jarvis the confidence that he needed, the breakthrough which convinced him that he could bat for a long time whatever the conditions.

Jarvis spent a long time, too, showing that day in day out he was one of the finest fieldsmen in the side. He sometimes lacked Vivian's incredible brilliance, or Burgess' stunning speed, but Jarvis was never less than very good and sometimes downright courageous as he threw himself at the ball.

He had, too, an enormous capacity for enjoying himself, and when Jarvis enjoyed himself life was seldom dull and never quiet. Yet underneath all the noise and horseplay Jarvis was a sympathetic soul, and a pushover for kids.

One night at St Vincent there was a barbecue at the hotel and Jarvis and I were tippling at the rum while listening to the steel band on the ocean shore. There was a stir among the St Vincentians who were watching, with a youngster as the centre of attraction.

"That kid's hurt," said Jarvis, as he darted away. So he was, with a fishhook embedded behind his knee and with everyone clucking away and no-one doing anything. Jarvis took over. He told the boy he had to be brave, and that bravery could mean New Zealand autographs, an old cricket ball, anything. While Jarvis prattled on, the boy stood stoically as someone eased out the hook. The autographs, the ball and a handshake were exchanged. Jarvis returned to his rum.

When Richard Collinge went home the call was not for another medium-fast bowler, but for a batsman who could bowl a bit, and ROSS MORGAN seemed the best available replacement. He looked it, too, when he top-scored with 75 against Barbados, thus foiling the super-confident Bajans from gaining what looked like an easy win.

The moderate bounce of the pitch seemed to suit the low-slung Morgan, and he was unlikely to get out, as he sometimes does in New Zealand, by pushing away from his pads and being caught at slip or gully. Also his off-spin, with his exotic hop-skip run-in, would be useful as a foil for Howarth.

Unhappily not all these things came to pass. Morgan seemed to develop some flaw in his footwork, which left him more cramped than usual. He got very few chances for his favourite cuffs through midwicket, and the spinners soon traded on his fondness to hit across the line. He got the occasional wicket, but his newly-developed looped delivery seldom worried the better batsmen.

So Morgan did not have the happiest of tours, and will have to regain much lost ground if he is to play for New Zealand again.

If you wanted to know anything about everything, BRUCE TAYLOR was your man, the walking Baedeker. What time did the plane go, what kind of plane was it, how much postage from here to there, how do you handle the local TAB, what room is so-and-so in, what's a good thing in the first at Union Park? Taylor, surely the best organised traveller of all time, would know.

Taylor, the champion tourist, soon developed into Taylor, the champion bowler. He was keenly disappointed when dropped for the first test, one of the few times when Taylor and the tour seemed out of joint. He cracked hearty about it afterward, saying that he had learned more watching than by getting hit round Sabina Park by Rowe and company.

If so, he learned quickly and soon had the records tumbling in what even West Indians regarded as one of the great series bowling efforts they had ever seen. By mid-tour Taylor was honed down to a peak of fitness. No matter what the state of the pitch or the ball he could, with his high action, coax out a little movement.

Against West Indies at Bridgetown he was superb. There was bite and bounce in the pitch, to be sure, and the West Indians' technique was indifferent. But Taylor struck one of those inspired patches which come perhaps once in a lifetime. He was good enough to realise that he had struck a purple patch, and to make the most of it.

As the tour went on Taylor got even better. His control was such that he seemed to have every ball at his command—the bouncer, the ball moving in or away, the yorker. Taylor maintained the ball which removed Rowe first-ball at Bridgetown was the best he had ever bowled. I would disagree. In the second innings of the fifth test he laid down Sobers' off-stump with the most perfect yorker you could ever see.

Apart from an invaluable 46 when Congdon was repairing the first innings of the second test, Taylor's batting seemed to fall away—until he and Wadsworth walked down into history with their fifth-test stand which saved the game and the rubber and the tour.

At other times, Taylor, who is regarded as a lucky man, did me the service of providing the statistics for this book, perhaps as repayment for the one time we were partners at euchre and he managed to get euchred 13 times.

At all times, Taylor enjoyed life, his cricket, his touring. He is talking of retirement. A pity; a tour could not be quite the same without Taylor.

GLENN TURNER has come a long, long way from the wispy Otago Boys High School lad who propped up one end of the Otago crease for many more minutes than he had runs.

The Turner of the tour was a mature man, every inch the cricketer. There are other changes. The broad flat Dunedin accent now has a tinge of Worcestershire, the still-slim frame is now all sinew and muscle, the young-looking face is wiser round the eyes. But the concentration, the determination are still there.

Turner's tour achievements are now history, the incredible run of four double centuries, the slip catches taken in with deceptive ease, the confident skill with which he led the side against Barbados. Yet there was one achievement less notable, but perhaps more valuable to the touring side than all the records he achieved.

Turner lives for cricket, and by it. He has succeeded in the toughest grade of all, county play in England. At the start of the tour, then, it was noticeable that Turner had the slightly detached air of the English professional amid the New Zealand amateurs. He seemed slightly of another world, which was not surprising.

Yet by mid-tour Turner had slipped smoothly and quietly into the core of the team. After his fourth double century Turner talked of his past career, and of the criticisms which had been piled upon the youngster in his early days for Otago. He had then built round himself a hard shell to ward off the slings and arrows. He was concerned that he still might be judged as being a hard, uncompromising young man. Turner need not concern himself. He won a bat at Guyana. He gave it to Chapple as a gift. I would be surprised if Chapple has been more touched by any other gesture from a cricketer.

Turner is turning into a mellow, matured man, and into a very fine cricketer whose run of centuries for Worcestershire a few years ago and heavy scoring in West Indies may only be a prelude to the bravura passages to come.

Turner scored so heavily because, with his logical cricket brain, he worked out quickly the things he could do and could not do under the conditions of the time. He sometimes played some handsome strokes, especially through the covers. He would doubtless have liked to play them more often. But he disciplined himself. He batted within himself, the better to keep in control of the bowling and his innings. The physical strain of his long innings must have been enormous, let alone the toll on his mental resources.

I had some fine old arguments with Henry Blofeld, the English writer-broadcaster who covered the tour, especially after Turner and Jarvis shut West Indies out of the fourth test. Blofeld said that he could never think of Turner as a great cricketer in terms of his long innings of that test. I was inclined to agree. Turner was great value for the New Zealanders, but he might not be a great cricketer—yet. But Turner has worked a long, hard path from the pale frail lad at Carisbrook. He still has some way to go, but perhaps greatness is just over the next, rocky climb.

The sight of GRAHAM VIVIAN sprinting about the outfield, his hands swooping down on the ball with perfect timing, the blurred thrust of his right shoulder as the ball hurtled back will live as long in the memory as Turner's batting or Taylor's bowling.

Vivian was a very fine field when he left New Zealand. By the tour's end he was quite superb, poetry in motion as he made fielding an art. Many of the others were very good. Vivian was brilliant, day in day out. He took fearful risks, plunging into the netting with his shoulder as he flicked the ball back from the boundary edge, turning a four into a two or three.

Vivian set the standard for the New Zealanders' wonderful fielding, and the others were spurred on to greater efforts as they tried to keep up his class. He took some wonderful catches, and his diving forward for a low stinging drive by Kallicharran in the fifth test was one such. That catch was not recognised by the umpire and Vivian furiously punted the ball away. He was chided for his lack of manners by the local press. Perhaps they were right, but Vivian threw his whole being into fielding and firmly believed he had held the catch. His explosive reaction was forgiveable, perhaps, on the grounds that his fielding was too good. No-one else would have got within a foot of the catch.

Vivian's batting did not always match his fielding, and there were reasons for this. He was shabbily treated at the start of the tour by being left out of any action in Jamaica. He did not have a long, solid innings until the Trinidad match, virtually in mid-tour. By then it was apparent that both the nature of the pitches and the New Zealanders' big-match tactics would not allow Vivian to tear into his strokes—as he did in a furious blast against Tobago in a second-class frolic.

Like Hastings and Burgess, Vivian needed speed from the pitch and freedom to attack. He got neither and except for a fine 61 against Barbados Vivian had to hold his rich strokes back.

For an hour on the second day against Barbados Vivian batted sublimely. He savaged Boyce. A square cut for four, a slice for another, a cover-drive for three and then a magnificent square cut to the fence which had the Bajans, even Boyce, applauding the majesty of the stroke. Alas, Vivian had few chances to cast away his chains, and we must still wait for him to mould the patient defence he showed on tour with the dashing strokes he left behind in New Zealand.

Vivian's bowling was still an exotic mixture of sharp wrong'uns and the occasional double-bouncer. While his action remains so jerky his bowling will probably remain a mystery to everyone, including Vivian.

A thoroughly likeable and good-mannered man, Vivian enjoyed touring, especially when surrounded by the creature comforts. In Los Angeles en route to Miami and Kingston the team was quartered for an hour or two at the airport Sheraton. There Vivian discovered a massage bed, 15 minutes for a quarter. Being Vivian he had a dollar's worth of agitated bliss.

Yet on the field he drove himself mercilessly hard. I did not think I would ever see a fieldsman to compare with Colin Bland, the Springbok. Vivian is fit to rank in that company.

The best time to talk to KEN WADSWORTH was about 10 a.m. Somehow Wadsworth and the breakfast table did not agree. When he was sounding off about the service, or lack of it, the food, weather, news, cricket reporters, etc., it was best to close the ears and cover the milk before it turned sour under the barrage.

By mid-morning Wadsworth would be restored—the super-confident, aggressive fellow likely to break into a soft-shoe shuffle or to belabour the air with what cannot be the smoothest voice to echo out of Nelson.

Amid the gloomy times of the Jamaica match and the first test Wadsworth's was one of the few New Zealand voices that could muster any confidence. When he woofed his way out, in his usual frustrating fashion, in the first innings against Jamaica we had words about it.

Don't worry, said Wadsworth, they would not get him cheaply again. They didn't, for he got 35 not out in 96 minutes in the next innings, and a week or so later came his 295-minute innings for 78 as he and Turner built their 220-run stand for the sixth wicket which made the test safe. To prove his point Wadsworth batted 124 minutes for 36 not out in the second innings.

About this time, too, Wadsworth refused to be bowed by the Rowe-fever that hit the New Zealanders after his two double and one single centuries. "Don't worry," said Wadsworth, "we'll get Rowe, and they will be as scared of Turner as we are of Rowe."

This was typically confident Wadsworth, and later events proved him completely right.

It was fitting, too, that he should add the final trimming to the tour with his last-ditch stand with Taylor in the fifth test. This gave Wadsworth an average of 44 in the tests, and pride of place behind Turner and Congdon.

While Wadsworth's batting improved remarkably during the tour his wicketkeeping became a little ragged round the edges. He still got the catches that mattered, apart from one or two that got away, and he made a very good job of taking Congdon, who is not the easiest man to take standing up. But too often Wadsworth fumbled what should have been straightforward takes, and this tended to give his keeping an untidy air.

Wadsworth is the type of genial (after 10 a.m.) man who would vastly enjoy a cricket tour of Antarctica. If there was fun, noise or music about, Wadsworth would not be far away.

Captain Abe Bailey, the thoroughly delightful Jamaican army officer who was the New Zealanders' liaison man in Kingston, organised a fine party poolside at his officers' mess. There was music, dancing, and that was the place for MURRAY WEBB.

"My," cooed a sweet young thing watching Webb as he danced, "isn't he supple?"

At dancing, yes. At bowling, batting and fielding, not always. The heat and the heartless pitches soon took the sting out of Webb's bowling and the tall young man who had bounded like an uncaged lion at Carisbrook and the Basin Reserve was reduced to a less ferocious bowler who could get neither speed nor bounce —and who seemed to sense he would not get wickets either.

There were various theories propounded, and Webb is something of a theorist himself. Perhaps he was too stiff, perhaps his feet weren't landing properly, perhaps he was too square on at delivery.

Webb worked hard, and very often stayed behind to train by himself in an effort to get back his old hostility. He bowled very well against the President's XI and against Guyana he somehow got some lift and life out of a hopeless pitch. Unfortunately, it was too late. If Webb had bowled on the lively third test pitch, when Taylor did the damage, he might have blown the West Indians to smithereens, but by then he was almost out of test reckoning.

Webb the batsman seldom appeared for long, apart from a solid stand of 50 with Wadsworth at Antigua. Like his fielding, Webb's batting depends whether he can assemble what seem to be yards of arms, legs, elbows and knees in the right order at the right time.

Off field Webb spent much time working on his thesis—the effects of newspapers on early New Zealand life and times—for his Master of Arts degree. He spent a lot of time, too, speaking with whatever stranger came within range, young or old, coloured or black or white. He is a serious young man, clear and concise of expression and intellect when given the chance. You could almost see him storing up the knowledge he gained as he talked with the local people. You could be just as sure that sometime, somewhere, the knowledge he gained will be put to good use.

The same might well apply to his cricket. He learned the facts of cricket touring the hard way. He is much too intelligent a young man not to profit from the experience.

Among the outriders of the party were Alan Richards, who covered the tour diligently and, I am sure, extremely well for the New Zealand Broadcasting Corporation, Henry Blofeld, an English freelancer who both wrote and broadcast on the whole tour, and myself as the New Zealand Press Association representative.

Frank Mooney, that delightfully puckish man from Wellington who is also a national selector, saw the first half of the tour, and Arthur Cutler, the Invercargill umpire, was there for all but the last act.

Separately or together they were good company. The way of a travelling broadcaster is not always easy, but Richards battled through nobly. Cutler, full of Southland charm and good sense, was as unflappable as Alabaster. Mooney, surely the most dangerous 16-handicapper in the world, formed an unholy alliance with Chapple and invariably finished in the money.

Blofeld knew his cricket and his crafts. He had played for Cambridge, might have played for England but for a boyhood accident, and had travelled the world writing and talking about cricket. The New Zealanders looked sideways at him when he caned them after the Guyana test, but no-one could be cross at the amiable "Blowers" for too long. For a man who, recovering from hepatitis, covered the tour without taking solace in alcohol, Blofeld kept his humour remarkably well. He took particular delight in finding that many of the West Indian listeners regarded his crisp, very-English speaking as being the typical New Zealand accent.

He had distant association with the use, by Ian Fleming, of the name of Blofeld as the specially evil villain in the James Bond sagas. Fleming, while searching for his villain's name, cast his eye down the members' list at his club. There were several Blofelds, and Fleming regarded that as the most suitable name he could find.

"Blowers" was sometimes agitated about what New Zealand and West Indies were doing to the game he loved. Nasty, never.

From time to time, too, there appeared Roy Lawrence, the cricket broadcaster of Kingston, a fine gentleman, Tony Cozier, the writer- broadcaster from Barbados and Brunell Jones, cricket writer for the *Trinidad Guardian* and *Evening News*.

Jones once accused me of slandering the Queen's Park groundstaff when I wrote about the odd nature of the second test pitch. Otherwise he was most courteous. Lawrence could reel off cricket stories superbly in his muscular Jamaican accent. Cozier is a fortunate man, with the charm of his wife Gillian competing with the beauty of his beloved Barbados.

# 3

# *The West Indians*

"I have been watching West Indies cricket for 40 years," said Roy Lawrence, the Jamaican broadcaster, during the fifth test at Port of Spain. "And never has the insularity in West Indies cricket been as bad as it is now."

Being a new chum to the Caribbean I could only make polite noises at Lawrence's sad proclamation.

Three months beforehand, at the test dinner in Kingston, Cecil Marley, the president of the West Indies board, said that since the failure of the visionary West Indies political and social federation some ten years beforehand, cricket was the major factor in uniting the West Indies. Perhaps the truth lies somewhere between the two fervent statements. Certainly one of the great weaknesses of West Indies cricket, especially in a home series, is the parochialism that exists at all levels of the game.

This stems partly from geography. Jamaica, the largest and most distant of the West Indies cricket nations, is very much an island apart. "Because of our size and distance," said Charles Mills, a delightful University of West Indies professor and a sturdy worker for university and Jamaican cricket, "the other islands tend to scorn Jamaica. Perhaps as a reaction, Jamaicans might look down on the other countries."

If the other three major territories, Trinidad, Guyana and Barbados, seem united in their dislike of Jamaica, they are also not wildly enthusiastic about one another.

There are various aspects of this insularity. Quite the most striking, and influential, is the West Indies board system of having a large selection panel comprising delegates from Jamaica, Trinidad, Barbados, Guyana and the combined Windward-Leeward Islands with, at the moment, Gary Sobers co-opted as the captain.

Last season the full panel selected the first test team—after some difficulty in having Sobers present—and thereafter the second, third and fourth test sides were picked by a subcommittee of three selectors, plus Sobers. Considering the distances and expense involved this sub-committee system might seem the best way of covering the widespread islands.

However, the West Indies board compounded the complaints of insularity by keeping to its policy of having the resident selector of the time as chairman. Thus Alan Rae was chairman in Trinidad, Jeff Stollmeyer in Trinidad, Keith Walcott in Barbados and Joe Solomon in Guyana. The other selector was Frank Thomas, of St Vincent, the combined Islands' man.

I do not wish to infer that the various chairmen plump solely for the players of their own territory, even if the West Indies team seemed to change character once or twice in the series. But the system is both unfortunate and unwieldy. Unfortunate because it implies bias by the respective chairmen, even if it does not always exist. Unwieldy because, in one prime case, Keith Walcott was chairman of selectors for the Barbados test when it was not possible for him to see any of the play in the previous test at Trinidad.

The obvious answer is a less unwieldy selection panel divorced from territory representation. Tony Cozier, Walcott and myself talked over this one morning in Guyana.

Cozier and I held to the theory that a sole selector, provided he had the time, was the ideal answer. Cozier likened him to Sir Alf Ramsay of English Soccer, and other West Indians, with their liking for the grandiloquent expression, talked of a "supremo".

Walcott was not completely convinced. Imagine, Walcott said, himself being a sole selector from Guyana, and picking a test team for Bourda without a Guyanese in it.

"Imagine that," said Walcott. "If that happened they would burn my house down."

This is another part of the insularity problem: the zealous patriotism for their own players among the territories. This tends to be aggravated by the partiality of the various newspaper and radio cricket experts. Just before the final test there were doubts about the fitness of Clive Lloyd and Lawrence Rowe, and vivid speculation about their possible replacements. The Trinidad afternoon paper, the *News*, came out with a bold heading naming Joey Carew, the Trinidad skipper who was dropped after the third test, as the replacement. Way, way down in the story was a paragraph suggesting, and only that, that Carew could replace either Rowe or Lloyd.

This partiality, or variations of it, occurred in each of the four main territories. In Jamaica, for example, they were pressing for a handful of Jamaicans in the first test, including Desmond Lewis, the wicketkeeper-batsman, Sam Morgan, the opener, and Clive Campbell, the young off-spinner. When none of these three was included in the first test side the newspaper reaction was that the selectors could not have spread the selection more evenly among the five cricket areas if they had tried.

The home-town feeling is quickly transmitted to the crowds at the matches and here the parochialism is even more emphatic. The most obvious example was after the running out of Lloyd, the Guyana hero, in the Bourda test. The hostility toward Charlie Davis was quite violent and the bottles flew.

A few weeks later Roy Fredericks was even more comprehensively run out by Alvin Kallicharran in the fifth test at Port of Spain. The crowd jeered, but were not hostile—after all, Fredericks came from Guyana, not the crowd's beloved Trinidad.

In the second test, on the same ground, Rowe had a miserable first day when catches tumbled from his hands. Davis dropped a catch, too. Rowe was booed off the field, Davis was not. Rowe was booed when he went out to bat, and booed again after Congdon had bowled him. Rowe was booed again after a "snorter" of a delivery from Taylor undid him, first ball, in the third test at Barbados.

No wonder Rowe expressed to the New Zealanders his unwillingness to play in the fifth test at Port of Spain. In the event he was injured some days beforehand, a genuine injury let it be said, and realising his feelings the selectors did not press him too hard to play at Port of Spain again.

This feeling persisted throughout the tour. Much of it was directed at Sobers, even in his native Barbados. The *Gleaner*, in Jamaica, one day came out with the curious remark that the West Indies board of control members were the high priests of West Indies cricket, and that Sobers was their altar-boy.

Amid all the criticism of Sobers' captaincy I could not find anyone who could agree on his replacement. Again the insularity. David Holford had skippered Barbados outstandingly, building up a wonderful spirit among his players, to win the Shell Shield. To some of us New Zealanders Holford seemed the man with the skill, balance and ability to knit some of that spirit into the West Indies side.

But mention that in Guyana, and you found that Holford's bowling and batting were regarded as a joke there. Mention it in Trinidad and the reaction was even more marked. Barbados had already had Worrell and Sobers as the most recent West Indies captains. The idea of Holford, another Barbadian, as skipper, could not be entertained. Why not Carew, who just happened to come from Trinidad. Or, if you were in Guyana, why not Lloyd?

If, as Lawrence lugubriously suggested, the divisions among the West Indies nations have never been wider, then I feel that West Indies will take a long time to climb back to their proud position of world champions. Perhaps something can be done, at WIBC and selection levels, to present West Indies cricket with the tight knit, combined strength which the late Sir Frank Worrell generated.

Something should be done, for West Indies abound in very good or very promising players. Giving in a weakness in genuinely fast bowling, West Indies have any amount of polished or raw material.

The New Zealanders, for example, were staggered at the large number of talented spinners put out against them. There were the senior men, Gibbs and Holford—and the New Zealanders could hardly disguise their glee when Gibbs was dropped for the third test and not recalled. Inshan Ali, and Raphick Jumadeen, the young Trinidad left-armers were astonishingly skilled and mature for players in their early twenties.

Tony Howard, the Barbados off-spinner, got one test and did not do very well, mainly because he had the fault of bowling rather too much at or outside the off-stump. He took four wickets in each innings for Barbados against the New Zealanders, and the New Zealanders quietly spread the word that they had been very impressed with Howard's ability. The bait was taken, Howard got two for 140 in the Guyana test, and was then discarded.

But the New Zealanders kept very quiet about Rex Collymore, the tall Guyana slow left-armer who took six wickets for 115 against them. Considering the docility of the Bourda pitch this was one of the outstanding bowling feats of the tour and the New Zealanders were happy that Collymore was not promoted to the fifth test at Trinidad.

There were other spinners of quality. Arthur Barrett, the Jamaican leg-spinner, looked decidedly useful, and so did his team mate Campbell, the off-spinner.

The Leeward Islands had Elquimedo Willet, the teen-age left-arm spinner who was perhaps the best finger-spinner of all the left-armers the New Zealanders struck. Trinidad are developing another youngster, Imtiaz, a right-arm wrist-spinner.

All of these spinners are very talented and the pity is that only a few of them will rise to test level.

Glenn Turner at his finest — cover-driving David Holford for four during his magnificent 223 not out in the first innings of the first test at Sabina Park. Michael Findlay is the wicketkeeper while at the right Gary Sobers is in his favourite position to close the trap when Holford bowls his googly.

The first of the many, and the first of the few: at the top Bevan Congdon gets the first of his 13 test wickets with Joey Carew lbw for 43 in the first innings of the first test at Sabina. Below, Glenn Turner swoops on a snick from Charlie Davis off Bob Cunis' bowling at Sabina. Sadly for Cunis, the merciless pitches seldom allowed him similar moments of triumph.

Inshan Ali is the most striking of these and, properly handled, could be a match-winner against the Australians when they tour the Caribbean next summer.

He is a small, slim man with short fingers; after a brisk little run his left-arm flipped through quickly. I watched him through the binoculars for hours and was never completely certain whether I could pick his usual chinaman or his wrong'un which was a leg-break to the right-hander. Judging by results, not all the New Zealanders could "read" Ali all the time, either.

Ali has one annoying habit of running across the line of the stumps, especially when he senses a caught-and-bowled chance. The New Zealanders were several times moved to complain about this habit, and not always as a matter of gamesmanship, for Ali did tend to make a scrape too close to the line of the stumps for comfort. The umpires were fairly lenient, even one at Guaracara Park who told Ali he could not rule on an lbw appeal because Ali had run across the umpire's line of sight.

In other places Ali might have stricter action taken against him, but it is a small problem and one he could solve himself without too much difficulty.

Jumadeen, who played in the fifth test, is more in the Hedley Howarth mould, although he lacks the New Zealander's high fluent action and his tight command of direction. Jumadeen bowled very well for much of the fifth test and only in the crunch, when Wadsworth and Taylor held out in the last two hours, did Jumadeen bowl rather too much wide of the off stump.

Gibbs is still a very fine bowler, especially with his peculiar looped flight which made the ball turn and bounce unusually high. Unluckily for him, Gibbs bowled mostly at Turner and Congdon. They devised a counter which had an extraordinary number of balls clipping their outstretched pads and ballooning away to Gibbs' close-in leg-trap. The New Zealanders were content to survive against Gibbs, to stifle him in any way possible.

These were not pretty tactics, but they were effective and Gibbs did not get past the second test.

While in St Vincent, rather off the beaten track for accurate publicity, the news came to the New Zealanders that Gibbs had been included in the 13 for the fifth test. Next day came the news that Gibbs was not in the fifth test squad and there were some sunny New Zealand smiles. Looking back, a combination of Ali and Gibbs in that critical test would have been too much for the New Zealanders in their battle for survival.

During the series Geoffrey Greenidge, of Barbados, and Kallicharran, of Guyana, emerged as batsmen of particular promise, and fit to rank with the senior men, Fredericks, Davis, Carew, Sobers and Lloyd.

Greenidge, a tall slim young man, was good enough to get a hundred for Barbados Colts against MCC in 1968, and good enough, too, to battle to the top in county cricket for Sussex. An intense, dedicated young man, Greenidge is unlike most of the West Indies batsmen in that he has kept his county cricket technique intact even on home pitches which allow a freer, more risky style. This is not a bad fault. Greenidge plays straight and sensibly, and could well develop into an admirable foil for a more explosive batsman at the other end. In addition he is gifted as a runner between the wickets and quite outstanding—in the Vivian-Burgess class in fact—as an outfield.

Kallicharran is more a product of his West Indies upbringing. A small, darkly attractive man, Kallicharran has the typically flamboyant touch to many of his strokes. He loves to cover-drive, all flowing artistry which does not always allow for such mundane matters as getting into the line of flight before playing the stroke. There is the flush of joyous youth about his batting, and on West Indian pitches he can discard some of the essentials of batting technique. He is now off to county cricket, and if he picks up the essentials as quickly as, say, Greenidge has done Kallicharran may well become—as his admirers maintain—the best thing to happen to West Indies cricket since Rohan Kanhai.

Rowe started sensationally with two doubles and a single century against the New Zealanders on his home pitch at Sabina. During one of those incredible innings a tired New Zealander asked Rowe whether he ever got out. Rowe replied that this was his home pitch, and he had no right to get out on it.

Rowe on other pitches—Trinidad, Barbados and Guyana—was another matter and by the end of the fourth test Rowe's technique and confidence were in ruins.

In this Rowe was just as much a victim of his own environment as of the New Zealand bowlers.

The test dinner at Kingston came after Rowe's wonderful 214 in his test debut. None of the speechmakers could resist remarking on Rowe's wonderful exploit, or on his wish to share an impromptu collection with Roy Fredericks, his partner in a 269-run stand for the second wicket. Out rolled the praise, so lavish that Rowe was being mentioned in the same breath as Sobers and George Headley.

A New Zealander—say, Bryan Williams after some sensational

All Black performance—would have been embarrassed beyond endurance by such fulsome praise and, indeed, Rowe looked during the dinner as if he would gladly have slipped out of sight under the tablecloth.

But this is the West Indies way of things, for Kallicharran and Ali received similar adulation later in the tour. Only one speaker had the wit to remark that while Rowe was on the mountain-top of achievement he should beware that there were valleys below.

That night no-one seemed to care about valleys. In the grand old English custom the various speakers "took wine" with someone present whom they wished to honour, and Rowe was toasted in this manner. In fact, the New Zealanders were so impressed by the praise poured on Rowe that for sometime afterward, whenever glasses were full, someone rather cynically called for "a toast to Lawrence Rowe".

Rowe gives every impression of being both an exceedingly fine batsman and a level-headed young man. But such was the praise thrust upon him then and for days afterwards in the newspapers, that he could be forgiven if he regarded centuries as being matters of almost divine right.

When, at the next sighting, Congdon knocked down Rowe's middle stump for only 22 at Trinidad the crowd were struck as if by lightning—and Chapple was moved to call for free beers for anyone within earshot. That dismissal, and the boos which greeted his dropped catches in the same test, plunged Rowe into the valley and he never, even during a stout 51 in the third test, looked likely to climb back to his mountain-top.

If Rowe's feats at Sabina had been kept in better perspective then he might have become the dominant man of the series. For Rowe has the makings of a remarkable batsman. His basic technique, especially his footwork, is superb. He has a wonderful off-side drive, either straightish or through covers, and is just as proficient at chipping the ones and twos on the on-side. He is equable of temperament and pleasant of manner.

If he has one fault it is the West Indian habit of playing through the line of the ball rather than getting feet and body into the line. This is a common West Indian habit bred by pitches which seldom allow a delivery from anyone of medium or fast pace to deviate once it has bounced. It produces some handsome strokes, forward or backward of point. It also produces, when the ball does move from the pitch, the possibility of the ball getting an outside edge or nipping in through the "gate" between bad and pad.

Given time and experience away from West Indies, Rowe will

adapt his technique. Given time, too, the scars to his confidence will heal and he will be better equipped to handle the praise which West Indians love to lavish on their successful players. I would suspect that Rowe against the Australians next year will not stroke the ball so handsomely as he did against the New Zealanders. But I also suspect that he will be much harder to dislodge on all kinds of pitches and that he will get back to the single and double hundreds on the mountain-top. He has too much natural talent to be down in the valley for long.

Round and about, too, there were other promising batsmen. Morgan, the Jamaican opener, batted pleasantly for his country and the President's XI against the New Zealanders. His development will depend on whether he can continue playing the strokes which come so easily on his native Jamaican pitches, but not so readily when the pitches give a slower and lower bounce.

Trinidad have a beefy young man, Richard de Souza, who was regarded as uncommonly promising when played as a colt against the 1965 Australians. Since then de Souza has not developed as quickly as, say, Kallicharran. His critics, and he has them even in Trinidad, maintain that until he fines down a bit, de Souza will have neither the stamina nor concentration to play long innings.

But de Souza appealed to me, especially during his 100 for Trinidad at Guaracara Park, because he was one of the few young men the New Zealanders encountered who was prepared to graft and scrap for his runs. At the end of his century it was difficult to recall any special stroke that gave de Souza's innings a touch of class. He took his time, 288 minutes, and was overshadowed by the explosive batting from the other century-makers, Carew and Davis. Yet de Souza got his hundred, and got it well. There were many more promising batsmen the New Zealanders met who flitted brightly across the scene for 20 or 30 and then disappeared.

Sobers spoke feelingly after the fifth test at the absence of genuinely-fast bowlers in West Indies. Just as feelingly, he blamed the pitches for not giving them encouragement. Yet Sobers, curiously enough, did not want pitches with grass on them, for he maintained that if these were provided they would have four-day games finishing in two or three days.

As Cunis, Webb and Taylor would testify, West Indies at the moment is no place for a bowler of anything below the Tyson, Hall or Snow class. The drab pitches offer them no help at all.

Vanburn Holder, the tall, well-built Barbadian, did well in the four tests he played in because he had some speed, and the craft he had learned playing for Worcestershire. Sobers, somewhat below his old sharp speed, had some useful bursts in the tests. Uton Dowe, the Jamaican, had one test where he bowled rather well. Grayson Shillingford, the tall man from the Windwards, had two tests with occasional success.

Dowe was the fastest of these four and on his home Sabina pitch had the New Zealanders worried with his fast, low bounce. I had a private thought that Dowe might have been recalled, with some profit, for the fifth test, but in the meantime he had become involved in a squabble with his captain Easton McMorris and the Jamaica authorities and by the end of the tour seemed to be definitely *non grata* in high places—although hardly the "moron" one high official called him.

Guyana had a big strapping fellow named Adonis who caught Jarvis napping with his second ball, and had him playing on. Speed was one thing, accuracy another and Congdon happily hit him for six fours in the next two overs so Adonis retreated quickly into the undergrowth.

Oddly enough, two of the most effective new-ball bowlers the New Zealanders faced did not appear in the tests.

One was Keith Boyce, the Essex pro, who used the lively Bridgetown pitch extremely well. Boyce is of moderate speed, but like Holder can "do a bit" with the ball and bowled most accurately—rather in the way Taylor extracted some movement from the heartless pitches.

The other was Andy Roberts, the whippy young man from the Leeward Islands. The Antigua pitch was livelier than some of the others and this helped Roberts get both lift and life. He had an exceedingly nasty bouncer and, late on the third day when most of the sting had gone from the pitch, still made the ball fizz up nastily round Vivian and Campbell's ears. There were some that thought Roberts had a slight kink in his action, but if so this was a minor flaw. He did have, more than anyone the New Zealanders met, genuine speed and, like his team-mate Willet, deserves encouragement.

A third prospect could be Cecil Lawson, the Jamaica left-armer. He can hardly love Jamaican pitches, and he did not take a wicket against the New Zealanders either for Jamaica or for the President's XI at Montego Bay. A tall slim man, Lawson has a smooth action and a useful burst of speed. He could well be effective on a tour of England or Australia, where he could get either swing or seam. For the moment, though, he must toil on Jamaican pitches and there is not much profit there for a man of his type.

West Indies are singularly fortunate in their wicket-keepers. Michael Findlay, the gracious and aristocratic St Vincentian, kept in all five tests and, apart from the early problem of reading Inshan Ali in the second, was safe and sound. Findlay also is developing as a solid batsman, giving in a slight weakness against spin.

For variety you could have the Leewards jack-in-the-box, Auckland Hector, probably the quickest stumper the New Zealanders saw. Milton Pydanna, of Guyana, was another only a shade below international class. Lewis, of Jamaica, was sound if unspectacular, while David Murray, of Barbados, will obviously be a very fine keeper when he loses his frilly touches and concentrates on the ball.

Many West Indians were glum when they failed to win the series against New Zealand. As far as stroke-play and spin-bowling were concerned they were superior to the New Zealanders. With Greenidge and Kallicharran and Lloyd they could quickly develop into a fielding side every bit as good as the dashing New Zealanders.

Quite plainly, West Indies have the manpower with which to defeat Australia next summer. They have Fredericks, Greenidge, Rowe, Davis, Lloyd, Kallicharran, Carew and Foster as their leading batsmen. They have Holder as a first-rate seamer, Findlay as a wicketkeeper, and a host of spinners of whom Gibbs, Holford, Inshan Ali and Jumadeen would rate the highest at the moment.

What they need is the drive and the spirit with which the New Zealanders foiled them in the test series. These things will only come when West Indies are properly selected, and properly led.

They will only come, too, when officials and selectors and players and the news media discard their insularity—when they are mature enough to recognise a player purely on his ability and not on which territory he comes from. This is a problem only West Indies can solve for themselves. Until they do West Indies will find, as they unhappily did against New Zealand, that even under their own peculiar conditions they can come to grief against a team less gifted in everything except a unified spirit.

# 4

# *Crowds Can Be Lively*

Over the years it has been possible to gain the notion that West Indian cricket crowds are made up of carefree islanders, full of fun and sometimes half full of rum, liable to dash off a snatch of calypso here, sparked by gaiety and humour and quick to go into ecstasies at some brave deed in the middle.

This is not quite accurate. The first impression one gains of West Indian crowds—at Sabina, Queen's Park, Kensington Oval, Bourda and Guaracara Park— is that they are fenced in. It is an irritating sight with the crowds in the public areas held back either by large steel-mesh fences or high barriers of chicken-wire.

Just as unhappily, such barriers seem to be necessary for if there is one common denominator for West Indian crowds it is that they are liable to explode into action. Sometimes the action is good-humoured, especially when the hepped-up folk of Queen's Park launch into an impromptu "jump-up".

At other times it is less than amusing, such as the harsh cries from the crowds at Sabina, the bottle-throwing at Bourda, or the deadening chorus of the bottle-bangers at Kensington Oval.

Fights among the crowd were not uncommon. Sometimes these were harmless, isolated punch-ups between two men. However, in one case a man at Queen's Park tried to beat another senseless with a steel seat. These fights seemed to act like detonators. Within seconds hundreds of people would rush to the scene of the incident. By and by the police would sort out the mess and if the police took the culprits away they had a comet's-tail of gawking spectators. Usually the police were extremely tolerant, but one spectator who had his head cut open by a security guard's truncheon at Bourda later started proceedings for an assault charge.

The ugliest scenes of all came with the bottles at Bourda when the crowd were so incensed at the run out of Lloyd, one of the local heroes, that they screamed abuse at Davis for being a silent partner to the run out and then stopped the game for 20 minutes with their bottles.

The bottles were not thrown at the New Zealanders, although there were some near misses, but were more an expression of the crowd's anger at Davis.

The crowd were in an ugly mood, even if they chortled when a young woman dashed out on to the field, heading for Davis who was sitting on the ground near the pitch waiting for the storm to subside. Perhaps she wanted to hug Davis, more likely to indicate her displeasure.

Suddenly came the even uglier sight of a mounted policeman, his long club hoisted high, pursuing the woman. The policeman drew alongside and for a sickening moment appeared to be ready to club her down. Perhaps he relented, or perhaps the woman's swerving run carried her clear of danger. She doubled back to the stand, the policeman's horse stumbled and lost ground when turning and the woman escaped unscathed. So it passed off as a diverting part of the incident. But if the policeman had hit her with the club I feel sure the crowd, steel barricades and all, would have swamped the ground.

Fortunately, most of the other crowd-participation was kept behind the barricades, but it was not always amusing.

At Kensington Oval, for example, there is an old wooden double-deck stand and it is the local habit for a noisy bunch to take their bottles to the top deck. Once the bottles are empty the noise begins. The bottles are banged on the wooden floor and the racket resounds from the sound-shell of the bottom deck. The noise thunders out—"boom, boom, boom-boom-boom"—a savage, head-thumping beat which after 15 or 20 minutes leaves the nerve-edges raw.

There are a variety of triggers for the crowd explosions. Liquor is one, perhaps the most potent. Betting is another, and large amounts change hands. When Lawrence Rowe was bowled for 22 in the first innings of the second test one spectator was $50 richer—he had bet that Rowe would not reach 25. Transistor radios are another factor. They blare away all day and if the announcers suggest that some umpire's decision was doubtful the crowd are likely to react. Cecil Kippins, the stately umpire from Guyana, spoke feelingly about this problem. If Kippins had his way radio broadcasters would be consigned to some distant spot, preferably square on to the pitch, so they could not second-guess or adjudicate on the umpiring decisions and thus excite the crowd.

Umpires sometimes have to work under unusual strain. In the

past they have been threatened with violence, and it was a sad moment when Douglas Sang Hue, one of the finest umpires it would be possible to see, was booed and verbally abused after he had turned down several lbw appeals against the New Zealanders as they fought to save the fifth test on the last afternoon.

When Rowe was heading for his second century in his test debut at Sabina Park the New Zealanders were upset when a very good lbw appeal by Cunis was turned down, and a few minutes later when an even better run out appeal was denied. Rowe was in the 90s at the time, and the crowd were baying for his second historic century. If either appeal had been granted the crowd reaction would have been bitter, and quite possibly physical.

I am not suggesting that the umpires of the time, Sang Hue and Johnny Gale, were influenced by any possible crowd reaction. They are fair and square gentlemen. But they would not be human if they did not think afterward what would have been the reaction if Rowe had been judged out with his second century just round the corner. The newspapers and radio—and Rowe's brilliant form—had built up the image of a superman and the crowd would have reacted, possibly violently, if their latest hero had been given out so close to glory.

Fortunately, not all the crowd reaction was a matter of bottle-throwing and hysterics. They were parochial, unashamedly so, and sometimes they were vastly amusing. Queen's Park, in Port of Spain, could when it wanted produce a special flavour unmatched anywhere in West Indies.

Little Inshan Ali batted bravely in the first innings of the second test. When he came off the field the 1500-odd people in one grandstand greeted him not with the usual rippling handclapping. Instead they clapped in a distinctive, cha-cha-cha kind of rhythm, a quite astonishing impromptu chorus with every clapper strictly in time with the beat.

The New Zealanders, and most other people, came to like a particular bouncy section of the Queen's Park crowd who usually congregated to the left of the broadcasting tower. This was the place for fun, humour and rhythm. Like crowds the world over they liked looking at girls. Whenever some comely lass, usually in bright pants and tight sweater, walked in front of them on her way to a seat this happy bunch would cheer and chortle and cavort—and quite often gallantly escort the girl to her seat. As the day wore on they would form their band. The steel seats were upturned and used as drums. Bottles tapped with knives formed the tenor section.

Anything else that would make a noise was pressed into service. Then off they would go, between overs, when wickets fell, when some local hero did well. Incredibly, this Heath Robinsonish collection could belt out a stunning rhythm in the steel-band manner. Men and women, caught up in the rhythm, danced on the concrete cycling track in front of the band. When it rained they would pound away for hours.

Here, then, might have been the essence of the West Indian cricket crowd—humour, rhythm, music and sheer delight. They should be standard equipment on all grounds.

While the comments and jibes from the spectators lacked the wit and flavour of those which roll down from "the Hill" at the Sydney Cricket Ground, at least one of them was interesting.

When Clive Lloyd was pounding away at the New Zealand bowling in the Guyana match Jack Alabaster had to field one of the thunderbolts. "Did that hurt, Alabaster?" asked a man in the crowd. On being assured by Alabaster that it had, the man replied: "Yeah, man, that's power—Black power."

This was one of the few times that racialism was mentioned in public on the tour. One or two of the players were chided for the fact that there were no Maoris in the side. An invitation for the complainer to nominate a Maori good enough to play usually squashed that argument, and if the discussion persisted the selection of Tom Puna, the Indian-born off-spinner six years ago was the final clincher.

Rebs Ferreira, a Guyana broadcaster and a most helpful man, gloomily predicted that controversy raging over the invitation to the South African Rugby team to tour New Zealand next year could result in the cricketers being regarded with some disfavour in Guyana. Fortunately the prediction came to nothing.

However, most of the West Indies countries were aware of the Springbok tour controversy, and the threatened ban of the 1974 Commonwealth Games if the Rugby tour took place. In fact the threats of CARE and HART were among the few pieces of New Zealand news that appeared in the Caribbean newspapers.

Just after we left Jamaica came the threat from that country that Jamaica would not go to the Games if the Springboks toured, with the hint that other Caribbean countries in the Commonwealth would follow suit. I mentioned this soon afterward to Dr Eric Williams, Prime Minister of Trinidad and Tobago. He seemed unimpressed with Springboks or Commonwealth Games and was more concerned with West Indies chances of beating New Zealand at cricket.

Still, as a visitor from a country apparently under fire from the UN downward for maintaining sporting ties with South Africa, it was not uninteresting to regard discrimination in reverse in some of the West Indian countries.

In Guyana, for example, several Indians spoke to us of the discrimination against them by the Negro party controlled by Forbes Burnham. It was Burnham who in 1970 wanted to ban Gary Sobers from playing in Guyana after Sobers had competed in a double-wicket tournament in Rhodesia. The Indians, so they told us, were discriminated against in employment in both the civil service and police.

In Barbados a white broadcaster was politely told that he could not be engaged by a local radio station. If he had not been white, he was told, the problem would not have arisen.

So, as we travelled about the Caribbean perhaps we were entitled to a wry smile at the reports that New Zealand was condoning, if not encouraging, discrimination in South Africa by maintaining sporting contacts with the Springboks.

# 5

# *Jamaica: Land of Soon-Come*

Jamaica, the land of contrasts, of confused impressions—of people with great wealth and heritage in a country of unsurpassed beauty living together with the impoverished, the unemployed and the unemployable of the packing-crate shacks.

I do not wish to pose as a three-week expert on Jamaica, for I doubt whether the confusions and contrast would meld into a single impression given three years or three decades.

First impressions, they say, are lasting. On that basis I should have left Kingston and Jamaica as quickly as I arrived. Immediately after landing in the stifling heat of Palisadoes airport I taxied to the offices of the *Gleaner* newspaper, and from there intended to go at about 9 o'clock at night to the cable office. A *Gleaner* reporter said it was a short drive, along such-and-such a street, turn right, left and there you were. I said I would walk. He frowned, summoned a company driver and instructed him to drive me to the cable office, back to my hotel, and not to let me out his sight.

This gracious man, Campbell, whose father had been, he said, a great singer, drove me to the cable office bemoaning the violence of down-town Kingston. As we passed down narrow streets, with dark figures loitering in the doorways, I could see what he meant. I had a typewriter and briefcase with me and asked Campbell what chance I would have walking those streets at night.

"No chance with those hags, sah," said Campbell, "no chance at all. Maybe it be OK if you drop the bags and run, but just as likely they knock you down and then go back for the bags. There are bad people, bad young people in this town."

Campbell, bless him, delivered me safely to the cable office and to my hotel which was placed in a rather quieter part of Kingston.

Contrasts. The next day, as the New Zealanders trained at Sabina Park, there were a group of elderly men watching. One came and stood close to me. Five minutes passed. Then he asked if I was a New Zealander, and if I could tell him the names of the players batting and bowling. This I did, we chatted for a while and he left to join his friends.

Five minutes later he and his friends were back again.

"I have come," he said, "to introduce my friends as a mark of respect for your kindness." With courtly grace he introduced each in turn, wished me a happy stay in Jamaica and left.

Contrasts. Driving round the Beverly Hills area on the heights overlooking Kingston, a place where architects and open cheque-books meet to form houses of remarkable style and cost. Or walking (quickly) past some of the dives and hovels of indescribable stench a chain or two from the cricket ground at Sabina Park.

Such contrasts, such confusions—at least to the middle-class New Zealander knowing little of opulence or real poverty—were vivid, raw impressions, repellent to the mind as well as the nostrils.

Yet it was not long before the subtle charm of the Land of Soon-Come began to take hold. I spoke, I hope not with disgust, to well-educated Jamaicans of these sights and sounds of such marked inequality.

It was ever thus, they said. Over the years of colonial rule, with money pouring in from the vast sugar-cane estates, and in the recent years of self-government, inequality was the common denominator. There had always been haves and have-nots, and if much of the British wealth had gone, Jamaicans themselves were still building a two-tier society. There was still talk of graft in high places, and poverty in low places.

There was unemployment and slum housing, they said. But many of the unemployed did not want work and, as the local government had recently found, many slum-dwellers refused to move from their tar-and-paper ghetto to little concrete boxes that were being provided for them.

Behind it all, so it seems, is the Jamaicans' inbuilt respect and reliance on the family-system. A member of the family without work or bed was provided for by the rest of the family. There is a strong matriarchal backbone to this society, with the family group frequently dominated either by the mother or grand-mother. The mother had become the dominating factor over several generations, perhaps because over those same generations not every child could be sure who the father was.

So, under this charm of the Land of Soon-Come the raw edges of the first impressions of Kingston and Jamaica began to soften and to heal; and with the healing the realisation that here was a land of culture, of tradition, of quite remarkable pride in a country built of people of many races.

The New Zealander is not normally a time-conscious bird, no matter how often the New Zealanders' bus waited while someone—"if Jarvis is here, we are all here" quite often was the cry—came along late. But within a day or so of arrival we were, as the Americans say, getting uptight about the slap-happy Jamaican attitude toward time. The waiters at the Courtleigh Manor Hotel seemed to take ages to fill the simplest order. We thought this was because they were to be rewarded from an overall service charge, and not from individual tipping.

Chapple came in beaming a few days after we arrived. He had, said Chapple, been talking with the manager of the firm that produced the local beer, Red Stripe. In his tactful way Chapple had said, and quite truthfully, that the boys enjoyed Red Stripe very much. This brought from the manager the glad news that tomorrow the team would receive not only a generous free supply of Red Stripe, but that it would be stored in a refrigerator outside Chapple's room. Naturally, Chapple spoke of this promise, soon to become a fact, with some pride. A day went by, another, no beer and words were spoken about Chapple.

Being a man of action Chapple phoned the brewery. The truck bearing the manna had been organised, in fact it had left the day before. That it hadn't arrived did not disturb the brewery. Perhaps the truck had broken down, or some other calamity had befallen it.

In a word, the beer would arrive, soon-come. And so it did.

Soon-come to the Jamaicans is what the day after manana is to the Mexicans.

The subtle charm of the land and the people began to take effect. Within a week any delay in the team arrangements, any waiter who had disappeared without trace, anything that did not arrive on schedule. . . . Ah, well, soon-come.

The charm is also insidious. The late-comers to the bus would shrug their shoulders. "Sorry I'm late, chaps, soon-come."

So within a week or so of this blandishment it was possible to sit back and enjoy Kingston, Jamaica, Jamaicans—even the fact that it seemed impossible to dismiss their Sabina Park fixture, Lawrence Rowe. "We'll get him out, soon-come."

And there is much to enjoy in Kingston, for cricket and cricketers are held in high esteem. There was time to eat grilled shrimps with the stars twinkling up from the swimming pool while the local combo twisted tunes into Jamaican tempo. Time to sit in the balmy night air, and be introduced to the ways of rum-drinking by Allan Rae, one of the many gentlemen of Jamaican and West Indies cricket.

There was time to sit on the terrace of the Casa Monte and look over the lights of Kingston, to nibble at Red Pea soup and barbecued lobster and to sip benedictine with what must be the best coffee in the world.

You could even sit back in the taxi and wonder whether this latest son of Henry Morgan would rob you blind, or disarm you by charging a dollar or two less than the previous rogue who had taken you on the same trip the day before. Taxi-drivers in Kingston are a special breed of men. They have nerves much harder than the steel in their cars for Kingston must be a panel-beaters' paradise. They have a raucous horn which can run though a whole scale of imprecations, abuse, warning, greetings . . . or which can be blown for no reason at all. They can knife through the smallest gap, one hand on the wheel, the other on the horn . . . or they can stop with a shuddering halt if a dog runs in front of them.

And in daytime downtown Kingston need not be a nerve-wracking hole in the corner place. The Jamaican has a distinctive walk, head up, shoulders back, arms swinging almost military fashion past slim hips. It is a proud, almost insolent walk and when you see a Jamaican lass go by, straight of back, slim of hip and leg, with a micro-mini skirt flouncing from her chubby derriere your realise that midis and maxis will never overtake this land.

Perhaps we didn't really appreciate Jamaica, Kingston-style, until the New Zealanders spent five days at Montego Bay for the match against the President's Eleven.

There are some Jamaicans who look upon tourism as the last economic hope of a land with dwindling natural resources. There are those who regard tourism, at least Montego Bay style, as an evil, however necessary, which must not be allowed to strangle the Jamaicans' natural existence.

After spending a short time at Montego Bay, with its beach-side hotels, its crystal-clear water and its depressingly drab town-ship I am inclined to agree with the latter hope. Winter-bound Americans flock to places such as Montego Bay, money-minded Jamaicans devise ways of separating the Yank from his dollar.

One cricket official there spoke with pride of the home he was building amid the magnificent native bush on the hills over-looking the Montego Bay airport. It would cost him 90,000

Jamaican dollars. Then he would rent it to Americans for $700 a week in the winter and $400-$500 a week in the summer.

There are various ways of lightening the tourist's wallet. The Montego taxi-drivers made the Kingston variety seem like Boy Scouts doing their good deed for the day. You can find a hotel bill blithely charging $2.50 for lodging a collect overseas call, or charging $3.50 a day for the use of the garage, even if you do not have a car and there is no garage in sight.

It is a frenetic and, to the casual Kiwi eye, unhealthy atmosphere with pale and often querulous Americans and other tourists paying through the nose for a brief and artificial glimpse of Jamaican life.

The whole point of the exercise was brought home to me by one Montego Bay hotel-keeper.

"This place only needs two things to really make it go. One is legalised gambling. The other is legalised abortion. If we had those we would really be in business."

When I asked if legalised gambling and the setting up of casino concessions might not attract the syndicate money and influence from the States he replied: "Sure, and why not. So we get the Mafia. So you stay in line and make it. Or you don't stay in line and get dead. We have got our own little Mafia here already."

There is a strong under-current of violence in the land and, to the New Zealand mind, a blase attitude to the value of human life. Some houses still have grillwork which prohibits entry to the bottom storey of their house, and some businessmen still carry revolvers in the glove-box of their car.

And it came strange to New Zealand eyes to see the crowd at Sabina Park being patrolled by policemen bearing truncheons, very often with grim crash-helmets cramping their faces into some Neanderthal primitiveness. Some would have bags of tear-gas grenades, others a cylinder of Mace on their belts and, on one occasion, bearing riot guns.

Yet this could be taken almost as a microcosm of Jamaican life. At one end of the ground the fashionable members' pavilion, with waiters bearing drinks, with billiards rooms and other evidence of upper-crust life. At the other end of the ground people who could stand with their hands hooked into wire-netting for hours on end without moving a muscle, as some passive demonstration that they could expect nothing more. And always the policemen with their truncheons as if to indicate that even at such a great sporting occasion violence lurked not far below the surface.

ɩawrence Rowe (above), all poise ɩnd power, and Roy Fredericks, ˈith everything flying, hitting ɩrough the covers during their 69-run stand in the first test at abina. Rowe scored 214, redericks 163.

Holford has the ball; Davis who dropped the catch, wishes the ground would swallow him up and Burgess sighs with relief at his escape. West Indies dropped seven catches that day, the first of the second test at Queen's Park.

Mark Burgess, Terry Jarvis, Graham Vivian, Glenn Turner and, at far right, the bowler Bruce Taylor, raise their arms as Ken Wadsworth catches David Holford during the West Indies first innings of the third test.

Jamaicans will cram every inch of Sabina Park. They will hang on the fence, sit in the trees, perch anywhere that can give a view of their great love. I liked the several hundreds who used to thread their way up the 150ft floodlight pylons skirting the ground. If it is symbolism you want, take the brave soul who climbed to the very top, sat astride the highest bank of floodlights and there, in the sun and wind, flung his arms wide in defiance at the groundlings below. Symbolism, perhaps, the spirit of Jamaica rampant.

Sabina Park, too, meant a press box with the best view possible and, when the air-conditioning worked, a Shangri-La of cool, clean air amid the heat and smells outside. The press box, too, meant meeting Jack Anderson, the doyen of Jamaican cricket writers, a man of charm to match his bulk. Jack is a large man, with kindly eyes crinkling below his curly greying hair. While working at the *Gleaner* office I had much to do with Jack, and no man could be kinder or more in love with cricket.

There are many facets to the diamond that is Jamaica. The rich, the poor, the mansions, the hovels, the crisp lasses in the street, the prostitutes in abundance (including one large lass with a bellow that announced at 40 yards range that she was "Josephine, the sex machine"). On one hand the superb University of West Indies campus at Mona, a place of liberal ideas as spacious as their surroundings. On the other hand primary schools with 60 to a class, not enough teachers to go round and producing waifs who would scrounge for "ten cents Misteer" as you quit Sabina Park, and who mutter some unintelligible curse at you when you pass them by.

Yet my one lasting impression of Jamaica was of children. The schools were shut on the Friday the New Zealanders played at Montego Bay. From everywhere came the schoolchildren, the boys all dressed in light cotton khaki, the girls in brightly coloured smocks of different hue.

Compared with New Zealand children of the same age they were as crisp and clean as a spring day. I remarked on this to a Montego Bay man. Ah yes, he told me, the children take great pride in their appearance. They might only have one uniform but it was always spotless. They would stand in a bus rather than crease it by sitting down.

If those children became as proud of their country as they are of their uniforms Jamaica, for all its inequality, its pangs of nationhood, its violence, will become a place far richer than tourist dollars can make it. Perhaps, and soon-come.

First match. —— v. University of West Indies, Mona, Feburary 3. New Zealand won by 104 runs.

This became a pleasant, if one-sided romp against a keen but not very strong side not well versed in the arts of limited-over cricket—and it might also have produced the first skirmish of the tour.

Amid the hustle and bustle of settling down in Kingston and casting off their travel weariness, the New Zealanders looked forward to this one-day game as their first real workout before the game against Jamaica, the Shell Shield leaders, two days later.

So there were a few frowns when the UWI officials, headed by a kindly man, Charles Mills, asked that the game be played on a 40-over basis. Not good, said the New Zealanders. A limited-over match might not allow all the batsmen adequate time in the middle. It could also mean a loss, something the New Zealanders thought would affect their image so early in the tour. So on and so forth the discussions ranged.

But good sense prevailed. Chapple and Dowling, rather than promote the slightest unpleasantness at such a sensitive time of the tour, agreed to play a 40-over game. It was a good piece of public relations and, in the event, New Zealand were never in danger of being embarrassed.

There were more frowns after the game. One of the umpires complained that Cunis, after being no-balled, had used what could loosely be termed unparliamentary language to the umpire. Cunis demurred. The various officials discussed the matter, and within a few minutes all was forgotten and forgiven. Next morning the *Gleaner* mentioned the incident and remarked that Cunis had apologised to the umpire. This did produce a fruity word or two from Cunis, especially after he had been telephoned by a free-lance columnist and been given a free and lengthy lecture on how cricketers should behave in the West Indies.

Chapple's face took on an interesting hue, words were said in the right ears, the ripples in the tea-cup subsided and all was peace again.

In between the frowns the cricket was interesting without being exciting. The UWI campus at Mona is expansive and they are justly proud of its beauty and facilities. The cricket oval is a fine one, too, with a backdrop of wooded hills and mountains, and in the middle is a pitch more suited to a 40-day rather than a 40-over match.

In the pre-match warm-up the New Zealanders, especially the new chums, regarded this hard-baked, smooth, grassless strip with interest (if they were batsmen) and horror (if they were bowlers).

Still, the UWI captain did the right thing and put New Zealand in to bat, and one sensed that this might have been a result of Chapple's diplomacy of a few days before.

The UWI bowling was enthusiastic, but of no great speed or menace. Dowling and Turner started pleasantly enough, with Turner looking decidedly interesting as he adjusted quickly to the conditions and was soon driving "on the up", to show that on these pitches the ball was unlikely to deviate off the pitch.

Both were gone by 87 after scoring at a crisp rate, and then Congdon and Burgess let fly, the runs came in at five an over, Congdon reached 50 in an hour, 50 runs came in 27 minutes and by lunch New Zealand were 146 for two wickets.

Burgess was even quicker than Congdon, with 50 in even time and he had hit 13 fours before he took aim at the sightscreen, under-clubbed a little and was caught near the boundary. He had batted only 76 minutes for his 78 runs and his power of stroke, especially off the back foot, gave the immediate impression that he would be one of the successes of the tour.

Congdon was no less impressive for he found that on such a true pitch he could play some of his more exotic strokes with safety—especially some meaty thumps through midwicket from outside the off stump and those special cuts when he seems to be heading toward the square leg umpire.

By 2.45 New Zealand were 238 for three when they ran out of overs—a striking rate of almost six an over—and the UWI batsmen would have to hit furiously to catch up with that target.

Curiously enough, the UWI batting had little of the usual undergraduate enthusiasm, especially after Taylor had dismissed Sebastian and Ishmael with consecutive balls with the score at 12. Jarvis stopped a hot drive, fell as he knocked the ball down and then fired in a superb return to run out Narayansingh at 20, thereby giving Campbell, the apprentice wicketkeeper, his first taste of blood.

Thereafter UWI buttoned up. Their captain, Howell, who had played Shell Shield cricket for the Combined Islands, scored a solid 59 but the rest muddled along without any apparent idea about the special techniques of limited-over games.

Vivian picked up two quick wickets, Jarvis wangled his way to the crease long enough to bowl his quaint leg-breaks and Campbell made Jarvis' bowling look even more respectable with a snappy stumping of Howell at the fag-end of the game.

So UWI were 134 for eight at the close and in their droll way some of the students regarded the result as a draw, so everyone was happy.

The New Zealanders enjoyed their entree to the tour, for if the pitches were to be as hard and unsympathetic to bowlers as this one was the batsmen, at least, would flourish.

They also had their first taste of the boisterous West Indian crowd. The grandstand was small, but it was packed and every boundary, every thump on the pad, every catch produced a booming staccato roar from the lusty throats around us.

From time to time, too, someone would leap up with a banknote in his hand and challenge someone else, usually 10 or 15 yards away, to some sort of bet. Money changed hands frequently, and never quietly.

We were interested, for perhaps we could have had a small flutter ourselves. Alas, the local patois was delivered at machine-gun velocity, and the time the offer had been translated for us someone else had accepted the bet.

New Zealand: (40 overs) 238 for three wickets (B. Congdon 89 not out, M. Burgess 78, G. Turner 38; C. Alleyne one for 31). University of West Indies: (40 overs) 134 for eight wickets (A. Howell 59, A. Daisley 24; B. Taylor two for 20, G. Vivian two for 31).

New Zealand won by 104 runs.

Second match. —— v. Jamaica, Sabina Park, February 5, 7, 8, 9. Drawn.

There was a test team look about the New Zealand side for the first big tour game, except that Taylor was still waiting in the wings. Collinge and Alabaster had looked most promising in the net practices and the Jamaicans, who have a healthy regard for size, were already talking of the 6ft 5in 16-stone Collinge as the danger-man in the coming tests.

Collinge, they said, was just the kind of bowler to make the most of the early life and speed of the Sabina Park pitch. Then, with the same regard for size and weight, they got the biggest roller they could find and for a week did their best to squeeze the life out of the bare, bony pitch.

The New Zealanders were jumpy as kittens before the match. This was a key game, the first chance to make the kind of impression that would influence their play, and possibly their crowd appeal, for the whole tour. Dowling spoke before the game of a cautious outlook. He had planned for several months for the tour and took the realistic view that the accent should be not to lose a game in Jamaica. There would be time afterward to work out plans and tactics. For the moment the cautious view was the best.

Jamaica, on the other hand, were buoyant and confident. They were leading the Shell Shield competition after topping Guyana on the first innings a day beforehand. At some time or another eight or nine Jamaicans were nominated as possibilities for the first test side the following week.

Funnily enough, one of the names mentioned only seldom was Lawrence Rowe.

## FIRST DAY

"Phew, it's hot," said Wadsworth after the knock-around in front of the large, boisterous crowd. Sabina Park is very enclosed and the heat beat down fiercely.

"Phew, it's going to get hotter," said someone else when Dowling came back to say that he had lost the toss and that Jamaica were batting.

There was a growling buzz round the ground as Collinge bounded in for the first ball of the match and you could almost see the New Zealanders quail when the ball, of reasonable length and speed, went through at about bail-height and had Wadsworth taking it near his shins. Collinge tried a bouncer and Samuel Morgan played it off his hip. So much for the early speed and life of Sabina.

Morgan, a slim lad, batted pleasantly. He hooked another Collinge bouncer for four and a backfoot drive off Cunis through mid-off had Cunis' mouth drop open, as if this was scant respect for a bowler recently playing for the Rest of the World.

After an hour it was obvious that in such stifling heat heavily-built bowlers such as Collinge and Cunis could not keep up their vigour for more than half-a-dozen overs, so Congdon took over and soon had Desmond Lewis, apparently only a shade of the man who had kept wickets and opened for West Indies the year before, lbw at 68.

Enter Rowe and soon it was 84 for one at lunch, with Morgan gliding along smoothly to 51. Not bad, thought the New Zealanders, for the bowling had been tolerably accurate and the fielding on the hard, bumpy surface looked keen and competent.

Not at all bad, they said, when a brilliant stop and throw by Burgess ran out Morgan at 121. Better things to come. Maurice Foster, another West Indies batsman, tried to cut the first ball he received from Alabaster, did not pick the googly and Turner held the catch at first slip.

Another Alabaster googly, or perhaps the top-spinner, and Easton McMorris, veteran of many a test, was leg-before. Four for 138. The Jamaicans munched their peanuts and were strangely quiet.

Soon they had something to shout about. Rowe, his dark face impassive, started to hit for the boundary. There were nine fours in his 50 and a meaty whack for six off Alabaster soon afterward.

Yet the New Zealanders did not seem disturbed for Rowe's partner, Renford Pinnock, a stocky little man, was given to so many nudges and miscues that he seemed certain to disappear at any moment. He jumped about as if he had stones in his shoes and when Collinge whistled a short ball past his tummy Pinnock looked as if he would prefer to be elsewhere.

But suddenly Pinnock was forgotten as Rowe took control. By tea they were 197 for four and Rowe looked magnificent. Cover drives of sublime timing made mock of Dowling's field-settings. There were deft little cuts and bread-and-butter chips for ones and twos through mid-on. Alabaster smiled a little when Rowe swept a leg-spinner for four, for it looked a risky stroke and perhaps the first chink in his armour. So Rowe, still Sphinx-like of face, kept on sweeping, the wrists rolling over perfectly, the ball never leaving the ground and whoever was fielding at long leg soon had to sprint this way and that as Rowe swept where he wasn't.

By now the Jamaicans had forgotten their peanuts and were greeting each Rowe stroke with a baying roar. Inevitably came his 100, in 198 minutes and only then did we find that Rowe's employers, an air-conditioning firm, had promised him a dollar-a-run bonus whenever he scored a century.

A minute or two later there was another forbidding sight—Collinge limping through his long run, and gesturing as if he had tweaked a hamstring muscle. He tried his short run, but was lame and had to go.

With Rowe so much the attraction everyone forgot about Pinnock. Somehow he acquired runs and by stumps, at 280 for four wickets, he was 52 not out, a shadowy innings compared with Rowe's 124 not out, but already Pinnock had helped in a 142-run stand for the fifth wicket, so perhaps his batting was not quite as eccentric as it looked.

The New Zealanders had time to lick their wounds that night and during the next day, a rest day. They talked of the phenomenal Rowe, of the heartless pitch, the heat, the noisy crowd. Some of them whistled in the dark that Rowe would disappear next day. But no one could think how.

## SECOND DAY

After 35 minutes delay while the soft run-up dried there was the encouraging sign of Collinge, apparently restored to health, pounding in with the new ball. That was all the encouragement the New Zealanders got.

Rowe went on and on, even more implacable than on the first day, his strokes even more assertive—and Pinnock just as adhesive. Jamaica were 329 for four by lunch.

After lunch Rowe was 150, with 82 in boundaries. Jamaica were 350 . . . where would it end?

Howarth was recalled, Pinnock prodded forward inside the right line and Turner dived to his right for a splendid catch. Rowe and Pinnock had added 222 in 266 minutes and Jamaica were 360 for five.

Still Alabaster could flight and turn the ball. He undid Barrett with a leg-break, and Haye with a top-spinner, but Rowe went commandingly on, reached his 200 in 415 minutes and, for the first time, relaxed. He banged away four fours, cut at Alabaster, Wadsworth held the catch and the New Zealanders applauded as warmly as anyone—and probably with more feeling—as Rowe marched off.

Howarth finished off the tail, tea-time, and the next big test as Turner and Dowling went out to see if they could lead New Zealand to somewhere near Jamaica's mountainous 451.

Dowe, a sturdy short man with the inevitable chain and medallion round his neck, immediately made it hard for he skidded one through, Dowling played back and was lbw with the total at three. Fortunately Turner stayed firm, so did Congdon after a nasty whack in the tummy from a Dowe bouncer and New Zealand fought through to 44 for one at the close.

More talk and theory that night as the New Zealanders rested their weary muscles and tried to analyse how to bat Jamaican style. There was a touch of confidence to the talk. The New Zealanders felt they were technically as good, if not better, than the Jamaicans—Rowe always accepted. What the Jamaicans could do New Zealand might well do better.

## THIRD DAY

For 90 minutes it seemed as if the New Zealand theory was right. Congdon breezed along to 50 without much trouble and Turner handled Dowe and Lawson very tidily.

Suddenly things went wrong, very wrong. Turner was taken at the wicket from the off-spinner, Campbell. Burgess steered a full toss from Barrett straight to Dowe. Hastings gave Foster a sharp return catch. Congdon swung across Foster's line and was caught. Wadsworth blasted one four and was caught trying to do it again. Dowe removed Jarvis and Cunis with skidders. Collinge was run out and Alabaster hit himself out.

In just over two hours New Zealand had lost nine wickets for 70 runs, and this on a pitch that was supposed to be a batsman's joy. To make it worse at least half the wickets were offered up with bad shots, mad shots or no shots at all.

The Sabina crowd howled with glee at New Zealand's humiliation, and howled even louder when Dowe had Turner taken at the wicket in his second over of the follow-on. Another wicket and it could have been a calamity, so Dowling and Congdon dug in and were 45 for one at stumps.

That night the talk among the players became urgent, for New Zealand were 250 behind and defeat was round the corner. Forget Dowe, Lawson and Haye. The spinners, Barrett, Foster and Campbell were the problems.

Frank Mooney wondered aloud how Foster and Campbell, bowling quickish off-spin with a drift away to the slips, could be scored from through McMorris' shrewd field. This was a new dimension, a new type of attack backed by a field shrewdly placed and demanding risky shots if runs were to come. Barrett, with his turn and bounce, was another problem. But how to score runs under these conditions? For if the New Zealanders did not score runs they would almost certainly get themselves out trying to break the cordon. It was not one of the happiest nights of the tour.

## FOURTH DAY

By now none of the New Zealanders remarked on the stifling Sabina heat. It was there, it would have to be endured.

Soon McMorris was at the New Zealanders' throats again. Dowe and Barrett, then Foster and Campbell. Congdon, brave Congdon, clipped and chipped a few fours, reached 50 in 161 minutes and then extracted from Foster his first boundary in 16 overs. Grim, tough going, with the crowd screeching for blood, but Congdon and Dowling stuck fast and posted a 100 together in three hours.

Dowling, still searching for his old touch, got a four through the covers off Haye, burly and medium-fast. Out of the woods? Not yet, for Congdon walked round Foster and lost his leg stump at 126 for two and, as if in sympathy, Dowling hit a full toss back to Barrett and it was 129 for three.

Burgess and Hastings after lunch, and almost no Burgess when Haye dropped a cut off Lawson at gully. Something had to give.

After so much spin McMorris took the new ball after 82 overs. Perhaps he had not picked that Hastings was not happy against the spinners, or that Burgess could not find the gaps. Or perhaps he thought that Dowe would do the job.

Five overs and 25 runs later McMorris certainly regretted his ploy. Relishing the freedom Burgess and Hastings scored 50 in 55 minutes as they counter-attacked superbly.

Gone was Hastings' hesitancy, out came Burgess' back-foot power. Within an hour they broke Jamaica's grip. Back came Foster and away went Burgess, missing as he hit across the line and Jarvis, playing back, went to Dowe at 229 for five with 100 minutes to go.

More tremors, then, for out came the wayward Wadsworth to stand with Hastings. I had chipped Wadsworth after his brief, lusty first innings. "Not again," said Wadsworth, as his strong jaw jutted out. "Next time I won't be so easy."

He wasn't. Seldom has anyone played so straight so often. Speed or spin, they bounced off Wadsworth while Hastings, taking heart, did the right thing and played shots. Within 40 minutes the crisis was over, and all that remained was the question whether Hastings would have time for his 100. He cut it rather fine, for as Foster bowled the last over Hasting marched straight out at him, hit the ball superbly and it sailed over the sightscreen for the six and the century.

It was a good, bold and brave blow—the perfect finish for such a fine innings. It showed, too, that there was some fight in these New Zealanders . . . for they would obviously need it in the harder days ahead.

That night, gaiety. Some of the mysteries of Jamaica-style cricket—the bowling pattern, field-settings, the batting methods —had been seen, even if not completely solved. The New Zealanders knew they had escaped defeat by a narrow margin. But, more than that, they felt they had learned a tremendous amount and were quite prepared to analyse and store the knowledge away.

## JAMAICA

| *First Innings* | | | *Bowling* | O. | M. | R. | W. |
|---|---|---|---|---|---|---|---|
| S. Morgan run out | 62 | | | | | | |
| D. Lewis lbw b Congdon | 24 | | Collinge | 24 | 6 | 80 | 0 |
| L. Rowe c Wadsworth b Alabaster | 227 | | Cunis | 32 | 8 | 70 | 0 |
| M. Foster c Turner b Alabaster | 0 | | Congdon | 17 | 1 | 60 | 1 |
| E. McMorris lbw b Alabaster | 11 | | Alabaster | 37 | 2 | 130 | 5 |
| R. Pinnock c Turner b Howarth | 84 | | Howarth | 27.3 | 3 | 94 | 3 |
| A. Barrett b Alabaster | 10 | | | | | | |
| W. Haye c Turner b Alabaster | 2 | | | | | | |
| C. Campbell not out | 11 | | | | | | |
| U. Dowe b Howarth | 0 | | | | | | |
| C. Lawson c Collinge b Howarth | 3 | | | | | | |
| Extras (b4 lb8 nb5) | 17 | | | | | | |
| Total | 451 | | | | | | |

Fall: 68, 121, 124, 138, 360, 391, 399, 446, 447.

## NEW ZEALANDERS

| *First Innings* | | *Second Innings* | |
|---|---|---|---|
| G. Turner c Lewis b Campbell | 31 | c Lewis b Dowe | 7 |
| G. Dowling lbw b Dowe | 0 | c and b Barrett | 43 |
| B. Congdon c McMorris b Foster | 66 | b Foster | 73 |
| M. Burgess c Dowe b Barrett | 13 | b Foster | 36 |
| B. Hastings c and b Foster | 0 | not out | 100 |
| T. Jarvis lbw b Dowe | 8 | b Dowe | 5 |
| K. Wadsworth c Lawson b Barrett | 8 | not out | 35 |
| R. Cunis b Dowe | 7 | | |
| J. Alabaster c Lawson b Barrett | 9 | | |
| R. Collinge run out | 4 | | |
| H. Howarth not out | 4 | | |
| Extras (b5 nb1) | 6 | (lb9 nb1) | 10 |
| Total | 156 | (for five wickets) | 309 |

Fall: 3, 86, 113, 114, 115, 129, 136, 141, 151. — 7, 126, 129, 200, 229.

*Bowling*

| | O. | M. | R. | W. | O. | M. | R. | W. |
|---|---|---|---|---|---|---|---|---|
| Dowe | 18 | 7 | 31 | 3 | 29 | 7 | 69 | 2 |
| Lawson | 13 | 3 | 20 | 0 | 13 | 1 | 35 | 0 |
| Barrett | 29 | 13 | 40 | 3 | 32 | 10 | 73 | 1 |
| Campbell | 18 | 3 | 35 | 1 | 22 | 7 | 31 | 0 |
| Haye | 3 | 0 | 10 | 0 | 10 | 2 | 30 | 0 |
| Foster | 12 | 6 | 14 | 2 | 33 | 15 | 42 | 2 |
| Morgan | — | — | — | — | 5 | 1 | 17 | 0 |
| Rowe | — | — | — | — | 1 | 0 | 2 | 0 |

Third match. —— v. President's Eleven, Jarrett Park, Montego Bay. February 11, 12, 13, 14. Drawn.

Shocks galore. No Vivian in the New Zealand side, no Campbell. What goes on, I asked Chapple as he released the side. That is the side, said Chapple blandly.

Not everyone was bland. Vivian and Campbell bit the bullet and took the blow bravely. They had played, but not batted at Mona. They had not played at Sabina.

If they did not play at Montego Bay they certainly would not play in the first test. This would mean that their first action would be at Antigua in the three-dayer against the Leewards—a month after the tour started.

Blofeld, the free-lancer, suggested that the tour selectors were being dense, for Blofeld is not given to the more earthy Kiwi slang.

It mattered not that the President's XI looked strong, with a crop of bright young men of West Indies cricket knocking on the test door—or, in Findlay's case, knocking again after being dropped the previous year. The selectors had decided that the first test team must be built as quickly as possible. Jarvis figured in their test plans. Vivian and Campbell did not. Ergo, Jarvis in, Vivian and Campbell out—with Cunis and Alabaster put on ice to be fresh for the test.

So to the fleshpots of Montego Bay, with its scads of tourists, piratical taxi-drivers and a pleasantly spacious ground made all the more pleasant by the hordes of crisply-clean schoolchildren.

The pitch was something else. Hard, brown and shiny, and surrounded by a bare and quick outfield. The New Zealanders offered a silent prayer about the toss, and almost hugged Dowling when he won it.

The top brass of West Indies were there, too, for the test side would be announced during the game. They had come to watch Campbell, Lawson and Morgan, whom the New Zealanders had played at Sabina. Kallicharran, the little Guyanese was warmly spoken of as a test batting prospect. So was Jumadeen, with a healthy bag of Shell Shield wickets coming from his left-arm spinners, and there was always Bernard Julien, a batsman and left-arm bowler of such varied skills that he sounded like a budding Sobers.

## FIRST DAY

If the New Zealanders had learned something at Sabina they hardly showed it before lunch, even if they did not lose a wicket. In two hours they were 52, with Turner struggling along for 14 of them and Kallicharran regretting a dropped chance from Dowling the first time he played at Jumadeen.

After lunch it was a little better. The bowling was of modest quality, even if Matthews, a sturdy Guyanese medium-fast bowler, could glower and scowl and squawk whenever he forced a false stroke. There were not many, for the pitch was perfect, too perfect in fact, and as the afternoon roasted on Dowling and Turner made the most of it.

They weren't fast. Tea came at 161, by which time the President's bowlers were limp, and both had their centuries by stumps—Dowling in 300 minutes, Turner in 314 and by the end the score was 226.

So the New Zealanders went away rejoicing to look up the record books and dwell on the pleasure of the morrow. If this was the cream of West Indies' young cricketers, what must the milk underneath be like?

## SECOND DAY

The President's XI had some new ideas, so Jumadeen bowled to six on the leg side, but Dowling and Turner went blissfully on until, somehow, Matthews beat Dowling's stroke and had him lbw for 124, with New Zealand 268.

But there was no rest for the young hopefuls. They cast their field wide, so Turner and Jarvis dawdled on picking up singles when they could, but seldom taking risks.

Lunch, 308 for one, with Turner 158. The figures poured in, even if the runs did not. A 50 stand in 82 minutes, 100 stand in 134, then Turner's 200 in 530 minutes. Turner had set out to prove to himself and the team that what Rowe could do a New Zealander could do. So he did it, even if he only managed five fours in his second 100 after hitting 15 in his first.

Having proved his point, and worn himself completely out, Turner had a dip and the best his fatigued frame could do was to hit a catch as far as mid-on. Jarvis, 51 in 169 minutes, left five runs later at 390 for three. It was hardly a test-class innings, but he had a good long bat and that was what he needed after his brief appearances at Sabina.

Having reduced the President's bowling to pulp, New Zealand unkindly let Burgess and Taylor loose. They hammered away happily, taking 56 runs from five overs of the new ball, and had scored 96 in 59 minutes before Burgess was out and Dowling took pity and closed at 486 for four in 608 minutes.

Baichan, a left-hander, and Morgan were in at 4.50, and away at 5.22 when bad light stopped play. They had 19 runs and as neither Webb nor Collinge could do much with this incredible pitch they promised many more the next day.

## THIRD DAY

Webb and Collinge were not exactly menacing, but Taylor, at his first appearance, had Morgan taken at first slip and the President's XI were 48 for one.

They might have been 70 for three had the catches stuck. Jarvis put down Kallicharran when 15, and got a painfully bruised finger, and Wadsworth should have caught Baichan at 25. So it was lunch at 83 for one, and already Kallicharran was looking good and Baichan was becoming tedious, with 28 in 152 minutes and not a stroke to remember.

Dowling tossed the ball to Burgess, Burgess sent down a full toss to Kallicharran, Kallicharran hit to Dowling, and it was 134 for two. Burgess saw the joke, but Kallicharran did not, for it probably meant his chance of a test cap had gone, at least for the first test.

One could only admire Baichan's concentration, if not his methods. He arrived at 50 in 246 minutes while a burly young man, Irving Shillingford, looked liable to disappear at any moment.

They stayed to stumps at 219 for two even after a solid spell from Webb who was starting to look at something near test form. The first day brought 226 runs, the second 279, the third 200—this was adding-machine cricket gone mad, with the players and the pitch sharing the blame.

## FOURTH DAY

The weather was hot, but the catching was not. Shillingford gave chances at 54, 61 and 64, and the bowling lost whatever steam it had. Baichan, now an utter bore, ground on and on until, quite out of the blue, Congdon bowled almost at yorker length, Baichan missed and his off stump toppled down. He had batted 444 minutes for his 96. It was bad luck about his hundred, but he was not really regretted.

Shillingford was another matter. The longer he lasted, the better he got. His century arrived, with a crisp drive for four from Howarth, in 284 minutes. Slow going, but still the fastest of the match.

So Shillingford decided to enjoy himself. He banged a four through the covers and then picked Collinge off middle stump and whacked him over midwicket for six. The crowd roared,

Collinge fumed, so Shillingford did precisely the same to the next ball.

This rich stuff was like a shot of adrenalin to everyone, especially Collinge. He bowled de Souza and soon Julien was run out. Still the President's XI were 356 for five, with two hours to play. Nothing much else could happen on this pitch.

Up came Howarth and bowled Shillingford with a quicker, flatter ball. Six for 359. At the same score Howarth bowled Matthews, then Campbell and, first ball, Jumadeen—who seemed to refuse to believe it until Howarth pointed at his broken wicket.

Lawson foiled the hat-trick simply by hitting his first ball for four, escaped to the other end where Taylor bowled him. In 21 dizzy minutes Howarth had taken four wickets for no runs in 11 balls, all bowled on a pitch that seemed to make hitting the stumps a lost art.

Burgess and Congdon had batting practice for 90 minutes, scored 101 most pleasantly and that was that.

Sabina's pitch gave the bowlers a little hope. Jarrett Park was quite hopeless. The New Zealand batsmen were happy, but the bowlers wondered whether this would be the pattern for the tour.

The West Indies selectors weren't so happy. Only Findlay went from the President's XI to the first test and most of the other candidates must have taken a couple of steps backwards.

NEW ZEALANDERS

| *First Innings* | | *Second Innings* | |
|---|---|---|---|
| G. Turner c de Souza b Morgan | 202 | | |
| G. Dowling lbw b Matthews | 124 | | |
| T. Jarvis b Jumadeen | 51 | | |
| M. Burgess b Julien | 51 | not out | 51 |
| B. Taylor not out | 47 | | |
| B. Congdon did not bat | | not out | 39 |
| Extras (b1 lb2 w2 nb6) | 11 | (b2 lb3 w6) | 11 |
| Total (4 wickets decl.) | 486 | (for no wicket) | 101 |

Fall: 268, 385, 390, 486.

*Bowling*

| | O. | M. | R. | W. | O. | M. | R. | W. |
|---|---|---|---|---|---|---|---|---|
| Matthews | 30 | 7 | 102 | 1 | 4 | 1 | 5 | 0 |
| Lawson | 30 | 8 | 93 | 0 | 5 | 1 | 21 | 0 |
| Julien | 29.4 | 9 | 79 | 1 | 6 | 1 | 23 | 0 |
| Jumadeen | 40 | 9 | 116 | 1 | — | — | — | — |
| Kallicharran | 7 | 2 | 16 | 0 | 2 | 1 | 4 | 0 |
| Campbell | 30 | 7 | 53 | 0 | 1 | 0 | 4 | 0 |
| Morgan | 4 | 0 | 16 | 1 | 2 | 0 | 9 | 0 |
| Shillingford | — | — | — | — | 2 | 0 | 9 | 0 |
| de Souza | — | — | — | — | 2 | 0 | 11 | 0 |
| Baichan | — | — | — | — | 1 | 0 | 4 | 0 |

PRESIDENT'S XI

*First Innings*

| | |
|---|---|
| S. Morgan c Turner b Taylor | 32 |
| L. Baichan b Congdon | 96 |
| A. Kallicharran c. Dowling b Burgess | 51 |
| I. Shillingford b Howarth | 124 |
| R. de Souza b Collinge | 32 |
| B. Julien run out | 2 |
| M. Findlay not out | 3 |
| S. Matthews b Howarth | 0 |
| C. Campbell b Howarth | 0 |
| R. Jumadeen b Howarth | 0 |
| C. Lawson b Taylor | 4 |
| Extras (b12 lb4 w1 nb3) | 20 |
| Total | 364 |

Fall: 48, 134, 275, 352, 356, 359, 359, 359, 359.

*Bowling*

| | O. | M. | R. | W. |
|---|---|---|---|---|
| Webb | 30 | 9 | 52 | 0 |
| Collinge | 20 | 7 | 74 | 1 |
| Howarth | 52 | 16 | 102 | 4 |
| Taylor | 30 | 9 | 57 | 2 |
| Congdon | 14 | 5 | 24 | 1 |
| Burgess | 6 | 1 | 28 | 1 |
| Jarvis | 2 | 0 | 7 | 0 |

Fourth match — FIRST TEST, Sabina Park, Kingston, February 16, 17, 18, 19, 21. Drawn.

Blofeld and I, with one eye on approaching deadlines, waited about the Courtleigh Manor the day before the first test. Dowling, never very decisive about these matters, took his time about assembling the selection committee and more time to decide on what looked like a fairly straightforward task. With Vivian out of action the six batsmen picked themselves. Wadsworth for keeper, Howarth and Alabaster for the spin, Cunis for the donkeywork and Taylor for whatever delight took his fancy.

Then came the bombshell. No Taylor, and with Webb promoted above Collinge who looked something of a fitness risk. Taylor's face was a yard long, but he said nowt. It was a strange selection, even giving in that Taylor had missed the tests against England last year.

Still, no-one knew what to expect from the first test. Perhaps

Webb, with his extra speed, would be the answer and with Wadsworth looking so sound in his second innings against Jamaica having Taylor batting at eight might have been a luxury.

West Indies looked good, even without Lloyd whose ailing back had passed a fitness test, but the selectors wanted to give him more time to get back to form. Findlay had regained his test place which Lewis of Jamaica had taken against the Indians. The critics near and far raised only a few peeps of protest, mostly against the retention of the genial Carew. Jamaicans wanted Lewis or Morgan there, and from down Guyana way there was keening that Kallicharran was only the 12th man.

Otherwise most West Indians were happy, for they had a team of all-round strength, and with the exciting prospect that Rowe was a shining new star.

The New Zealanders were quiet on test eve. Montego Bay had been a boost to the morale so abruptly shaken by Jamaica. There was a feeling that they had already learned much about this new form of cricket. They wondered whether they had learned enough to get out of the first test with at least their colours still flying.

## FIRST DAY

There was no need for a public address announcement about the result of the toss. Sobers appeared from his lair, strolled out in that peculiarly aristocratic gait of his and once the coin had fallen he gave a quick gesture to the dressing room.

Suddenly there was a baying roar from the packed stands, a sharp staccato thunderclap of tumult as the Jamaicans jumped with glee—and the New Zealanders bit their lip and went in to prepare for what they knew must be a long hot battle.

It was a gay, crazy scene. The spectators had already taken up all the seating. Their gay colours splashed about in the harsh sunlight, and a few brave souls started what was to become a steady march of spectators up the floodlight pylons in the corners of the ground.

New Zealand started quietly, with Dowling posting deep fine leg and deep third man from the start. The pitch looked a little quicker than the one for the Jamaica game, but it was still hard and merciless for the bowlers.

Fredericks, with only a nervous show of white teeth occasionally breaking the blackness of his face, flicked Webb for four. Carew, eyes squinting under his odd jockey-type cap, put Cunis through the covers for four. Fredericks hooked a Webb bouncer for four. The battle was on, and it could be a one-sided fight.

Neither Cunis nor Webb could get any life or movement. Carew and Fredericks moved into their familiar pattern without fuss. Fifty runs in 73 minutes, too fast for New Zealand's comfort.

Congdon, bowling his medium-pacers with his usual apologetic air, came in and Cunis went out after Fredericks and Carew had plundered 12 from an over. Alabaster, immediately on a length, slowed them down as lunch approached.

Suddenly Congdon broke the stand, tricking Carew with his slower ball and getting a quick lbw decision, and three minutes later the New Zealanders went not too unhappily to lunch, for one for 80 seemed a useful start under such circumstances.

Soon Rowe rocked them back. Webb pitched up, and Rowe glanced a four. Webb dropped short, Rowe hooked a four. He did not play himself in, he merely seemed to continue from where he had left off in his double-century of a few days before.

Fredericks was another matter. Dowling put down a sharp chance when Fredericks was 46. Howarth had him bamboozled, for try as he might Fredericks could not drive him properly and to cut across Howarth's slight angle was risky.

He looked as permanent as a poplar leaf in an autumn breeze, but was scenting his first century after 19 tests and was not going to miss the chance. At 84 Burgess dropped him off Alabaster, at 91 a snick fled between Turner and Wadsworth.

Then came Fredericks' hundred, in 276 minutes, and with Rowe growing better minute by minute they put on the third 50 of their 150 stand in only 43 minutes. New ball or old, it did not matter and by stumps West Indies were 274 for one wicket, with the inevitable Rowe 94, Fredericks 126. The brief joy that Congdon's wicket brought just before lunch must have been a very distant memory for the New Zealanders.

They slumped about the dressing room afterward, wondering how Fredericks had survived, and how they would ever get Rowe out. The bowling had, by recent standards, been good but the fielding on the bumpy ground and the catching had been indifferent. They had learned, the hard way, that chances come few and far between on such plumb pitches, and that they must be taken.

## SECOND DAY

The sun seemed hotter, the Jamaicans' chatter even noisier, the piles of peanut shells in the grandstands even deeper as the New Zealanders went out to face what looked like another ordeal.

Rowe, impassive as ever, reached his century (227 minutes, eight fours), gave his cap a tug as the jubilant crowd signalled his wonderful feat, and settled down as if to score another.

If Rowe looked everlasting, Fredericks was every bit as exasperating. Wadsworth put down a snick off Fredericks, then 142, from the first ball that Howarth bowled. Eight runs later another chance to Dowling. Seven runs later poor Howarth drooped in dismay as Cunis dropped Fredericks at deep mid-off.

The gallant Howarth tried again, Fredericks drove at the next ball and up went Howarth's left-hand for a superb caught-and-bowled, for the hit looked as if it would go for six.

West Indies 347 for two, with Rowe and Fredericks scoring 269 runs in 291 minutes for the second wicket—where would it end?

By lunch Rowe, utterly in control and stroking his cover drives majestically, was an even 150. Afterwards Davis pottered about, flicked away those wristy square drives which are his trademark and then, wonder of wonders, got an edge to Cunis and Turner held the catch at first slip. The look on Cunis's face, streaming with sweat and with his Viking-blond hair awry, was pure bliss, even if a quick look at the scoreboard told of the first bowling "hundred" of his career.

The crowd hummed, and then sighed, for it was Foster, not Sobers marching out in time to see Rowe clip away his 17th four to reach his double century.

Once again the triumphant roar from the crowd. Rowe permitted himself a quiet smile and relaxed, banging away happily at Howarth and Burgess who had been pressed into service. Rowe hit Howarth out of the ground, hit again but this time he sliced and at deep extra cover Dowling hugged the precious catch to chest.

Away went Rowe, bat held high as the whole crowd stood and cheered. It was a great and affecting moment until some eager spectators rushed out to acclaim him. They patted Rowe, pushed him, poked him and then tried to carry him away shoulder high.

The idea was right, but the execution was dreadful, and poor Rowe, instead of coming back to a welcome befitting a young god, was half-carried, half-dragged by the mob for the last 25 yards. It was a sad end to a magnificent innings, and I wondered why all the policemen about the ground had not given him the chance to stride off under his own steam.

Enter Sobers at last, to be met by the bowling from a rather mystified Burgess, who seemed bemused that he should be bowling at the great man.

Sobers gave a couple of flourishes, including a stunning drive through extra cover and then, at 508 for four cried enough and let the weary New Zealanders get some rest.

They had little time for it. In his second over Dowe made the new ball skid, Dowling played back, missed and was lbw.

Out came Jarvis, not Congdon. A mistake, this, even if Congdon was tired after bowling 23 overs. Jarvis, who had fielded mightily in the hottest corner of the ground, was hardly fresh either and his recent form was indifferent.

Still, Jarvis it was, but only briefly for at 25 he edged a full-pitched ball from Shillingford into his off-stump. Turner went phlegmatically on, in no trouble with his defence and Burgess was just starting to look good when he edged a full toss from Dowe into his stumps.

By now the crowd were in a frenzy and Congdon, none too happily, held out to stumps at 49 for three.

It took a brave man to crack hearty that night. Even Wadsworth, the super-optimist, was subdued. All the planning and scheming to get through Jamaica unbeaten now seemed only a pale memory.

## THIRD DAY

Once again the stifling sun and, as if in tune, Sobers brought on Gibbs and Holford and tried to smother Turner and Congdon with a close-set leg trap.

Turner, his squinting eyes sinking deeper into his boyish face, showed his faultless technique, but Congdon had troubles. He took a swat at Gibbs, Fredericks at short leg ducked instinctively and the catch lobbed just in front of him.

At the same score, 11, Holford just got a finger to a sharp return catch from Congdon. Two balls later Holford bowled a full toss and Congdon hit it straight back. Four for 75, and Hastings almost made it five as he offered no shot to a wrong'un and, it seemed, half of Kingston roared for lbw.

The pressure from the spinners and Sobers' hostile field-setting was even more intense. Turner made a brave show by lofting Gibbs for one four and cover-driving the next for another.

Again Turner drove at Gibbs, but not accurately and the catch curled out to extra cover. Across moved Carew. He was not the most popular man in Jamaica at the time. He was even more unpopular as he jabbed one hand out for the ball and spilled the catch.

Turner was 47, the score 103 for four. Had Turner gone New Zealand must have tumbled to defeat. He stayed but Hastings went, for as he tucked down one of Gibbs' floaters Sobers' hand snaked out and held the catch.

Five for 108, the wayward Wadsworth with Turner, and soon after it was lunch at 128 for five.

Back came Dowe with the new ball and Turner watched interestedly as he swayed under three bouncers in succession. Wadsworth, his rather angular jaw jutting out arrogantly, handled Dowe and Shillingford sensibly and soon the real battle was rejoined—Gibbs and Holford and Foster, with a forest of men waiting for Wadsworth to put up a catch.

Turner went quietly and steadily on. He rested for patches, and then would hit two or three fours, before resting again. The crowd, rapt in the struggle, applauded mightily at Turner's 100, a wonderful example of 320 minutes' courage and concentration.

Wadsworth seemed to take heart at this, picked up a four and by tea New Zealand were 217 for five wickets. It seemed like a miracle, while Wadsworth wiggled his head in his own odd way and blissfully announced that the bowling was a piece of cake.

Then came another crisis. Gibbs bowled, the hungry hands clustered round Wadsworth and somehow he survived. He did everything except butt the ball with his head, but he kept it on the ground. For half an hour Wadsworth and Turner foiled Gibbs.

Suddenly, in one of those inexplicable actions of his, Sobers removed Gibbs, brought back Shillingford and the crisis was over. The crowd sighed at the change, and you could almost hear Turner and Wadsworth whistle with relief.

New Zealand were 250, and then Turner hit Carew through cover for four and the stand was worth 150. Carew had a seven-two field, but Turner and Wadsworth were not under pressure. Just before stumps Turner, by now completely composed and in command, had his 150.

A few minutes later Turner and Wadsworth went off, an arm about each other's shoulder. Already their stand was worth 172, the score was 280, the follow-on mark was within reach. No wonder, as the gallant pair went off, that those New Zealanders lucky enough to be there had to swallow a lump of pride.

The West Indians and New Zealanders drank together that night. It was a nice point, for in those blistering four hours New Zealand had shown that they could fight, that this was becoming a match between equals.

## FOURTH DAY

Wadsworth opened the day with a meaty clout for four off Gibbs and in half an hour New Zealand were 300.

As a final ploy Sobers took the new ball, and Turner and Wadsworth enjoyed it immensely. Gone was Wadsworth's dutiful defence, out came the old Wadsworth of the flashing blade.

Shillingford pitched up, Wadsworth hit him straight for four, the stand was worth 200, the follow-on mark of 308 had been passed and at my elbow Blofeld, forever with the right words at the right time, said: "Bloody magnificent."

So Wadsworth flicked Shillingford for two fours, hooked Dowe for another and looked very much as if he would get to 100 before the eternal Turner got to 200. Five for 108 seemed a long way away.

Sadly, Wadsworth did not reach his hundred. At 78 he hooked again at Dowe, the ball got a bit of glove, a bit of bat and 25 yards away Fredericks spurted in for the catch.

Wadsworth had batted for 295 minutes, helped Turner score 220 for the sixth wicket, got New Zealand past the follow-on—and most important of all showed that good sense and a brave heart could thwart and then command the West Indies bowling.

Perhaps unused to such a long wait with his pads on Cunis stayed briefly, and one run later, at 329 for seven, tickled a Shillingford outswinger and Findlay did the rest.

There was a touch of alarm in the New Zealand camp. Was Turner, after all his wonderful work, to be left high and dry short of his 200? The alarm was unnecessary. The ball plunked solidly into the middle of Howarth's bat. Dowe bowled bouncers. Howarth looked angry, but did not flinch.

Turner took over. A flowing cover drive off Holford made him 191. Rather than expose Howarth he turned down a single. A single made him 192, a drive at Dowe was worth two. Another single, a cut for two off Holford. Three short, and a shudder as Turner just dug out a Holford top-spinner that skidded through low and very, very straight. Holford bowled, Turner swayed back and cut, Dowe chased like a demon but the ball beat him to the fence.

The Jamaicans thundered their praise. Turner, the man who had foiled them, was a hero of cricket and for all their cantankerous behaviour beforehand the crowd seemed to realise this.

Turner had batted 520 minutes, scored 200 of 360, and had, rather remarkably, hit precisely 100 in fours.

Howarth, his job done, went lbw to Holford for 16, Alabaster had an aimless woof at Gibbs and was caught and while Webb admired in scoreless wonder Turner went on to 218 (of 380 for nine) at lunch.

Turner tried to protect Webb, at some cost to his personal score, and did it well until Webb, after 37 minutes of faithful service, missed a straight ball from Shillingford and was lbw.

So Turner went back to even more acclaim, West Indies led by 122 and Carew and Fredericks, in default of any special instructions, went out and pounded away at Webb. His first over was a maiden, his next four cost 34 runs.

Enter Congdon, again Carew was deceived and back went his off stump. Fredericks swung and missed, Congdon bowled him and it was 57 for two.

Rowe was, once again, another matter. Completely in command, never appearing to hurry, he still reached 50 in 77 minutes (breakneck speed for this match) and a brisk 41 by Davis had West Indies 168 for three at stumps.

When would Sobers declare tomorrow? The advice came in thick and fast that night and in the papers next morning. Already 290 on, Sobers might have declared overnight and taken a risk. Obviously he would bat on tomorrow, but would he allow Rowe time for the incredible feat of a double and single hundred in his first test? Would Sobers set a time-limit on the batting tomorrow and stick to it, with Rowe short of his century? Would Sobers get tarred-and-feathered if he did? Yes sir.

## FIFTH DAY

Rowe solved all these questions simply. For 25 minutes he batted like a charm to 90. At 90 Cunis roared for lbw against Rowe, a very likely-looking appeal. At 91 the New Zealanders claimed that Rowe was run out when Howarth fielded brilliantly. Who would be an umpire in a situation such as this?

Rowe was not out, three singles, three twos and this incredible young man had his second hundred—and Sobers called them in with West Indies 218 for three, 340 runs on with about 310 minutes remaining.

West Indies hardly had time to bowl New Zealand out, so it seemed, for Dowling survived two narrow escapes against Dowe. Davis dropped Turner off Sobers and at lunch New Zealand were 50 for no wicket. Victory was out of the question, but an honourable draw was there for the taking.

Almost. Two balls after lunch Holford bowled Dowling with a googly. One run later Turner tried to cut a Holford googly and was bowled. Fifty-one for two and Burgess got an outrageous edge for four from his first ball, and celebrated by hitting Gibbs for two fours.

Just when Congdon, back at No. 3, and Burgess seemed to be

taking command, Burgess sent Congdon back from a short single, and Davis' throw beat Congdon home. This was 96 for three, and more tremors when Holford bowled Hastings at 131 and had Jarvis lbw at 135 for five.

Two hours to play—would New Zealand, after their wonderful first innings recovery, collapse into defeat? Not while Wadsworth was there they wouldn't. Burgess did the hitting, Wadsworth the defending. Burgess, hitting powerfully, put Gibbs away for six over midwicket and raced up into the 70s and then the 80s. Old ball or new, it mattered not. The Wadsworth chin jutted out once again, the flashing Burgess blade struck and struck.

The last hour, 20 overs remaining and Burgess 89. Dowe bowled a good length and Burgess hit him through the covers. Dowe bounced and Burgess hooked him for four. Dowe bounced again, Burgess airily wafted him over slips for four. No nervous nineties for Burgess, with his century coming in 183 minutes, with a six and 15 fours.

The applause had just subsided when Burgess drove at Dowe, the ball zoomed up and neatly into Dowe's hands as he ran through. A wonderful Burgess innings, full of power and confidence, but as Cunis came out to join Wadsworth I could not help feeling that Burgess should have batted longer, for minutes were more important than runs.

The criticism seemed to lose its point when Cunis, broad and stubborn as ever, dug in. Wadsworth, rather ambitiously, tried a light appeal with 12 overs to go, without intimating whether the sun might have been getting in his eyes. Back to the battle, but it was really only a skirmish. Fredericks and Holford, Sobers and Holford, Carew and Dowe—Sobers shuttled his bowlers about with no apparent plan or purpose, and Wadsworth and Cunis held out safely.

WEST INDIES

| *First Innings* | | *Second Innings* | |
|---|---|---|---|
| R. Fredericks c and b Howarth | 163 | b Congdon | 33 |
| M. Carew lbw b Congdon | 43 | b Congdon | 22 |
| L. Rowe c Dowling b Howarth | 214 | not out | 100 |
| C. Davis c Turner b Cunis | 31 | b Howarth | 41 |
| M. Foster not out | 28 | not out | 13 |
| G. Sobers not out | 13 | | |
| Extras (b1 lb11 nb 4) | 16 | (b9) | 9 |
| Total (4 wickets decl.) | 508 | (3 wickets decl.) | 218 |
| Fall: 78, 347, 428, 488. | | 44, 57, 155. | |

*Bowling*

| | O. | M. | R. | W. | O. | M. | R. | W. |
|---|---|---|---|---|---|---|---|---|
| Webb | 25 | 4 | 86 | 0 | 5 | 1 | 34 | 0 |
| Cunis | 34 | 3 | 118 | 1 | 20.4 | 2 | 87 | 0 |
| Congdon | 23 | 2 | 55 | 1 | 11 | 2 | 45 | 2 |
| Alabaster | 25 | 4 | 110 | 0 | — | — | — | — |
| Howarth | 44 | 6 | 108 | 2 | 17 | 6 | 43 | 1 |
| Burgess | 2 | 0 | 15 | 0 | — | — | — | — |

NEW ZEALAND

| *First Innings* | | *Second Innings* | |
|---|---|---|---|
| G. Dowling lbw b Dowe | 4 | b Holford | 23 |
| G. Turner not out | 223 | b Holford | 21 |
| T. Jarvis b Shillingford | 7 | lbw b Holford | 0 |
| M. Burgess b Dowe | 15 | c and b Dowe | 101 |
| B. Congdon c and b Holford | 11 | run out | 16 |
| B. Hastings c Sobers b Gibbs | 16 | b Holford | 13 |
| K. Wadsworth c Fredericks b Dowe | 78 | not out | 36 |
| R. Cunis c Findlay b Shillingford | 0 | not out | 13 |
| H. Howarth lbw b Holford | 16 | | |
| J. Alabaster c Dowe b Gibbs | 2 | | |
| M. Webb lbw b Shillingford | 0 | | |
| Extras (b10 nb4) | 14 | (b5 lb6 nb2) | 13 |
| Total | 386 | (for six wickets) | 236 |

Fall: 4, 25, 48, 75, 108, 328, 329, 361, 364. | 50, 51, 96, 131, 135, 214.

*Bowling*

| | O. | M. | R. | W. | O. | M. | R. | W. |
|---|---|---|---|---|---|---|---|---|
| Dowe | 29 | 5 | 75 | 3 | 13 | 3 | 46 | 1 |
| Shillingford | 26.5 | 8 | 63 | 3 | 11 | 2 | 32 | 0 |
| Sobers | 11 | 3 | 20 | 0 | 13 | 5 | 16 | 0 |
| Holford | 44 | 18 | 64 | 2 | 33 | 12 | 55 | 4 |
| Gibbs | 45 | 9 | 94 | 2 | 21 | 8 | 42 | 0 |
| Foster | 14 | 8 | 20 | 0 | 9 | 5 | 12 | 0 |
| Carew | 9 | 0 | 29 | 0 | 4 | 1 | 6 | 0 |
| Fredericks | 4 | 1 | 5 | 0 | 4 | 0 | 14 | 0 |
| Davis | 5 | 3 | 2 | 0 | — | — | — | — |

# 6

# *To Antigua and Tobago*

Ah, man, those are places for history, said Jamaicans as we set off across 1,000 miles of ocean to Antigua and, a week later, to Tobago. History perhaps, but laced with hysteria, at least in St John's, Antigua.

Antigua is virtually on the threshold of the Atlantic, made famous years ago as the site of Nelson's dockyard established before Trafalgar, and now renowned as an island of wonderful coral-sand beaches and liquor cheap enough to make it an alcoholic's paradise.

More prosaically Antigua is a vest-pocket democracy which, amid a declining agricultural economy, depends largely on tourist dollars from cruise ships, cheap liquor and on being the last major airport before Northern America.

Yet, like Jamaica, Antigua and its capital St John's had its own peculiar charm. The town is a place of narrow streets, footpaths like miniature Giants Causeways, of centuries-old wooden houses rubbing shoulders with crisp new office buildings. If for nothing else St John's is memorable for its cathedral, sitting on a slight mound in the centre of the town, its sandstone exterior crumbling, its vast interior coolly lined with pitch-pine—an oasis of reverence and incense compared with the cramped life outside. Antiguans are working to restore it. I hope they succeed for it is a place of beauty.

There are other places in St John's, such as the hotel the New Zealanders stayed at. Michael's Mount Hotel is just that, a hotel built on a 500-foot mountain by the Michael family. It sits there alone, looking like some latter-day hilltop monastery, a vast bluff of stone and brick and concrete frowning down on the township. Once inside where the incessant north-east Trade Wind takes the place of air-conditioning, you can, by subtle adjustments of the louvres on windows and doors, produce moaning and unearthly groaning suitable for the sound-track of *Wuthering Heights*.

But, at least for the New Zealanders, St John's and Antigua will remain in the memory for a cricket match that would require A. G. Macdonell, or perhaps Gilbert and Sullivan, to do it justice.

The cricket field, like the sun, rose in the east and set in the west and to the naked eye the drop seemed something like 10 to 15 feet. There were bumps and hollows, places of thick grass and other of bare soil laced with old bottle tops and pieces of glass. In the middle, in rather lonely level splendour, was the pitch which, like most of them in the West Indies, had been hammered into submission by hours of rolling. The men who did the rolling had time to spare, for they were the convicts from the gaol across the road and ground-staff duty was almost as welcome as parole.

Their uniform was a blue peaked cap, cream blouse and longish dark blue shorts—for all the world they looked like a bunch of overgrown schoolboys.

They were, their solitary and not too concerned guard told me, a fairly harmless lot. One had just missed a murder rap and was doing five years for manslaughter, but generally they were burglars, car converters and the like.

As ground staff they were champions. They could not do much about the undulations of the outfield or the sudden drop away to the western boundary, but when it came to removing or replacing the covers they were world-class. Without a command they would fasten to one edge of the cover and hurtle across the field, the cover billowing like some giant yellow butterfly behind them. Except once.

There was rain the night before the second day's play, with Leeward Islands at the fag end of their first innings. The New Zealanders arrived a little more than an hour before the starting time of 11 a.m. The covers were still on, and on the covers were puddles Dowling looked at Chapple, who looked at the book of words and then, without success, for the umpires who were in control of such matters as removing covers. No umpires.

Chapple looked at Dowling, Dowling looked at the puddles. Rocks were lifted, covers were slid away and, more by good luck than good management the pitch was affected only by two damp patches which looked dangerous but which served only to delay the start for an hour. The umpires had been summoned by an SOS call over the local radio station, and no-one seemed terribly upset that the covers had been removed, not strictly according to Hoyle. The prisoners, we later found, were not released until 10 a.m. that day, and so the covers had stayed.

So unfolded one of the more diverting games of cricket. Amid the fuss and bother over the covers, the drying-out of the patches and the late start, one of the umpires forgot the ball. On another occasion the bails went missing.

On the last day, when most of the sting had gone out of the game, Bob Cunis, promoted none too willingly to 12th man, had to field. The game went on, Cunis called for the ball, solemnly measured out his run, handed his hat to the umpire and made ready to bowl. He would have, too, had not the Leewards batsman realised what was happening and marched menacingly out of his crease.

On the last day, too, came the strange case of the early tea. The drinks had been taken out, an over bowled, and suddenly Bevan Congdon could be seen waving to his deep-set players to leave the field. Words were obviously being said in the middle. There was a flutter of interest in the pavilion. Had the Leewards declared, and left New Zealand a cakewalk to victory? Or had Congdon, as his agitated signals suggested, summoned his men from the field because of some dispute—thereby provoking another of the incidents to which the Leewards are not strangers?

Alas for hopes of victory for New Zealand, or sensational stories for the cricket presses of the world. The umpires had simply mistaken the time for tea, actually some 25 minutes distant. So there was time only for a brief laugh in the dressing room before the umpires and players marched out again.

Yet there was more to Antigua than this strange cricket match which, to be perfectly truthful, the New Zealanders did not play well.

There was, some miles to the south, a magnificent natural harbour which is known as Nelson's Dockyard, for Nelson spent much time there first as a junior officer and then as a captain in the King's Navy. Some of the original dockyard and buildings remain and if, like the elegant old cathedral in St John's, they are ever restored to their original state this harbour will rank as one of the wonders of the Caribbean.

The hinterland is not without beauty, either, and from any of the hills or small mountains you can see acres of rippling sugarcane, with every now and then one of the old limestone crushing mills standing like sentry-boxes about the landscape.

Antiguans we met complained that they lived in a quiet backwater that the rest of the world passed by. Judging by what was going on in other parts of the world and, indeed, among their neighbours of the West Indies, perhaps being a quiet cosy backwater is not a bad idea.

Fifth match. —— v. Leeward Islands, Recreation Ground, St John's, Antigua, February 25, 26, 27.

Among the preliminaries to the game was the Turner double-shuffle. He was in the New Zealand team when we left Jamaica, he was out of it when we got to Antigua and, sadly, was back in at the last moment when Dowling first noticed a recurrence of his back trouble.

At long last Vivian and Campbell were in action and Cunis, who might have relished the idea of some cheapish wickets after his thin time in Jamaica, was out.

The Leewards were not regarded as stern opposition. Antiguans spoke warmly of their favourite son, Vivi Richards, a dashing young batsman. There was also a young left-arm spinner with the resounding name of Elquimedo Willet, who had played with distinction for Combined Islands in the Shell Shield matches.

But the general idea seemed to be that, even allowing for the scenic-railway ground, the New Zealanders would have both a pleasant romp and the first win of their tour.

## FIRST DAY

And so it seemed, for after Congdon had lost the toss Webb knocked over one opener and Collinge knocked over the other. Two for two.

Alas for high hopes. The New Zealanders had to wait until just before lunch for their next scalp. Richards looked as good as his reputation and when Taylor fired a bouncer at him Richards leisurely hit it over the fence—which brought a marked increase in the rum consumption round the ground.

Eventually Alabaster removed Jim Allen just before lunch, which came at 87 for three.

Alas again for high hopes. Livingstone Sergeant, also of Combined Islands, reached 32 by hitting eight fours, with the rum bottles gurgling with each boundary. Richards hit Alabaster for six. More gurgles.

Then Sergeant obliged by hitting a Congdon full toss to Jarvis, and Alabaster chimed in by bowling Richards and by stumps Webb with the new ball had Leeward 229 for eight.

## SECOND DAY

Came the rain, Dowling supervised the removing of the covers, Jarvis looked with concern at the wet patches on a length at both ends and after an hour's delay Taylor and Webb mopped up the tail—Leewards 243 and happy with their score.

Jarvis and Turner started pleasantly enough. Then, at 37, they were both gone, with Willet having Jarvis stumped and, at 44, getting Hasting caught.

Vivian, trying to find form pottered round until Willet fed his sweep shot and he was caught near the downside fence. Congdon went, also sweeping at Willet, while Taylor had time to hit a six out of the ground before he went, too.

Campbell, on 13, was dropped and someone with a mind for graveyard humour observed that at 94 for six New Zealand had avoided the follow-on.

Campbell and Wadsworth soldiered on sensibly to stumps at 135 for six after what would hardly rank as one of the great days of New Zealand cricket.

## THIRD DAY

There were high hopes that Campbell would carry on for a big score in his first full game for New Zealand. This was no game for high hopes. Campbell was out for 42, at 147 for seven, and Alabaster and Collinge hardly sold their wickets dearly when they both went at 154.

Fortunately Wadsworth was still there and Webb, organising his elbows and kees and feet into position, stayed put while they added 50 runs for the last wicket which gave New Zealand a faint tinge of respectability at 204.

Willet was as good as his figures looked—43 overs, 15 maidens, 65 runs and five wickets. Andy Roberts, a whippy young man, bowled very quickly and looked most promising.

It was pleasant to hear, too, that Derrick Robins, the cricketing philanthropist from England who was in Antigua at the time, was prepared to take Willet to England for a short time. West Indies cricket had been good to him, said Robins, so perhaps by taking Willet away for more experience he could do some good for West Indies. Salt of the earth, men like Robins.

The rest of the match tottered along. Alabaster got three wickets at bargain rates and Leewards declared, leaving New Zealand 20 overs to score 150.

Roberts made sure they didn't by bombarding Vivian and Campbell with bouncers and the match fizzled out.

It was, overall, a grim performance by the New Zealanders. If they had learned lessons in Jamaica they forgot then in Antigua. Had there, by some chance, crept in a casual approach both to practice and playing? By rights they should have beaten the Leewards, even the Leewards players maintained that afterward. But the New Zealanders, on that form, would not have beaten anyone. But at least they avoided the follow-on.

## LEEWARD ISLANDS

| First Innings | | Second Innings | |
|---|---|---|---|
| L. Williams c Turner b Collinge | 2 | c Campbell b Webb | 1 |
| S. Greenaway b Webb | 0 | c and b Alabaster | 11 |
| J. Allen c Congdon b Alabaster | 21 | c Congdon b Alabaster | 58 |
| V. Richards b Alabaster | 82 | lbw b Congdon | 0 |
| L. Sergeant c Jarvis b Congdon | 33 | b Alabaster | 8 |
| G. Allen c Congdon b Webb | 53 | not out | 18 |
| A. Hector b Taylor | 12 | | |
| G. Gould c Campbell b Webb | 17 | not out | 6 |
| A. Roberts lbw b Webb | 4 | st Wadsworth b Vivian | 6 |
| E. Willet c Wadsworth b Taylor | 5 | | |
| E. Carter not out | 4 | | |
| Extras (lb6 nb4) | 10 | (b1 lb2) | 3 |
| Total | 243 | (for 6 wickets decl.) | 111 |

Fall: 2, 2, 60, 141, 143, 170, 218, 226, 235.

Fall: 2, 71, 72, 72, 92, 99.

*Bowling*

| | O. | M. | R. | W. | O. | M. | R. | W. |
|---|---|---|---|---|---|---|---|---|
| Collinge | 14 | 7 | 33 | 1 | 1 | 0 | 1 | 0 |
| Webb | 19 | 6 | 42 | 4 | 6 | 1 | 24 | 1 |
| Taylor | 19 | 1 | 58 | 2 | 8 | 2 | 26 | 0 |
| Alabaster | 32 | 12 | 60 | 2 | 19 | 10 | 24 | 3 |
| Vivian | 1 | 0 | 15 | 0 | 8 | 1 | 15 | 1 |
| Congdon | 11 | 3 | 25 | 1 | 8 | 4 | 10 | 1 |
| Campbell | — | — | — | — | 2 | 0 | 8 | 0 |

## NEW ZEALANDERS

| First Innings | | Second Innings | |
|---|---|---|---|
| G. Turner c Sergeant b G. Allen | 15 | | |
| T. Jarvis st Hector b Willet | 21 | | |
| B. Congdon c Hector b Willet | 15 | | |
| B. Hastings c Greenaway b Willet | 5 | | |
| G. Vivian c Carter b Willet | 10 | not out | 9 |
| K. Campbell c and b G. Allen | 42 | not out | 12 |
| B. Taylor c Hector b Gould | 15 | (nb1) | 1 |
| K. Wadsworth c Hector b Roberts | 67 | | |
| J. Alabaster c Gould b Willet | 0 | | |
| R. Collinge c Sergeant b G. Allen | 0 | | |
| M. Webb not out | 8 | | |
| Extras (b3 lb3) | 6 | | |
| Total | 204 | (for no wicket) | 22 |

Fall: 37, 37, 44, 60, 72, 92, 147, 154, 154.

*Bowling*

| | O. | M. | R. | W. | O. | M. | R. | W. |
|---|---|---|---|---|---|---|---|---|
| Roberts | 20.4 | 7 | 41 | 1 | 5 | 0 | 11 | 0 |
| Carter | 10 | 3 | 25 | 0 | 4 | 2 | 6 | 0 |
| G. Allen | 39 | 18 | 37 | 3 | — | — | — | — |
| Willet | 43 | 15 | 65 | 5 | — | — | — | — |
| Gould | 8 | 2 | 30 | 1 | — | — | — | — |

Tobago just had to be a wonderful island. Once leaving Antigua airport the British West Indian Airways hostess, a lissome lass designed to restore anyone's faith that ministering angels still exist, looked sideways at me when I requested my second rum and ginger ale. Seawell airport in Barbados meant a brief meeting with Peter Shortt, a man with a luxuriant moustache and, after many years as a cricket administrator, a keen idea of how to look after tired and dry cricketing travellers. Then to Piarco airport in Trinidad, more friendly faces such as that of Russell Vogtherr, now assistant trade commissioner on the island and once a very useful Wellington under-23 cricketer.

Then into a propellor-driven Convair 440 for the short hop to Tobago, with a captain who called everyone "folks" over the squawk box, and kept the plane low enough for us to wonder at the sight of a Caribbean moon etching patterns into the smooth steel of the sea below.

Tobago, so far, is a beautiful island untouched by the bug of tourism. It has a tranquillity with its rolling green hills, narrow roads, mile after mile of beaches and palm trees. In a word Tobago looks precisely how a tropical island should.

Tobagoans are attached to Trinidad by government, but they are a hardy, proud race. An aged taxi-driver, who stunned me by asking me to nominate the fare before we started, told me gravely that he had been overseas but had returned to Tobago never more to roam. When pressed for details he allowed that he had visited Trinidad for a fortnight and could not get home quickly enough.

"We have peace here, all the food we want, a lovely country, we are content. We have food in the ground and in the sea and in the trees. What do we want with places like Port of Spain, all the time they rush about making money."

At the end of the ride the driver turned round, remarked that "you listen real good" and dropped two dollars from the fare.

Tobagoans, perhaps more than other West Indians (with the possible exception of Trinidadians) have music and rhythm in their blood. During the match at Shaw Park just out of Scarborough, a steel band set up business beside the grandstand. During any break in play the band was in business, bonking away like mad. The people did not just stand and listen. Within minutes all the crowd were dancing, jigging, slapping time with the rhythm. We had to pass through this crowd to the lunch room (and the first taste of such things as flying fish and dolphin) and it was hard to resist the heady, rhythmic beat of the band as you went by.

Mind you, Tobago also had two 20th century additions to its pastoral charm which did it no harm at all. One was the Mt Irvine Bay Hotel, a magnificent modern hostelry, to which all New Zealand travel agents should sometime wander so they can realise just what a luxury hotel really means.

It had what must be one of the great dining areas, an outdoor terrace with, as its centrepiece, an old limestone sugar mill in which reposed the bar and from which, from about two-thirds its height, a roof swooped out over the diners. There was even a swimmers' bar, set in a bay of the swimming pool where you could paddle in, sit on a concrete stool some 18 inches below the water and prop your elbows on the bar-top.

The New Zealanders' eyes goggled at such luxury, but those who were golfers—or thought they were—goggled even more at the sight of a superb golf course attached to the hotel.

There it was, with vast smooth fairways sweeping in and around groups or lines of palm trees, superbly-planned holes, large fast greens and, if the pocket was so inclined, those motorised caddy carts to trip around in. Nicklaus and the rest have played there and no wonder; it is a course for great golf or if you are the best 24-handicapper in the world, as Glenn Turner must very nearly be, a place where you can play five holes one under and very nearly trickle in your first ace.

One of these days, when the bank account goes up and the golf handicap goes down Tobago will seem like a second heaven.

Sixth match. —— v. Tobago, Shaw Park, Scarborough. February 29, March 1. New Zealand won by an innings and 40 runs.

Among the preliminaries was a cocktail party where it was possible to rub shoulders with the Duke of Norfolk and his family, with Colin Cowdrey also in the party, who were holidaying there.

Cowdrey, ever a friend of New Zealand, was as charming as ever. He even bore with a smile a withering piece in the *Trinidad Guardian* suggesting that Cowdrey was, in fact, on some sort of secret talent-spotting mission in the Caribbean. Cowdrey, said the paper darkly, had even rung up Bernard Julien, the Trinidad all-rounder? Why not? They both play for Kent.

Shaw Park is a pleasant ground, sitting on a rise just out of Scarborough, with the Atlantic pounding in at one side and attractive trees lining the ground.

The steel band was there, so were the Tobago players with a fresh issue of bright blue caps. Everything was, in fact, perfect except for a wandering scribe like myself who was at the mercy of the one-man morse-key which was the sole telegraphic contact with the outside world.

## FIRST DAY

Dowling took one look at the dry, dusty pitch, won the toss and decided to make runs before the pitch got too bad.

Within 90 minutes Garnet St Louis, the Tobago skipper and legspinner, was making the ball do crazy things and Jarvis, Burgess and Dowling had gone for 68.

Hastings was almost out first ball and Vivian had to survive an lbw appeal that could have been heard in Trinidad. They lived, and most pleasantly, defending sensibly for a while and then attacking to add 95 before Hastings was neatly caught at square leg. So Campbell, who needed the practice, was out first ball and Taylor loped in to join the fun.

What fun. Taylor hit three sixes from consecutive balls. One shattered a windscreen in the carpark, another knocked a spectator from a tree. Vivian blasted away, five sixes and six fours until he scored 90 in 100 minutes and Cunis was bowled just before the declaration at 262 for seven wickets, in four hours—good going on such a pitch.

Webb got one wicket, Taylor two and Howarth, on the kind of pitch he would love to take home, had three for 14 as Tobago dropped to 48 for six at stumps.

## SECOND DAY

A quick win, and golf afterwards. That was the theory at breakfast, but with the New Zealanders in their present erratic mood the theory sounded rather hollow.

In fact it was very accurate. Howarth and Alabaster rolled up the Tobago first innings for 97. Cunis, who had obviously spoken meaningfully to Dowling when he did not get the new ball in the first innings, had it in the second. He had both openers out by 52 and then the spinners took over. Vivian made the ball do extraordinary things as he got three for 30 and Howarth got four more cheaply.

Golf anyone?

New Zealanders: First innings, 262 for seven wickets declared (G. Vivian 90, B. Taylor 46 not out, G. Dowling 34, T. Jarvis 23, B. Hastings 57; A. Carter four for 47).

Tobago: First innings, 97 (W. Scotland 18; H. Howarth five for 24, B. Taylor two for 7, J. Alabaster two for 42); second innings, 125 (D. Solomon 37, W. Brown 26; Howarth four for 37, G. Vivian three for 30, R. Cunis two for 39).

New Zealand won by an innings and 40 runs.

# 7

# *Trinidad: Before the Carnival*

The Convair of Arawak Airways, one of those bright and breezy airlines, bounced jauntily into Piarco airport just out of Port of Spain—the ideal introduction to Trinidad, the friendly land full of bounce and rhythm, of people of sophistication, culture and gaiety, of a way of life unashamedly hedonistic.

There is an air, a panache, about Port of Spain, Trinidad's lively, lusty capital, that the other West Indian cities we visited have not acquired. It comes, I feel, from the multitude of cultures —Spanish and Portuguese, English and Venezuelan, Chinese and Indian, Negro and French—that have been absorbed into Trinidad over the centuries.

It is mirrored in the architecture, an astonishing jumble of Gothic, Tudor, Baroque, Olde English and what can only be described as 20th-century Metro-Goldwyn-Mayer. The buildings, like the people, are all tossed into one entrancing mixture. The sights are incredible. So are many of the people.

There was Dr Eric Williams, the Prime Minister, a man of extraordinary intellectual gifts and pursuits, or "Ossie" Gonzales, the New Zealanders' beloved liaison man who seemed to know everything about everybody in all of Trinidad. On the distaff side there could be the marvellously statuesque Negro women, gorgeous blondes that would put Scandinavia to shame, and stunning Indian-Chinese creatures as delicate as fine china.

Like the other countries, Trinidad has its problems. Less than three years ago there was a brief Army revolt and window-smashing marches in the streets. There is a Black Power element simmering below the surface and, as in many other parts of the world, there is violence and murder and cutlass-choppings.

Some Trinidadians regard these as comic-opera happenings, others as signs of growing and revolutionary unrest. Yet Trinidadians carry on whith their typical flair for living.

The Army revolt was one case. Three of the ringleaders were tried for mutiny and convicted. The Trinidad High Court quashed the convictions on a legal technicality. So the ringleaders were immediately re-arrested for treason. Just before we left the newspapers were urging some form of Government action or decision on the 20-odd soldiers still held in gaol some two years after being charged with treason and other crimes.

There were no visible signs of it, but a state of emergency existed while the New Zealanders were in Trinidad. There were no curfews or other obvious measures. But it did exist and allowed the Government to clamp down on any outlawed political meetings.

Dr Williams attended the excellent cocktail party—which gradually developed into a genuine New Zealand "hooly"—put on by Joe Campbell, the New Zealand Trade Commissioner, and his wife Yvonne, in Port of Spain.

The PM was chatting with some friends about political matters when one of them said: "But, after all Eric, you are a benevolent dictator."

Dr Williams gave a quiet smile: "A dictator, perhaps. Benevolent, not always."

While Dr Williams was in power and in complete command of the Government, while the money from sugar and rice and oil was pouring in, while cricket could be played on the vast Queen's Park Savannah—ah, well, life would go on, Trinidad style.

It was, perhaps, typical of Trinidadian life that amid the worries of the Malik murder trial and whether or not West Indies could win the fifth test the major item of news concerned none of these mundane things.

Carnival, the annual two days when anything goes in Trinidad, was just around the corner. The big question, posed from pulpit and street-corner was whether the Family Planning Association band members in the big march would be allowed to wear FPA propaganda ("Loop before you leap" and "Rubbers erase worries" were two of the slogans) on their T-shirts. They weren't, but the T-shirts already sold became prized collectors' items. And the FPA gloomily looked forward to another crop of carnival babies nine months later.

It was typical that, when Dr Williams threw a cocktail party for the New Zealand and West Indies teams, a steel band—and a very fine one—should be in the ballroom, too. It was typical of Trinidad that the band should often play with gusto. And it was just as typical of Trinidadians that they should sip and nibble and, above the blast of the band, still talk, fortissimo. A little bit of musical noise wouldn't interrupt their enjoyment.

Unfortunately, the New Zealanders had to leave Port of Spain a few days before Carnival, which had been postponed from its usual pre-Lenten timing because of a polio epidemic. The preliminaries were impressive enough, with the floral displays springing up, the calypso kings heading for their tents, beauty contests and the like. This, apparently, is nothing compared with the real thing, the two days of Mas (masquerade), the bands, the parades, the jump-ups when the whole country goes whoopee.

Even before Carnival there was an infectious air in the streets, especially in the main shopping area skirted by Independence Square and bisected by Frederick Street. The shops are many and varied and the New Zealanders descended on one, Casa Edmundo, and bore away shirts of outrageous hues.

Or you could almost shop among the shoddy-droppers, who would sidle up and offer a watch here, a "genuine pearl necklace, Boss" there or some other gimcrack.

Even these folk had a sense of humour. One of them approached Jack Alabaster and offered for $25 a "genuine Bulova watch, Mister". Jack had an eye for a bargain, but a keener eye for the real thing. After beating the price down to $15 (about $6 in New Zealand currency) Jack pointed out that the inscription on the watch-face was "Bolivia" not the trade-name "Bulova".

"My goodness, Boss," exclaimed the wide-eyed rogue. "So it is, you are right. Five dollars, Boss."

Jack laughed, so did the peddler and even within earshot could be heard extolling the worth of this $30 watch to another tourist.

Queen's Park Oval, scene of the big games in Port of Spain, had a spacious atmosphere all of its own, with its backdrop of trees and wooded hills. And whoever decided to spoil the view by erecting massive floodlighting pylons on a neighbouring ground should be committed forever to bowl at Bourda.

Women's Lib has not swept through West Indies yet, and certainly not through the cricket grounds. Queen's Park, like Kensington Oval and Bourda, has a large members' pavilion giving a magnificent view of the pitch. There are bars and other amenities. It is strictly men only—the ladies have their own stand nearby and may join their menfolk on the steps of the pavilion, but not inside, after the match.

There may be political and social troubles lurking below the surface in Trinidad. It will take a strong man to maintain the grip that Dr Williams has, and apparently is keen to relinquish, on his country.

But on the surface, at least, Trinidad is a land of charm and of boundless good humour. While they have music and Carnival and cricket it is hard to imagine Trinidad being anything else.

Seventh match. —— v. Trinidad, Guaracara Park, Pointe-a-Pierre, March 3, 4, 5, 6. Drawn.

Before reaching the fleshier pots of Port of Spain the New Zealanders went first to Pointe-a-Pierre, some 30 miles south where Texaco have one of the largest oil refineries in the Commonwealth. To cater for their staff and the people of the district Texaco have also developed a splendid ground, Guaracara Park.

The New Zealanders were delighted to find a smooth, green outfield. They were less delighted to find yet another pitch as smooth and bland as a monk's head. They were even less delighted when Congdon, acting skipper after Dowling had stayed in Port of Spain for treatment to his back, lost the toss.

Carew, whose sunny disposition made him a great friend of the New Zealanders, smiled his quiet smile and batted.

Trinidad, Shell Shield winners in the two previous seasons, had fallen on leaner times and were not in the shield race. Still they had Carew and Davis of the first test side, de Souza, Jumadeen and Julien of the President's XI, and Jack Noreiga, an off-spinner who had taken nine wickets in an innings of a test against India the previous year. There was a tall medium-fast bowler with the engaging name of Prince Bartholomew.

And by now the fame of Inshan Ali, the left-arm mystery spinner, was beginning to spread and the only worry the Trinidadians had was whether Ali was in fact better than a teenage prodigy, Imtiaz Ali, a right-arm leg-spinner. In the event Imtiaz was left out, but Trinidad still had what looked like a potent spin attack.

The New Zealanders were without Dowling and Collinge, who had also stayed in Port of Spain for treatment. Jarvis and Webb were rested, although Jarvis' rest was brief for, after Turner strained a knee muscle just before lunch on the first day, Jarvis was on the field for the rest of the Trinidad innings.

## FIRST DAY

Carew declared war from the start. Cunis bowled the first ball, Carew slammed it at cover and Burgess fielded. War, most certainly, but a one-sided battle on this pitch. This was Carew country and he made the most of it. Cunis was hit this way, Taylor that. Howarth was on for the 10th over and immediately had Oscar Durity tickling a catch to Turner.

That only increased the tempo. Soon Davis was hitting Howarth over the square leg fence, Carew made a meal of Alabaster and in 34 minutes they added 50. Turner departed and by lunch Carew and Davis had breezed along to 107 for one and the New Zealand bowlers seemed powerless.

They had a 100 stand in 91 minutes and even though the admirable Howarth conceded only 47 runs from 20 overs Carew and Davis were completely in control. Carew hurried through the 90s with fours, reached his 100 in 190 minutes (with 16 fours) and then just as breezily hit himself out by slashing at Cunis.

Davis set his sights rather higher for, with de Souza going along solidly at the other end, Davis reached his 100 in 213 minutes, 60 of them in boundaries, and set off after another.

So, as the day simmered along to stumps, Trinidad were 297 for two, Davis still there on 137, de Souza 43 and the New Zealanders were drooping as low as they had been at Sabina a month before.

If it was any consolation they had taken the two catches offered during the day. But the bowling had been humdrum, Congdon's captaincy had been decidedly odd for he moved the bowlers about with no apparent plan and seemed to err by taking the second new ball 40 minutes before stumps, when neither Cunis nor Taylor seemed in any mood to make good use of it.

And, as the New Zealanders drifted away to the expansive hospitality of their billets provided by Texaco executives, there came the chilling news that Turner's injured knee might, with the second test just round the corner, prevent him from batting.

## SECOND DAY

Davis' big laugh echoed round the Trinidad dressing room before the start of play—he has the impish kind of humour that would find a postage stamp amusing—and he had some more chuckles in the middle. He snicked Taylor's first ball and Congdon, at first slip, muffed the chance. So Davis nicked Cunis, Congdon again dropped the catch and Cunis' face was a study —it was the first time in a week he had got an edge.

Davis smiled some more, at 150 in 308 minutes, but his luck could not last and four runs later Taylor again got the edge and Congdon scooped up the catch safely. Still Trinidad were 322 for three and would have been 349 for four had Hastings fastened on to a catch off Larry Gomes, a youngster of pleasant style.

Vivian repaired that with a rocket of a throw from cover that ran Gomes out and just before lunch Congdon had Roy Faria, the wicketkeeper, lbw.

Still de Souza soldiered on, playing any number of forgettable strokes until he reached his century (13 fours, 287 minutes) and then hit all over a straight ball from Cunis. Vivian got a rare wicket when Julien skied a big hit, and he almost got another with what looked suspiciously like a five-bouncer. Alabaster undid Bartholomew with a top-spinner, Congdon bowled Jumadeen and then the amiable Carew cried enough at 474 for nine wickets.

Turner did not bat so Campbell, after only one innings of consequence on the tour, was pressed into service as Congdon's partner. It was a tough task for Campbell, and some of the more senior batsmen should have taken his place. He handled the seam attack sensibly but the first sighting of Inshan Ali was enough, with the fourth ball nipping through and bowling him with Campbell quite obviously mystified by the whole affair.

Fifteen for one, and then 27 for two as Burgess on-drove, set off for the single and Congdon stayed at home. Burgess pounded his pad with annoyance as he stalked off and the chortling of the crowd prevented anyone from hearing if Burgess' bat had bounced off the dressing-room wall. It was bad cricket and hard words were said about Congdon for not moving in what might well have been a comfortable single. Just before stumps Hastings, then 19, was dropped by Julien off Noreiga.

So it was 70 for two (or three counting the injured Turner) and still 404 runs behind the Trinidad first innings. Some of the New Zealanders cracked hearty afterward—remember the first test, they said—but no-one cracked hearty about Inshan Ali for the little man with the quick run-in still had mystery in his fingers and few of the New Zealands could offer any solution.

## THIRD DAY

Congdon did not captain very well on the first day, and did not catch very well on the second, but, praise be for New Zealand, he batted very well on the third.

Hastings made most of the early play against the seamers and caught Congdon at 44 after giving him 46 minutes start. Hastings gave Ali a stiff catch-and-bowl chance in his first over, reached his 50 in 89 minutes and went four runs later, probing forward for the Ali chinaman only to have a leg-spinner flick across, take the edge and carry for Davis to make a diving catch.

The situation was grim, 121 for three, and Vivian spent 34 minutes over his first run, but had 18 and the durable Congdon 77 when lunch came at 165 for three.

Carew, for some reason, switched to off-spin from himself and Noreiga. Congdon celebrated by hitting Noreiga for two fours and reached 90. Vivian allowed himself the liberty of a six off Noreiga.

So the amiable Carew tried another tack, giving Julien and Bartholomew the new ball. Congdon reached 99 with a crisp four off Julien and then came his 100, with nine fours in 262 minutes—a brave innings and somewhere in the vast refinery someone sounded off with a steam whistle to mark the occasion.

Vivian snicked Bartholomew for four to bring the 100 stand in 148 minutes and the New Zealanders, at 221 for three, were happier for the follow-on mark of 325 seemed just round the corner.

But Carew was not done. After only nine overs of the new ball Ali was back, and Vivian was gone, lbw when trying to sweep. Wadsworth played forward for the off-break, but the legbreak hopped away and Faria had the stumping. Taylor got himself run out trying to make hay from an overthrow. Six for 235, and then seven for 240 as Congdon tried to cut Ali and Davis had the catch. Congdon had laboured mightily for 332 minutes, but had hardly taken off his pads before Howarth was the third to fall to the Ali-Davis trap.

Eight for 248 and while Cunis and Alabaster hit away happily Turner buckled on his pads in a last-ditch effort to avoid the follow-on.

Alabaster had a venerable old bat, probably one of the few Bobby Simpson autographs to be seen these days, but the middle was as good as ever as Alabaster hit Noreiga over the fence, admired the stroke for some seconds and repeated it.

The score started to race toward 300, but Bartholomew had Cunis lbw at 286 for nine and a tentative Turner helped Alabaster to reach 307 for nine at the close.

Alabaster, with his 39 not out, and Congdon were regarded as heroes, but Carew still had the game under control. His prize weapon, Ali, had already taken six wickets and if New Zealand did not avoid the follow-on Ali threatened to spin New Zealand to their first defeat.

## FOURTH DAY

Alabaster made a brave show. Davis dropped him at 310 off Ali, so Alabaster swept him for four. Then it was 319, six runs needed, Jumadeen bowled Alabaster, and New Zealand were faced with the follow-on.

Then curious Carew took charge. He did not make New Zealand follow-on, and instead chased runs. Taylor knocked over Durity quickly, Carew scored 30 out of 37 before Howarth made a brilliant diving catch to shift him and Davis nudged Cunis to Congdon at slip. Trinidad were 75 for three in an hour. Julien hit Taylor over the grandstand and was out trying it again, and Gomes lived only briefly. By lunch Trinidad were 98 for five, 253 on with 180 minutes and 20 overs to play.

Had Carew declared then he would have had New Zealand on toast. They must have tried to chase such a reasonable target, and might well have hit themselves out against Ali.

Instead Carew, after being happy as a sandboy for three days, became cautious. Trinidad battled on, and on, and on. There was time for Cunis to get Faria's wicket and for de Souza to be run out before Carew finally called them in at 147 for seven.

Cunis and Taylor were pleased, with three wickets each. So were the rest of the New Zealanders for they had no prospect of scoring 303 in about 190 minutes and thus were able to play out an honourable draw.

Campbell this time started better, Congdon could not be shifted and he scored 42 not out as New Zealand cruised to 120 for three at stumps.

But there was still time for the New Zealanders to try and make a point about Ali. With his angled, over-the-wicket delivery he tended to run down the line of the stumps, especially when he sensed the chance of a return catch.

Congdon quickly pointed this out to the umpire, who seemed unmoved, even after telling Ali that he could not rule on an lbw appeal because Ali had obscured his vision.

The New Zealanders persisted, Ali went off and changed his boots and Carew had the last laugh. By tea Ali had come down with some mysterious complaint which kept him off the field. Why give the New Zealanders a free look at Ali when he was an obvious choice for the second test a few days later?

Or almost the last laugh. That really belonged to the irrepressible Davis. He had bowled Burgess at the tail-end of the match. Listening to Davis explain all the vast and long trickery that had gone into that dismissal was more fun than the match itself.

## TRINIDAD

| First Innings | | Second Innings | |
|---|---|---|---|
| M. Carew c sub (Jarvis) b Cunis | 100 | c Howarth b Cunis | 30 |
| O. Durity c Turner b Howarth | 8 | b Taylor | 4 |
| C. Davis c Congdon b Taylor | 156 | c Congdon b Cunis | 24 |
| R. de Souza b Cunis | 100 | run out | 30 |
| L. Gomes run out | 14 | c Wadsworth b Taylor | 0 |
| R. Faria lbw b Congdon | 5 | c Taylor b Cunis | 4 |
| P. Bartholomew lbw b Alabaster | 28 | not out | 11 |
| B. Julien c Hastings b Vivian | 8 | c Hastings b Taylor | 26 |
| I. Ali not out | 20 | not out | 7 |
| R. Jumadeen b Congdon | 13 | | |
| J. Noreiga not out | 1 | | |
| Extras (b1 lb3 w1 nb16) | 21 | (b4 lb1 nb6) | 11 |
| Total (for 9 wickets decl.) | 474 | (for 7 wickets decl.) | 147 |

Fall: 36, 173, 322, 358, 380, 410, 428, 449, 473. — 27, 37, 75, 89, 96, 101, 138.

*Bowling*

| | O. | M. | R. | W. | O. | M. | R. | W. |
|---|---|---|---|---|---|---|---|---|
| Cunis | 31 | 7 | 74 | 2 | 13 | 0 | 74 | 3 |
| Taylor | 23 | 3 | 62 | 1 | 11 | 0 | 49 | 3 |
| Howarth | 42 | 10 | 117 | 1 | 2 | 0 | 13 | 0 |
| Congdon | 18 | 2 | 44 | 2 | — | — | — | — |
| Alabaster | 35 | 7 | 116 | 1 | — | — | — | — |
| Vivian | 4 | 0 | 22 | 1 | — | — | — | — |
| Campbell | 4 | 1 | 18 | 0 | — | — | — | — |

## NEW ZEALANDERS

| First Innings | | Second Innings | |
|---|---|---|---|
| B. Congdon c Davis b Ali | 119 | not out | 42 |
| K. Campbell b Ali | 8 | c Davis b Jumadeen | 21 |
| M. Burgess run out | 3 | b Davis | 22 |
| B. Hastings c Davis b Ali | 54 | c Faria b de Souza | 24 |
| G. Vivian lbw b Ali | 46 | not out | 4 |
| K. Wadsworth st Faria b Ali | 0 | | |
| B. Taylor run out | 1 | | |
| R. Cunis lbw b Bartholomew | 16 | | |
| H. Howarth c Davis b Ali | 4 | | |
| J. Alabaster b Jumadeen | 48 | | |
| G. Turner not out | 8 | | |
| Extras (b6 lb3 w1 nb2) | 12 | (b1 lb4 w1 nb1) | 7 |
| Total | 319 | (for 3 wickets) | 120 |

Fall: 15, 27, 121, 231, 233, 235, 240, 248, 286. — 32, 62, 111.

*Bowling*

| | O. | M. | R. | W. | O. | M. | R. | W. |
|---|---|---|---|---|---|---|---|---|
| Bartholomew | 25 | 3 | 47 | 1 | 2 | 0 | 7 | 0 |
| Julien | 14 | 1 | 33 | 0 | 6 | 0 | 13 | 0 |
| Ali | 37 | 11 | 79 | 6 | 3 | 1 | 9 | 0 |
| Noreiga | 25 | 4 | 80 | 0 | 15 | 4 | 30 | 0 |
| Jumadeen | 28.4 | 5 | 54 | 1 | 16 | 6 | 25 | 1 |
| Carew | 7 | 2 | 13 | 0 | — | — | — | — |
| Gomes | 2 | 1 | 1 | 0 | 1 | 0 | 4 | 0 |
| Davis | — | — | — | — | 5 | 2 | 5 | 1 |
| de Souza | — | — | — | — | 3 | 1 | 8 | 1 |
| Durity | — | — | — | — | 3 | 0 | 12 | 0 |

Eighth match.—SECOND TEST, Queen's Park Oval, Port of Spain, March 9, 10, 11, 12, 14. Drawn.

Not unexpectedly, after his wonderful bowling at Guaracara Park, Ali was promoted to the West Indies side. So was Vanburn Holder, the tall Barbados and Worcestershire medium-fast bowler.

Otherwise the West Indies team was unchanged, and looked the stronger even if Dowe and Grayson Shillingford had hardly played themselves out after the first test.

Dowling was not well, but he set his lean jaw and announced he would play. Sadly, Collinge had to go home. Neither Webb nor Campbell had the form to demand a test place and Vivian, the firebrand in the field, won the out-of-form Jarvis' place after his solid 46 against Trinidad.

The pitch, so everyone said, would take turn and produce shooters, probably from the third day onward. The day before the test the pitch was a drab thing, very hard and dry and with an abrasive surface that promised turn from the start.

The crowd of some 25,000 buzzed with noise as Sobers walked out with Dowling to toss, and then seemed to shriek with alarm when the announcement came that Sobers had put New Zealand in.

Around the members' pavilion people wondered aloud at Sobers' sanity. Surely he was tempting fate. I managed to catch his eye before he went out. "Why?" said Sobers. "Well if there is any life in the pitch it will be at the start."

## FIRST DAY

Having made his guess Sobers, in his own incredible way, made it work. After 18 minutes he made the ball bounce sharply up near Turner's ribs and it flicked off his glove for Carew to take a catch high to his right. Another Sobers special, the ball swinging sharply into Dowling, and Carew had his second catch.

New Zealand 16 for two and the crowd now greeting Sobers as a genius. They might have acclaimed him even more if Davis had held a snick from Burgess only one run after Dowling had departed.

So, after an hour and 15 overs New Zealand had struggled to 26 for two, and precious few of those 26 had come from the middle of the bat. Sobers had to rest, two for 10 from eight overs before he launched his spinners, Gibbs, Ali and then Holford.

A genius, Sobers? Perhaps, but then he seemed to err. Rowe, the Jamaican, was regarded as a first-rate slip field, and so he was posted to first slip. However, neither he nor Findlay, the 'keeper, had stood behind Ali before and they seemed to read him as uncertainly as the New Zealand batsmen.

At Guaracara Park a few days before Davis had taken three catches from Ali at first slip, and had had much experience reading the little Indian's bewildering spin. But Davis was posted elsewhere, Rowe stayed at first slip and this tactical mistake may have cost West Indies the test.

Just before lunch Congdon, then 22, prodded gingerly at Ali, the wrong'un got the edge—and Rowe dropped him simply because he was taken by surprise.

Burgess went immediately after lunch, at 66 for three, making a quite unnecessary slash at Holder. Congdon, 27, jumped out at Ali, missed, but Findlay did not read the spin and missed the stumping. Rowe redeemed himself a little by taking a simple chance from Hastings off Ali, and at 77 for four New Zealand were on the edge of disaster.

They seemed to have plunged right in when Holder had Vivian lbw at 78 for five, but Congdon's rare streak of luck held. At 29 he edged Holder and poor Rowe, by now completely unsettled, never looked like holding it. Wadsworth, on three, was put down by Holder off Ali. Congdon, 33, repeated his edge and the ball squirted forward from Rowe's jittery hands.

Shuddering shouts of alarm swept down from the crowd, Rowe looked as if he hoped an earthquake would swallow him up—and Congdon went placidly on as if nothing untoward had happened.

Wadsworth was less durable and after struggling for 48 minutes sent a return catch to Holford. So it was 99 for six, with Taylor leading in the tail and Congdon, for all his outward assurance, looking liable to disappear at any moment. Taylor gave him heart by pulling Holford for four and he smiled vastly after hitting Holford for six.

By tea New Zealand were 129 for six, the unflappable Congdon 48 after four chances in 219 minutes and Taylor a breezy 24. Back came Holder with the old ball, and then the new one, which suited Taylor's generous strokes. They scored 50 together in 58 minutes. It does not sound much, but already the West Indians were starting to look a trifle ragged and those quick runs of Taylor's seemed to take the sting out of them.

Out of the blue Sobers gave Foster a bowl, Taylor tried to cut a straight one and was bowled at 168 for seven. This must be the beginning of the end, and it might have been had Findlay not dropped Congdon (64) off Ali.

So Congdon swept Ali for four, put Gibbs through the covers for another and Cunis announced his presence by twice pulling Ali for fours.

By stumps, then New Zealand had tottered to 211 for seven, with the remarkable Congdon 85 and Cunis 20. They were not out of the woods, but at least they could see a few chinks of light between the trees. And, if nothing else, the day produced two tasty pieces of byplay in the middle.

Congdon spent most of the time foiling Gibbs with his bat-pad technique, with many balls being taken on the pad.

"Who are you?" demanded Gibbs, "Pele?"

"Ah, no," drawled Congdon, "not Pele, I can only kick with one foot."

The other came when Ali, exasperated at beating Cunis' usually broad bat five times in one over, made some sharpish comment to Cunis about batsmen not good enough to get an edge.

"Well, my man," said Cunis, "why bowl at the bat when you are not good enough to hit it."

There were few other pleasantries about the day and Rowe, with one catch in four attempts, was heartily booed as he came off the field.

## SECOND DAY

Rowe got a cheer early in yet another hot, sunny day—he left the field for some minor repairs.

Sobers bowled, and then had Ali quickly back in business and Congdon, looking much more confident than on the previous day, hit him superbly through the covers. A few minutes later, on 91, he straight drove him for six—an immaculate shot with the ball travelling straight and true like a well-hit seven iron.

Cunis had his problems against Holford and might have been out for 23 had not Sobers, anticipating Holford's wrong'un from the leg trap, darted forward only to have the edge go behind him. So Cunis buckled down again, his long blond hair flying out like a battle flag.

Congdon got a single, then another, and with a sumptuous shot hit Ali through the covers for four to reach his 100. The crowd roared with praise, Congdon waved his bat briefly and got back to business.

By now the West Indies attack had lost its polish. Sobers switched his bowlers rapidly, a sure sign that the batsmen were taking command—and they were for they raised their 100 in 131 minutes and Cunis had done his part by scoring 31 of them.

He had some luck at 36 when Findlay dropped a difficult chance when Cunis swept at Ali, so Cunis celebrated by thumping Ali for four and by lunch they were still there, Congdon 129, Cunis 43 and New Zealand 284 for seven—the incredible stand already worth 116 and New Zealand very nearly out of danger.

After lunch Sobers continued his juggling, even trying some wrist spin himself. Holder was there with the old ball and then, as the final effort, with the new one.

It meant the end of Cunis. Holder's first delivery with the new ball was of genial pace and direction. Cunis, expecting something quicker, pushed forward for the umpteenth time, but the pace deceived him and Holder had an easy catch.

Back came Cunis, his hair awry, his swagger slightly more nautical than before. He had scored 51, the stand was worth 136 runs in 171 minutes, the match had virtually been saved.

Holder quickly had Howarth out at 307 for nine and the ground-staff gathered at the edge of the field with their brooms and rollers as a tacit vote of no confidence in Alabaster's batting.

By now, however, Congdon was in top form and even Sobers clapped when Congdon drove him straight for four, perhaps the best shot of his wonderful innings. Holder hit Alabaster with a bouncer, so Alabaster twice hit Gibbs for fours. It was fun, but it could not last and Alabaster, after a bonny 18, tickled Ali round the corner to Carew to finish the innings at 348.

Congdon, still immaculate with never a hair out of place or an unseemly crease on his shirt, returned and the crowd greeted him like the hero he was. He had distributed chances on the first day, he had batted like a champion on the second—with no outward change in his implacable attitude. He had batted 504 minutes, with 14 fours and a six. He had saved a test that was virtually lost beyond recall.

Instead of lambs to the slaughter, the New Zealanders were pulsing with energy when West Indies batted. Taylor beat Carew off the pitch and had him lbw at 18 for one. Howarth did everything but bowl Rowe in his first over to the Jamaican. Congdon came on, then Alabaster.

Congdon bowled at Ali's foot-scrapes almost in line with the off stump. Rowe played and missed, played and missed again. He played and missed yet again, but Congdon did not and the New Zealanders leapt for joy as Rowe's off stump was knocked out. Davis, as jittery as any new boy, prodded anxiously at Alabaster and the catch floated up, and dropped into vacant country at mid-off. If it had gone to hand West Indies would have been 65 for three. As it was they were 68 for two at stumps.

The New Zealanders did not quibble about that. From the edge of defeat they now could even catch a faint scent of victory with three days remaining and West Indies to bat last.

## THIRD DAY

Davis must have slept well, for he greeted Alabaster with three booming fours in one over. Exit Alabaster. Fredericks was tentative against Howarth, but held on while Davis charged. He scored 30 in even time, but then the New Zealanders tightened up and cut off Davis' favourite strokes.

Fredericks, meantime, could make nothing of Howarth, especially the ball angled away from him. He tried to drive, to cut, but could not fathom Howarth's subtle changes. Inevitably, Howarth got him, with Fredericks reaching across for the drive and Wadsworth, after an agonising juggle, holding the edge.

By lunch West Indies were 153 for three, Davis down to walking pace at 41 and Foster, equally at sea to Howarth, a tentative four.

Still, Foster fought on grimly, helped Davis score 50 in 72 minutes and then seemed to capitulate to Howarth, sweeping at a ball which hustled through and hit middle and leg stumps.

Enter Sobers, clapped all the way to the crease, and cheered even more when a miss-hit drive at Howarth went for four, and when another—no miss-hit this—went soaring away for six.

Congdon was more of a problem, tight of length, slow enough of pace to demand power in the stroke. Sobers tried to attack him, misjudged the line by an inch or two and Wadsworth, standing up, took a very fine catch from the outside edge.

Five for 239, but Davis was still there and batting superbly as he cruised toward his century.

In the over before tea Howarth tried one of his "specials" which demands extravagant wobbling of the wrist, but not always equally spectacular results when it pitches. This one was shortish, Davis pulled it savagely and at mid-wicket Turner

Not copybook, but courageous – Bevan Congdon (below) mothering and Bob Cunis cything during their epic 136-un eighth wicket stand which aved the New Zealand first in-ings in the second test at Queen's Park.

Pressure and power: Scenting victory in the third test the New Zealanders (top) huddle round Michael Findlay's bat as Hedley Howarth bowls. The next day Gary Sobers (left) and Charlie Davis (right) hit out during their match-saving 254-run stand in the West Indies second innings.

sprang up, pulled down the catch and in his businesslike way set off for afternoon tea.

Six for 245, with all the big batting guns spiked, and the New Zealanders pressed home their attack after tea. Holford fought stubbornly, but Congdon removed him at 270 for seven.

Findlay fought, too, but Taylor bowled him just before stumps which came at 288 for eight.

The game had now changed course completely, and on into the night went the theories. A New Zealand lead of, say, 40 runs, could lead to a 200-plus margin at stumps, giving Dowling time to plan a declaration on the fifth day.

## FOURTH DAY

So much for theories. The ball was 131 overs old—and in Queen's Park parlance that means the consistency of a wet bread roll. Dowling, still out of joint with his injured back, decided that Howarth and Cunis would winkle out the last two—with the old ball.

Howarth and Alabaster, perhaps, or Cunis and Taylor with the new ball. But not a mixture like that.

Dowling's ruse might have worked. Holder and Ali decided on short singles. One was very risky, and as Howarth ran in to take the throw at the bowler's end he collided with the umpire, Ralph Gosein, and a very good chance was lost.

Ali and Holder batted bravely and sensibly, but as the minutes wore on and the runs trickled in Dowling's plan had obviously misfired. But he persisted for 68 minutes before he took the new ball.

In eight minutes Taylor knocked over Ali and Holder. New Zealand had a seven-run lead, which mattered not. What did matter was that Holder and Ali, in their plucky fight, had used up 76 minutes which New Zealand could not afford to lose. Those minutes late in the game might have had West Indies deeper in trouble, perhaps in defeat.

But Dowling should not be criticised too keenly. He had a plan and it almost worked. The only criticism can be that he tried the one plan for too long.

Whatever the worries, Dowling and Turner filled in 13 minutes before lunch, with Dowling in considerable pain with his back, but still tight-lipped about the injury. The pain more or less forced him to hurry after lunch, for his time was running out. Ironically, he was out to a fine stroke, sweeping Gibbs off the meat of the bat only to see Holder hold a magnificent catch at backward square. Plainly, it was not Dowling's day.

Still, Turner was very much in command and Congdon started where his 166 of the first innings left off. They reached 77 for one at tea, with Turner passing his 1,000 in tests, and cruised comfortably on to stumps, 30 minutes early because of bad light, at 112 for one.

## FIFTH DAY

Contrary to all the predictions the pitch survived the rest day without visible harm and Congdon and Turner went effortlessly along before lunch. Congdon cracked Holford for six, they scored 54 in the hour and Turner was heading toward his hundred. Sadly, he fell five runs short. Sobers bowled a quicker one, Turner jabbed down but the ball trickled from the face of the bat on to his off stump.

Congdon attacked, a four off Sobers, a six off Gibbs and but for his urgency might have become the first New Zealander to score centuries in both innings of a test.

Instead Congdon kept attacking and paid the price for an off-drive at Ali floated up and Holford held the catch. He had batted 244 minutes, 19 fewer than Turner, and even if the celebrated double had eluded him Congdon still came out of the test with honours thick upon him.

After lunch Burgess and Hastings scored briskly until Dowling called them in at 288 for three, giving New Zealand a 295-run lead with about 200 minutes remaining.

It was a token gesture and when Carew and Fredericks reached 52 without effort by tea the game was going flat. Suddenly it sprang to life again as Vivian, after moving the wrong way, dived back for a stunning catch from Carew.

Rowe, the merest of mortals now, gave Howarth a simple return catch. Fredericks had a genial wipe at Taylor and Hastings caught it. Three for 68, Congdon threw in an attacking field and Foster obligingly turned Taylor to Burgess at short leg.

Twenty overs to go, and soon Sobers had an ugly swing at Alabaster and was bowled, at 95 for five.

It was very, very close to panic stations, and had not Davis batted coolly West Indies might have folded up completely. Fortunately for them Holford was equally as sound as Davis. Congdon flirted with Vivian's exotic spin, Howarth tried his hardest, but Davis and Holford could not be shifted.

A draw, then, but judging by the reaction a points win to the New Zealanders. Within an hour the critics were starting to bite. By next day they had their teeth into the West Indies side. Sobers bore the brunt, but Rowe got his share, too.

No wonder the New Zealanders smiled quietly. They came close to losing the test, and then came just about as close to winning it. For a team that had struggled out of Jamaica fortunate not to be one down in the series they had thrown a spanner into the West Indies works.

The were entitled to smile from the ringside as the West Indians seemed to be jabbing away at themselves.

NEW ZEALAND

| | *First Innings* | | *Second Innings* | |
|---|---|---|---|---|
| G. Dowling | c Carew b Sobers | 8 | c Holder b Gibbs | 10 |
| G. Turner | c Carew b Sobers | 2 | b Sobers | 95 |
| B. Congdon | not out | 166 | c Holford b Ali | 82 |
| M. Burgess | c Findlay b Holder | 32 | not out | 62 |
| B. Hastings | c Rowe b Ali | 3 | not out | 29 |
| G. Vivian | lbw b Holder | 0 | | |
| K. Wadsworth | c and b Holford | 7 | | |
| B. Taylor | b Foster | 46 | | |
| R. Cunis | c and b Holder | 51 | | |
| H. Howarth | lbw b Holder | 0 | | |
| J. Alabaster | c Carew b Ali | 18 | | |
| Extras | (b6 nb9) | 15 | (b3 nb7) | 10 |
| Total | | 348 | (for 3 wickets decl.) | 288 |
| Fall: | 5, 16, 66, 77, 78, 99, 168, 304, 307. | | 35, 174, 218. | |

*Bowling*

| | O. | M. | R. | W. | O. | M. | R. | W. |
|---|---|---|---|---|---|---|---|---|
| Holder | 32 | 13 | 60 | 4 | 15 | 5 | 17 | 0 |
| Sobers | 26 | 7 | 40 | 2 | 20 | 3 | 54 | 1 |
| Gibbs | 29 | 6 | 64 | 0 | 35 | 14 | 67 | 1 |
| Ali | 46.5 | 10 | 92 | 2 | 33 | 8 | 60 | 1 |
| Holford | 22 | 6 | 45 | 1 | 17 | 2 | 50 | 0 |
| Davis | 3 | 1 | 9 | 0 | 4 | 2 | 5 | 0 |
| Foster | 9 | 5 | 12 | 1 | 7 | 2 | 9 | 0 |
| Carew | 3 | 0 | 8 | 0 | 5 | 0 | 10 | 0 |
| Fredericks | 5 | 3 | 3 | 0 | 4 | 2 | 6 | 0 |

## WEST INDIES

| | *First Innings* | | *Second Innings* | |
|---|---|---|---|---|
| R. Fredericks | c Wadsworth b Howarth | 69 | c Hastings b Taylor | 31 |
| M. Carew | lbw b Taylor | 4 | c Vivian b Taylor | 28 |
| L. Rowe | b Congdon | 22 | c and b Howarth | 1 |
| C. Davis | c Turner b Howarth | 90 | not out | 29 |
| M. Foster | b Howarth | 23 | c Burgess b Taylor | 3 |
| G. Sobers | c Wadsworth b Congdon | 19 | b Alabaster | 9 |
| D. Holford | lbw b Congdon | 14 | not out | 9 |
| M. Findlay | b Taylor | 16 | | |
| I. Ali | c Burgess b Taylor | 25 | | |
| V. Holder | b Taylor | 30 | | |
| L. Gibbs | not out | 3 | | |
| Extras | (b12 lb9 w1 nb4) | 26 | (b8 nb2 w1) | 11 |
| Total | | 341 | (for 5 wickets) | 121 |

Fall: 18, 65, 143, 200, 239, 245, 270, 281, 327. 59, 66, 68, 73, 95.

*Bowling*

| | O. | M. | R. | W. | O. | M. | R. | W. |
|---|---|---|---|---|---|---|---|---|
| Cunis | 22 | 5 | 67 | 0 | 5 | 0 | 33 | 0 |
| Taylor | 20.1 | 9 | 41 | 4 | 12 | 2 | 26 | 3 |
| Howarth | 52 | 17 | 102 | 3 | 20 | 8 | 36 | 1 |
| Congdon | 39 | 19 | 56 | 3 | 1 | 1 | 0 | 0 |
| Alabaster | 21 | 7 | 49 | 0 | 4 | 2 | 5 | 1 |
| Vivian | — | — | — | — | 4 | 2 | 10 | 0 |

# 8

# *Barbados: A Lot of Beating*

You could hear the chant everywhere . . . amid the sumptuous lawns and gardens of Government House, in the hustle, bustle and smells of downtown Bridgetown, on the beaches of gorgeously creamy sand . . . "Barbados will beat you."

For cricket to Barbadians is what Rugby is to the Welsh, and used to be to New Zealanders—an intrinsic part of their heritage born out of Barbados' affection for England and things English, nurtured even more by the deeds of the fabulous Walcott-Worrell-Weekes trinity and more recently by Sobers, Hall and Nurse.

A few weeks before Barbados, skippered by Holford, had won the Shell Shield, so the "Barbados will beat you" cry rang even louder.

The New Zealanders had been warned of this fervent patriotism and took it willingly enough, for they still had their tails in the air from the second test at Trinidad.

The took it even more willingly when they found Barbados to be a place of sunny people and sunnier beaches. Their hotel, the Windsor, was a pleasantly quiet place populated by so many elderly people browsing round the lounge that it looked like the scene for a Somerset Maugham short story. Happily, the Windsor supplied a spare room for the team meetings. Even more happily the beaches were just across the road and within 24 hours Campbell was back with a tan that would raise envy among the goose-pimples of St Clair beach in Dunedin.

Perhaps the most affecting moment in Barbados came one night when, after being entertained by the local press club, I adjourned to a hotel where Barbadians, tourists and some rather unsteady journalists combined in a wow of a party. The band blared, everyone danced, the barmen seemed to have six arms each. The noise was incredible.

Suddenly, without warning, the band began the Barbados national anthem. It is an appealing, stately and melodious tune (making *God Defend New Zealand* sound something like a soap-powder jingle).

Two seconds later everyone was standing, silent and with heads erect, whether they were Barbadians or visitors. It was an affecting moment and when the band had finished and packed their instruments I mentioned this to my friend.

"Ah," he said, "we are not many, we have only a small country, but we are a proud people."

Proud was the word. Barbadians (the harsher, more popular word Bajan seems to grate in this pleasant land) walk tall, the mahogany-hued Negroes are quick to laugh, and away from the clutter of Bridgetown they have much to be proud of.

For, in the scenic sense, Barbados takes a lot of beating. On one hand, moving up the west coast, you can flit by superb, and expensive, hotels nestling among the trees, with golden beaches and impossibly blue water a few yards away.

To the east there is even more beauty, or perhaps a rugged charm as the hills and valleys and canefields meander down to where the Atlantic surges on to rocks and headlands and more superb beaches.

To the north-east are the hills, craggy outcrops frowning down with the brooding beauty of Scotland.

Tourism is big business in Barbados, yet the Barbadians have had the wit and the wisdom to make sure that the 100-odd hotels (on an island smaller in area than Lake Taupo) do not become gruesome concrete-steel-glass eyesores. The hotels are there, and some of them are very fine. But they are tucked away off the main roads and have, most of them, been blended into the natural surroundings.

Sam Lord's Castle, on the south-eastern bulge of Barbados, is the perfect example. Sam was a rascal in the early 1800s who would hoist lanterns on the palms along the seashore. Ships off-shore, thinking the lights indicated an anchorage, would head for them, pile up on the reef and Sam's lads would hustle out in their boats and collect the booty.

The original castle—perhaps manor house is the more accurate term—remains, surrounded by lawns, gardens, fountains and a long path to the golden beach below. On the fringes of the property, tucked in among the trees, are the modern hotel units, tennis courts, swimming pools and the like. Better such sensible beauty than some umpteen-storeyed monster to pull in the tourist dollar.

Further north there is fine old Lodge School, started in 1720 and still breathing a tranquil charm. Or the venerable St John's

Church, with a relative of Constantine in the graveyard, or the Codrington Hall seminary with a magnicent avenue of palms opening the way to architecture sublimely classical and beautiful.

There are many other things and places of beauty in Barbados. The roads, either skittering round the coasts or making cool valleys through the canefields, are narrow. It would be a horn-blower's paradise, but the Barbadians handle them with a caution that owes more to courtesy than self-preservation.

Barbados' proud ties with England—Barbados claims to be the first country to be at England's shoulder at the start of the Second World War—are slackening. The political influence is solidly in the hands of the Negro majority and some of the power is being weaned away from the white families that once held most of Barbados' wealth. Yet the political life seems stable and sensible. In the *Advocate-News*, the morning newspaper, it was common to see criticism of the Government that would have brought prompt reaction in a more sensitive political atmosphere.

Strangely enough, the one place which seems out of keeping with the natural beauty and charm of Barbados is the cricket field, Kensington Oval.

For a ground that held such men as the "three W's" and the more recent heroes, Kensington Oval is a commonplace, not terribly attractive ground skirted half the way round with grandstands of depressingly utilitarian and, in some cases, ancient aspect. The ghosts of the great cricketers should not be asked to haunt such a place.

Ninth match. —— v. Barbados, Kensington Oval, Bridgetown, March 17, 18, 19, 20. Drawn.

The New Zealanders, by now reinforced with a pale-faced Morgan—but with Dowling deeper in gloom with his bad back—set off for Barbados' sunny beaches still savouring the drama and excitements of the second test.

Barbados, too, were still reliving their Shell Shield win, and the fact that Sobers would not be in their eleven worried no one —after all they had won the shield without him—and Holford, as captain, had built up a superb spirit in his side. Holder was not to play, either, ostensibly so he could rest for the third test. As later events showed the New Zealanders were happy that Holder was not in the game for the pitch would have suited him.

Barbados, instead, put their faith in two promising medium-fast men, Colin Payne and Hallam Moseley, backed up by

Keith Boyce, the Essex all-rounder and former test player, Holford and an off-spinner, Tony Howard who Barbadians maintained was twice as good as Gibbs.

For batting Barbados had Seymour Nurse, who batted so well in New Zealand three years before and now relieved of test worries, Geoffrey Greenidge, the Sussex opener, Peter Lashley, a former test batsman and the promising youngsters Nolan Clarke, Winslow Ashby and the wicketkeeper David Murray.

Congdon, Wadsworth and Howarth were rested and poor Dowling was forced to mope about with his back in a corset.

So Turner was made captain for the first time, and the New Zealanders smiled broadly when he won the toss.

## FIRST DAY

They smiled less broadly when Moseley and Payne, in their opening overs, made the ball lift and move awkwardly. There was some grass on the pitch, a little moisture in it and even if it played rather like some New Zealand pitches, the New Zealanders found the change from the heartless strips of Jamaica and Trinidad disconcerting.

Fortunately for the New Zealanders neither Moseley nor Payne was accurate enough to make good use of the pitch and it took Boyce, with the craft he had learned in England, to have Turner caught at 37 for one.

Jarvis, looking much more resolute, battled on sensibly, Hastings survived a chance to Holford off Boyce, but then checked a drive at Howard and Nurse gathered in the catch. Two for 83.

Burgess, relishing the quicker, high bounce, played his old strokes again, but Jarvis found Howard a problem and went lbw to him at 128, with his hard-won 60 taking 215 minutes. Morgan looked useful, Burgess grew more powerful of stroke but, as he had done at Port of Spain, was out immediately after the interval —this time two balls after tea.

Morgan, hitting across the line, was caught at 176, Campbell at 200 and after a speculative appeal against the light—which at least forced the umpire to remove his dark glasses—Taylor was knocked over by Boyce.

So by the end of a day that had promised much New Zealand finished disappointingly at 210 for seven. The fight, the spirit of the second test was not there. Wickets were cast away. The Barbadians gleefully predicted victory for their side, and it was hard to find an argument in rebuttal.

## SECOND DAY

Vivian, 15 not out after 88 painstaking minutes on the previous day, decided to attack and for the first time on tour looked the gifted strokemaker that New Zealanders know.

Boyce, still lively, was hit square for four, over the top of slips for another and pounded through the covers for three. These were magnificent strokes, but looked insignificant when Vivian square cut, the ball flashing first bounce to the fence and with even Boyce applauding the majesty of the stroke.

Cunis held fast, extracted four overthrows from a mixed up short single, while Vivian made the stand worth 50 with another glowing cover drive.

Enter Howard, exit Vivian, lbw in his first over, with 10 fours in his dogged 61, and Boyce had Alabaster out before Turner declared at lunch, 301 for nine, in a bid to keep the game open.

Taylor opened it up more by having Ashby lbw in his third over and might have rattled Barbados even further if he had managed to get the edge as Nurse flashed away, missing as often as he hit the ball with his daring strokes.

Greenidge, very much the English pro in his technique, looked safe and sound and his on-drives were handsome strokes. With luck so obviously with him, Nurse decided to make the most of it. The small crowd whooped for joy as cuts and drives, pulls and hooks raced away to the fence. Nurse reached 50 in 58 minutes; with Greenidge he added 100 in 82 minutes.

Cunis, relishing the chance to move the ball off the pitch, at last finished Nurse's boisterous progress by bowling him for 76 (12 fours, 89 minutes) and the game returned to normal.

Vivian took a splendid catch to remove Lashley at 164 for three, and if Greenidge looked safe and sound Clarke somehow survived until stumps at 195 for three.

By now the New Zealanders were looking forward to another draw, but the news that evening was gloomy. As far as could be seen Dowling was not making progress. Alabaster had not been able to bowl, for his ankle was sore and a doctor's examination showed an inflamed Achilles tendon which removed any hope that he would be able to bowl in this match, and might rule him out of the third test.

## THIRD DAY

There was little joy for the New Zealanders next morning, with the pitch playing easily, Greenidge moving along gracefully and Clarke, restored to confidence, hitting extremely hard. Greenidge cruised to his 100 (283 minutes, seven fours and a six), Clarke hit Webb massively for six and did the same to Morgan, trying out a looped flight for his off-spinners.

The score bounded from 200 to 300 in 91 minutes, but just before lunch Taylor had the new ball and removed Clarke with his first delivery.

Soon after lunch Greenidge gambled against Burgess' fielding and lost, but his 126 had made the selectors take notice and, none too secretly, Greenidge was told to delay his departure to Sussex in case he was wanted for the tests. Taylor, now on top of his form, had Murray caught and Boyce lbw. Holford chimed in with 35 and then closed the innings at 400 for nine. In the 85 minutes before stumps New Zealand lost Turner at 21 and, in the last over, Hastings at 43 to a witless stroke which skied comfortably to Payne at long leg.

Still 56 runs behind, and virtually three wickets down for Alabaster was in pain with his ankle, the New Zealanders once again faced the prospect of defeat. By now the "Barbados will beat you" chant could be heard everywhere and unless the New Zealanders batted more sensibly the home side looked likely to have another international scalp on their belt, for they had the power-packed batting to win a run-chase on the last afternoon.

## FOURTH DAY

Burgess started the last day pleasantly, but Jarvis had his usual trouble with leg-before at 55. Morgan settled in, Burgess hit powerfully and they wiped out Barbados' lead without trouble. Fifty came in an hour, Burgess hit a booming four off Howard to reach 50 in 102 minutes and then, in his peculiar fashion, did his disappearing trick immediately after lunch. Howard snuffed out Vivian and Campbell quickly, taking three wickets in 33 balls after lunch for 11 runs, but Morgan hit three fours in a Howard over to reach 50 and Taylor, with spinsterish caution, helped in a 50-run stand in even time before falling to Boyce again.

By tea, with an hour and 20 overs remaining, New Zealand were 226 for eight, but Morgan lasted only two more balls, Webb existed only a few minutes and Barbados needed 136 runs, with 35 minutes and 20 overs remaining. The crowd were jubilant. Had not Barbados won the shield by scoring 200-odd in half as many minutes? This time they needed five runs an over—Nurse could do that on his own.

Taylor bowled, without a slip, and Greenidge and Ashby took six from the over without risk. Cunis to Ashby, a dab at the second ball and Campbell had the catch. In came Nurse, the crowd trumpeting with joy. In came Cunis, the first ball to Nurse pitching a trifle short, cutting in through the gate and rattling the stumps. The crowd were struck dumb, such things were not possible, Nurse out first ball. So it was two for six, and then three for 15 when Cunis tricked Greenidge into a return catch and four for 21 when Taylor had Clarke lbw.

Twenty overs to go, 115 runs wanted and Barbados threw in Boyce, the power-hitter, as their final bid. He hit Cunis for six, slashed him for four, but Taylor got him lbw with a skidder and Barbados, at 48 for five, were out of the race. Holford and Lashley dug in and, try as they might, Cunis and Taylor could not get their teeth into the Barbados tail that followed. Holford went at 65 for six, but time was running out and Lashley and Murray saved Barbados from embarrassment.

The Barbadians cheered the New Zealanders off the field. The "fighting Kiwis" became their nickname. Perhaps "fickle" might have been a better word. How else could a team be outplayed for nine-tenths of the match, and almost win it in the last two hours?

NEW ZEALANDERS

| | *First Innings* | | *Second Innings* | |
|---|---|---|---|---|
| G. Turner | c Moseley b Boyce | 10 | b Payne | 10 |
| T. Jarvis | lbw b Howard | 60 | lbw b Boyce | 25 |
| B. Hastings | c Nurse b Howard | 28 | c Payne b Holford | 5 |
| M. Burgess | c and b Holford | 44 | c Boyce b Howard | 68 |
| R. Morgan | c Holford b Howard | 21 | b Boyce | 75 |
| G. Vivian | lbw b Howard | 61 | b Howard | 2 |
| K. Campbell | c Nurse b Boyce | 10 | c Holford b Howard | 0 |
| B. Taylor | b Boyce | 4 | c Murray b Boyce | 17 |
| R. Cunis | not out | 22 | c Nurse b Moseley | 5 |
| J. Alabaster | lbw b Boyce | 5 | not out | 0 |
| M. Webb | not out | 8 | c Murray b Howard | 3 |
| Extras | (b2 lb13 w2 nb11) | 28 | (b4 lb10 nb10) | 24 |
| Total | (for 9 wickets decl.) | 301 | | 234 |
| Fall: | 37, 83, 128, 162, 176, 200, 207, 270, 283. | | 21, 43, 55, 151, 166, 166, 216, 224, 226. | |

*Bowling*

| | O. | M. | R. | W. | O. | M. | R. | W. |
|---|---|---|---|---|---|---|---|---|
| Payne | 16 | 8 | 27 | 0 | 12 | 2 | 35 | 1 |
| Moseley | 17 | 5 | 27 | 0 | 16 | 4 | 25 | 1 |
| Boyce | 30 | 6 | 78 | 4 | 17 | 2 | 45 | 3 |
| Howard | 34 | 4 | 75 | 4 | 31.2 | 9 | 58 | 4 |
| Holford | 29 | 5 | 66 | 1 | 18 | 5 | 35 | 1 |
| Greenidge | — | — | — | — | 3 | 0 | 12 | 0 |

## BARBADOS

| | First Innings | | Second Innings | |
|---|---|---|---|---|
| G. Greenidge | run out | 126 | c and b Cunis | 6 |
| W. Ashby | lbw b Taylor | 6 | c Campbell b Cunis | 2 |
| S. Nurse | b Cunis | 76 | b Cunis | 0 |
| P. Lashley | c Vivian b Cunis | 14 | not out | 23 |
| N. Clarke | c Campbell b Taylor | 76 | lbw b Taylor | 4 |
| D. Murray | c Campbell b Taylor | 3 | not out | 7 |
| D. Holford | st Campbell b Morgan | 35 | c Turner b Taylor | 15 |
| K. Boyce | lbw b Taylor | 17 | lbw b Taylor | 21 |
| C. Payne | run out | 11 | | |
| A. Howard | not out | 11 | | |
| H. Moseley | not out | 3 | | |
| Extras | (b6 lb5 nb11 | 22 | (lb5 nb4) | 9 |
| Total | (for 9 wickets decl.) | 400 | (for six wickets) | 87 |

Fall: 17, 130, 164, 313, 317, 321, 351, 381, 393. — 6, 6, 15, 21, 48, 65.

*Bowling*

| | O. | M. | R. | W. | O. | M. | R. | W. |
|---|---|---|---|---|---|---|---|---|
| Webb | 27 | 1 | 112 | 0 | — | — | — | — |
| Taylor | 32 | 5 | 88 | 4 | 10 | 1 | 28 | 3 |
| Cunis | 27 | 5 | 98 | 2 | 10 | 0 | 37 | 3 |
| Morgan | 18 | 4 | 65 | 1 | 3 | 1 | 6 | 0 |
| Burgess | 3 | 0 | 15 | 0 | — | — | — | — |
| Vivian | — | — | — | — | 3 | 1 | 7 | 0 |

Tenth match.—THIRD TEST, Kensington Oval, Bridgetown. March 23, 24, 25, 26, 28. Drawn.

Dowling, by now quite distracted by the pain from his back, was packed off to hospital and his going cast a gloom over the party. Alabaster, in his stoical way, made light of his ankle injury. In theory he was considered for the test, but obviously the selectors were not prepared to risk him in a five-day game. With the promise of bounce in the pitch Webb came under consideration, perhaps in place of Morgan or Hastings—the latter in patchy form.

In the end New Zealand placed Jarvis for the injured Dowling, and promoted Morgan into Alabaster's position.

The New Zealanders smiled quietly to themselves when Gibbs, the off-spinner, was dropped and replaced by Shillingford. "Pele" Congdon and Turner, with a little luck on their side, had stifled Gibbs at Port of Spain and the popular feeling that Gibbs was over the hill (to which the New Zealanders privately did not subscribe) was taken up by the selectors.

The pitch was examined minutely in the days before the test, and the New Zealanders were saddened when they found a five o'clock shadow of grass had been trimmed off on the final morning.

Both teams had a council of war. Congdon, a full test captain for the first time, suggested the night before that he would bat if he won the toss. A few hours before the toss Congdon and his lieutenants conferred again. Even with a two-man, Taylor-Cunis medium-fast attack, they thought it a reasonable risk to put West Indies in. There might have been a defensive thought, too, about West Indies' three-pronged attack of Holder, Shillingford and Sobers.

Sobers looked at the pitch, a bland-looking strip, poked, prodded, called correctly and decided to bat, and Congdon sighed with relief at not having to gamble himself. There was a damp feeling in the air, and play was held up for 34 minutes while the outfield dried out after a shower. It had all the classical features of being a toss anyone would gladly have lost.

## FIRST DAY

Cunis' eye sparkled when he made the ball bound in his first over. Fredericks' eyes gave a wicked glint when he pulled a ball in Taylor's first over so high it was almost six. Carew, by contrast, looked unhappy as Taylor made the ball snarl up at him; he failed to keep down a flier and Morgan, at leg gully, darted forward for the catch.

You could almost feel the shudder sweep through the West Indies' camp. The crowd, who would have preferred their local favourite Greenidge in the side, jeered Carew as he went and they hardly greeted the hapless Rowe as he shaped up to his first ball.

Taylor afterward maintained that it was the best ball he had ever bowled, forcing the stroke as it pitched about middle and leg and then lifting and whipping murderously away to the off, taking the edge as Rowe pushed hopefully forward and Wadsworth had the catch. Apart from a desultory boo or two for Rowe, the crowd were stunned into silence. Two for six, and then three for six as Fredericks cut viciously at Cunis and Hastings at gully somehow smothered the ball as it ripped into his midriff.

There were cheers for Sobers, promoting himself to No. 5 to meet the crisis he had provoked with his toss decision. Davis, meanwhile, was in grievous trouble. His first ball, from Taylor, belted him nastily on the hand. Another pounded him on the hip. Somehow he squirted a single, Sobers cracked a four, but

Davis could not get away from Taylor. Once more Taylor produced a snorter, rather like a fast leg-break, which whistled near Davis' face and he guided it neatly to Jarvis at second slip.

Four for 12, Taylor three for six from 13 balls, and the out-of-form Foster joined Sobers, with the field closing in like sharks for the kill. Taylor pitched short and Foster bravely pulled him for four. Sobers hooked Cunis for four, a masterly stroke. Foster blazed away at Taylor, bowling rather short, and three times hit him to the fence. It was brave, bold batting but it could not last. Taylor bowled a fuller length, Foster played hopefully and Wadsworth again swooped on the catch.

Lunch, 44 for five. The atmosphere in the New Zealand dressing room was electric. They had West Indies by the throat and only Sobers stood in the way. Davis could still raise a wan smile among the West Indians—otherwise they looked like men preparing for the firing squad.

Holford and Sobers, against Taylor refreshed, and the alarm among the New Zealanders as Holford got an edge and Wadsworth spilled the catch simply because he tried too soon to throw it triumphantly in the air. No matter. Three balls later Taylor repeated the ball, Holford the snick and this time Wadsworth caught it as carefully as if the ball had been fine crystal.

Taylor, his thinning hair plastered with sweat, the spring gone from his step, had to rest, five for 42 from 15 overs, Congdon shuffled Cunis and Howarth about, and then bowled himself. His second ball went away from Sobers, he drove far from the line and Wadsworth soared across for the catch. Seven for 83, and Taylor back to bowl at Ali, the man he had scared with a bouncer at Port of Spain. Taylor tried it again and then, with Ali expecting another flier, Taylor bowled him with a ball of full length. Eight for 99, and then nine for 102 as Congdon bowled Holder.

All the time Findlay had been battling along, watching the carnage. Now he struck out boldly, with Shillingford doing his bit at the other end. Taylor bowled and bowled, seldom with his old vigour, for he seemed to be bowling from memory. Findlay hit him for four, so did Shillingford, and no matter how close Taylor was to a record of seven wickets in a test innings his time was running out. He seemed to be in his last over, for he was stooped and drooping with fatigue, but one last fling got the ball to jump, Shillingford heaved at it and Morgan spurted in to hold the catch.

Slumped in his seat, his shirt and trousers stained with perspiration, the congratulations rolled over Taylor. He professed ignorance of the record he had just broken. I filed a story in which Taylor's operative word was "golly". Perhaps it was journalistic licence. The operative word was a trifle fruitier than that.

There was still work to be done, and Jarvis whistled with relief when Sobers dropped him off Holder with the score at two. Turner had his lucky moment, too. Shillingford bowled about leg stump, Turner gestured at but did not seem to hit the ball and Findlay dived forward. The roar and umpire Cecil Kippins' finger went up.

Findlay spoke urgently to Sobers, Sobers spoke just as quickly to Turner—who had dallied a second or two—and the upshot was that Turner was recalled. Findlay had announced that he had not caught the ball. Kippins later remarked that he had over-ruled his earlier decision.

Whatever the reason, it was a splendid gesture by both Findlay and Sobers. West Indians will maintain that Sobers is either a genius or a god with clay feet. The New Zealanders then, before and afterwards, were inclined to call him a gentleman.

So Jarvis and Turner fought on to stumps at 31 for none.

There was joy among the New Zealanders that night. For once fate had been kind. For once conditions had favoured them. Taylor had bowled superbly and Cunis and Congdon almost as well. The catching had been extremely good. For once New Zealand had started a test by getting a grip on the enemy and not relaxing until the life had been choked out of the innings.

## SECOND DAY

The talk was not so much of Taylor's incredible feat, but of Sobers' misreading of the pitch, which was blamed for West Indies' collapse. Fate still smiled sweetly at the New Zealanders, for the pitch had lost its moisture and even if Turner was hobbling with a bruised foot he and Jarvis started soundly.

Suddenly Jarvis was out, again lbw, at 54 and at 68 Turner was taken by Holford at gully off a most un-Turner-like slash, with the feet far from the line of the ball.

Congdon started slowly, scoreless for 26 minutes until he clipped Ali for four. It was grim, hard work, with 100 in 200 minutes, but by lunch Congdon and Burgess had reached 110 for two and the innings seemed on an even keel.

But once again an adjournment meant the end of Burgess, for from the first ball, from Sobers, he squeezed a catch to Fredericks at gully. Congdon, batting superbly, and Hastings saw New Zealand into the lead without further alarm and began to pick up speed. Hastings, a doubtful selection after his recent indifferent form, relished the freedom that the bounce and speed of the pitch gave him. Congdon reached 50 in 106 minutes, they brought in 50 together in 47 minutes and 60 in an hour—madcap scoring by their own standards.

Holder and the new ball slowed down the scoring rate, but Congdon pressed on eagerly. He greeted Foster with two fours, watched Hastings reach 50 in 133 minutes and then raced serenely on to his century. It took Congdon 210 minutes, with eight fours. It hardly was breakneck speed, but was some measure of Congdon's command that his 100 against Trinidad took 262 minutes and the first 100 of his unforgettable 166 of the second test took 366 minutes.

On and on they went, and however Sobers switched his bowlers he could not stem the flow of runs. New Zealand went to 250, the stand was worth 150 in 168 minutes and the only tremor came when Greenidge, fielding substitute, made a magnificent but unsuccessful dive when Hastings cut Davis high and backward of point.

Inexplicably, Congdon lost his scoring rhythm. Perhaps he was tired. Whatever the reason his timing became erratic, the good strokes no longer went through the gaps. He was dropped by Ali off Foster at 119, and lived only eight runs before Holder had him lbw.

Congdon had batted 259 minutes, with 11 fours, and with Hastings had scored 175 for the fourth wicket. The score had moved from a tentative 112 for three to 287 for four, putting New Zealand completely in command of the test. It mattered little that Morgan's first sight of Ali was his last, two minutes before stumps, for by then New Zealand were 297 for five wickets, with Hastings 81 not out and looking every inch the fluent, confident batsman that the pitches seldom allowed him to be.

New Zealand 164 runs on, six wickets in hand, a scent of victory in their nostrils although wise heads maintained that unless the pitch cracked up or produced shooters West Indies might well be hard to shift in their second innings.

## THIRD DAY

Vivian started blithely, hitting Ali's first ball for four. Hastings was less commanding, and Davis dropped a reasonable catch at second slip off Holder—the ball flicking through his hands and away for four. Good fortune thus restored, Hastings marched on, cracking Holder through the covers for four and then hitting

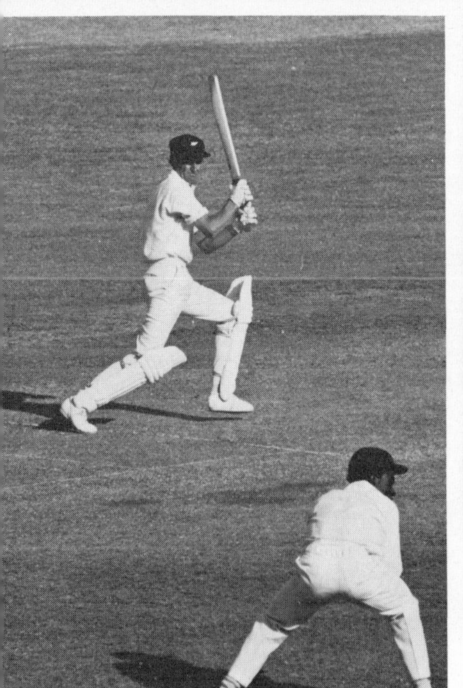

Third Test champions: Brian Hastings (top) drives, Bevan Congdon (left) cuts and Bruce Taylor bowls, the heroes of the Bridgetown test. Hastings scored 105, Congdon 126 and Taylor took his record-breaking seven wickets for 74.

The great stand: Top, Glenn Turner crunches to leg and, at the bottom, Terry Jarvis forces through mid-off during their 387-run opening stand of the fourth test at Bourda, Guyana.

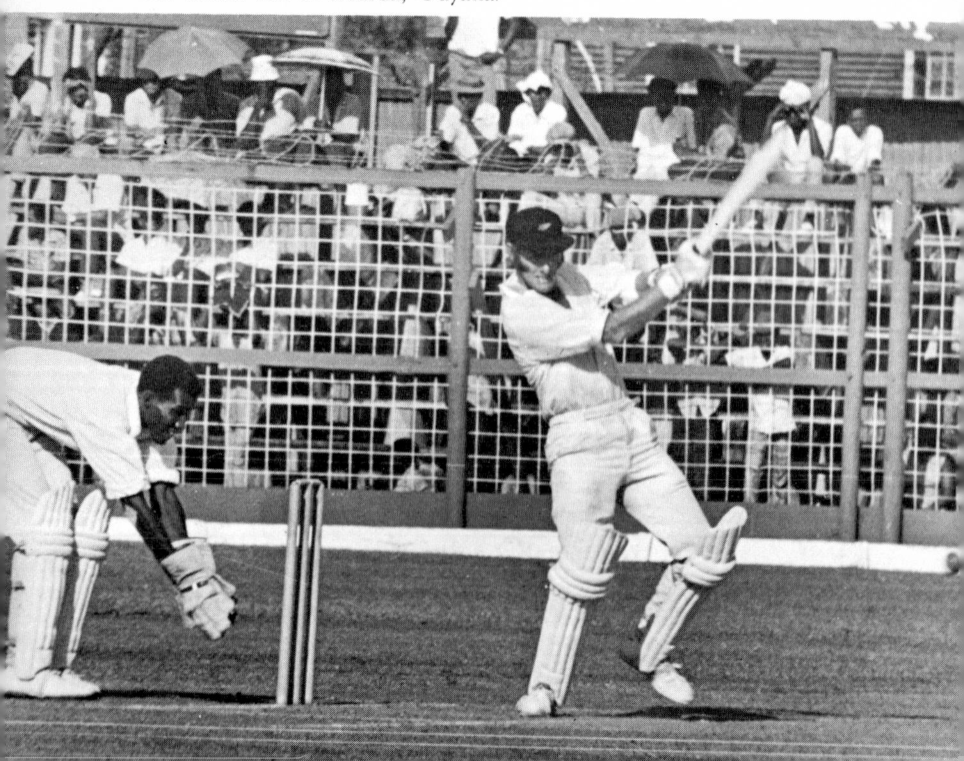

Sobers through the covers for his 15th four and his century in 260 minutes.

Sobers pressed on in a last defiant fling, making mock of those who claimed that if his shoulder didn't pack up under the strain his suspect knee would. He made one hurry at Hastings and got him lbw, a decision the New Zealanders thought marginal for the leg stump was barely within range. Sobers struck again, bowling Vivian, and put Taylor in his place by getting him lbw first ball.

Faithful Wadsworth and Cunis fought back stolidly, took lunch at 389 for eight, but Holder and Shillingford had the innings finished at 2.30. New Zealand, 422, had a lead of 289, with some 14 hours to play.

Taylor looked to heaven for justice when Fredericks put a bottom edge a fraction of an inch over the bails and away for four. By tea he and Carew had 37, but Cunis split them soon after, getting Fredericks very much in front as he played back. Rowe got a single first ball, and an ironic hoot or two from the crowd. Carew tried a light appeal, which missed, and then sliced Cunis to Jarvis, who juggled and missed, too.

On came Howarth, pitching into the bowlers' scrapes outside the left-handers' off stump, and Carew obligingly snicked him to Turner. Findlay became nightwatchman. Congdon shrouded him with catchers and Findlay somehow snicked the first ball between Wadsworth and Turner, and survived until stumps at 98 for two.

That night the kids clustered round the New Zealanders for autographs. The West Indian players slipped by unnoticed. Everyone loves a winner, and that is what New Zealand seemed sure to be—191 runs on, eight wickets to take, an innings to spare.

## FOURTH DAY

The New Zealanders were as jumpy as kittens before play. They had struggled hard to survive defeat on the tour, and now victory was within reach. They found it hard to realise.

Howarth had six men round the bat at the start, Findlay chopped one ball for four, but got an inside edge soon after and Morgan held the catch round the corner. Three for 105, Davis hit Howarth for two fours, Cunis for one, but was plainly baffled by Howarth. At 18 Davis got an edge, it fled past Turner, but it seemed only a temporary relief for Davis, as Howarth was in commanding form.

Rowe, however, looked solid, the score edged up to 150, they scored 50 together in 69 minutes and Rowe was 50 after 171 painstaking minutes of extremely sensible batting. Congdon changed Howarth to the other end, bowled himself and got Rowe lbw at 163. It was 171 at lunch, and Taylor had Foster lbw with the first ball after the break. Sobers, his head erect as if sniffing the scent of battle, joined Davis. Taylor was removed after one over and Howarth returned. Every time he pitched in the rough Sobers winced, but he was quick of eye and bat and managed to survive.

Soon the pattern emerged . . . Davis taking Howarth, Sobers at the other end. West Indies were 200 (310 minutes), Taylor took the new ball at 221 and Sobers twice hit him for four. Magnificent cricket, this, the New Zealanders bowling and fielding as well as they could, Davis and Sobers fighting for every run. By tea they were 243 for five. Sobers hit Taylor for four, Taylor beat Sobers completely, so Sobers hit Taylor for four again. A century stand, Congdon to Davis and two sparkling fours through the covers. The light was bad, Davis appealed and lost at 4.54, but by 5 o'clock the murk had deepened and that was that for the day. West Indies 297 for five, eight runs on, five wickets in hand.

Sobers was now regarded as the hero, but Davis had been, if anything, the more influential player for he had done most to foil Howarth, the outstanding New Zealander.

## FIFTH DAY

"Sobers must be fair dinkum," said one of the New Zealanders. It had become common practice for the players of both teams to have a knock-up on the outfield before play started in this and the previous tests. Common for everyone, except Sobers. He stayed in the dressing room. But there he was out on the field practising his batting.

Davis opened up with a crisp four through the covers, 300 arrived, Sobers cracked Taylor twice to the fence and soon the stand was worth 150.

Then the crisis. Taylor, with the pitch giving him little help, tried bowling round the wicket. Sobers fenced at the first ball, edged it and it flew straight to Jarvis, who spilled it on the ground.

Sobers was 87, the total 321, about 330 minutes play remained. A wicket then might have been the breakthrough the New Zealanders so dearly wanted. But the catch went down and Sobers and Davis carried on. Soon Sobers had his hundred, strangely his first against New Zealand and his 25th in tests. Not long afterward the gallant Davis joined him. Davis took 388 minutes, Sobers 248. Up came the 200 stand, by lunch the two heroes had lifted West Indies to 375 for five and time was running out for New Zealand.

Immediately after lunch Davis, 117, gave Wadsworth a difficult chance off Morgan. Two minutes later West Indies had 100 runs on and as the final move Congdon rested the gallant Howarth, 64 overs for 114 runs and two wickets, and took the new ball.

Sobers counterattacked magnificently. Three glorious boundaries came from his bat and there would have been a fourth had not Vivian made a splendid dive to stop it.

For 15 minutes Sobers was the king, the great player, but it was the fence or nothing for him. He flicked Taylor square, Vivian dived forward for a stunning catch and the great stand was over. Together they had scored 254 in 363 minutes, the time of Sobers' 142. West Indies were 136 ahead, with a little more than three hours left.

The New Zealanders, for so long so completely in command, seemed to slump for by now victory was out of sight. Davis, nearing the point of fatigue, battled onward and Holford stayed until 518 before Congdon removed him.

Now all that remained was Davis' quest for the double-century which would have given his epic innings even greater stature. Sadly he missed it. He was tired, desperately so, his lean face even gaunter than before after more than nine hours' vigilance. His strokes lost their power, his running became uncertain. He drove, straight to Turner at mid-on and set off, a hopeless run if Turner from short range hit the stumps. He did, and Davis was gone, 183 runs in 601 minutes with 19 fours. The New Zealanders knew something about match-saving innings . . . they applauded Davis as warmly as anyone.

Ali and Holder finished off the day, the New Zealanders flopped about their room and long after they had revived Congdon was still there, unchanged, wondering aloud that but for three balls and three dropped chances the game would have been New Zealand's.

The news that Dowling would have to go home hardly lightened the gloom. Still, no matter how keen their disappointment, the New Zealanders had come a long way. If anyone had said after the first test, or the first day of the second, that three dropped catches would stand between New Zealand and victory at Bridgetown he would have been laughed at.

## WEST INDIES

| First Innings | | Second Innings | |
|---|---|---|---|
| R. Fredericks c Hastings b Cunis | 5 | lbw b Cunis | 28 |
| M. Carew c Morgan b Taylor | 1 | c Turner b Howarth | 45 |
| L. Rowe c Wadsworth b Taylor | 0 | lbw b Congdon | 51 |
| C. Davis c Jarvis b Taylor | 1 | run out | 183 |
| G. Sobers c Wadsworth b Congdon | 35 | c Vivian b Taylor | 142 |
| M. Foster c Wadsworth b Taylor | 22 | lbw b Taylor | 4 |
| D. Holford c Wadsworth b Taylor | 3 | c Wadsworth b Congdon | 50 |
| M. Findlay not out | 44 | c Morgan b Howarth | 9 |
| I. Ali b Taylor | 3 | not out | 12 |
| V. Holder b Congdon | 3 | not out | 16 |
| G. Shillingford c Morgan b Taylor | 15 | did not bat | |
| Extras (nb1) | 1 | (b6 lb9 w1 nb8) | 24 |
| Total | 133 | (for eight wickets) | 564 |

Fall: 6, 6, 6, 12, 44, 52, 83, 99, 102.

48, 91, 105, 163, 171, 425, 508, 544.

*Bowling*

| | O. | M. | R. | W. | O. | M. | R. | W. |
|---|---|---|---|---|---|---|---|---|
| Cunis | 10 | 3 | 26 | 1 | 38 | 8 | 130 | 1 |
| Taylor | 20.3 | 6 | 74 | 7 | 33 | 3 | 108 | 2 |
| Congdon | 16 | 3 | 26 | 2 | 31 | 7 | 66 | 2 |
| Howarth | 3 | 1 | 6 | 0 | 74 | 24 | 138 | 2 |
| Morgan | — | — | — | — | 30 | 8 | 78 | 0 |
| Vivian | — | — | — | — | 8 | 2 | 20 | 0 |

## NEW ZEALAND

*First Innings*

| | |
|---|---|
| G. Turner c Holford b Holder | 21 |
| T. Jarvis lbw b Shillingford | 26 |
| B. Congdon lbw b Holder | 126 |
| M. Burgess c Fredericks b Sobers | 19 |
| B. Hastings lbw b Sobers | 105 |
| R. Morgan c Fredericks b Ali | 2 |
| G. Vivian b Sobers | 38 |
| B. Taylor lbw b Sobers | 0 |
| K. Wadsworth not out | 15 |
| R. Cunis c Findlay b Holder | 27 |
| H. Howarth b Shillingford | 8 |
| Extras (lb13 nb22) | 35 |
| Total | 422 |

Fall: 54, 68, 112, 287, 293, 369, 369, 412.

*Bowling*

| | O. | M. | R. | W. |
|---|---|---|---|---|
| Holder | 40 | 12 | 91 | 3 |
| Sobers | 29 | 6 | 64 | 4 |
| Shillingford | 24.2 | 7 | 65 | 2 |
| Davis | 10 | 3 | 19 | 0 |
| Ali | 35 | 12 | 81 | 1 |
| Holford | 9 | 0 | 20 | 0 |
| Foster | 14 | 2 | 40 | 0 |
| Fredericks | 2 | 0 | 7 | 0 |

# 9

# *Guyana: A Famous Pitch*

It did not take long to come down, from the blissful days of the vest-pocket paradise that is Barbados, to earth and the bothersome times of Guyana, tucked away on the northern coast of South America.

As had become usual the players and myself had simply noted "New Zealand" as our home address on the immigration cards before we returned our attention to the smoked salmon and other delicacies on the Air France flight to Georgetown.

As was usual we were diverted to the VIP room, to sip and natter while our baggage was cleared and it was time to move off to the hotel. Amid the sipping and nattering I was tapped on the shoulder.

"Are you Cameron?" asked a Guyanese, in the usual West Indian way of dispensing with given names. Assured of this, the official then requested that I fill in my home address, in detail. Having done so I asked the reason.

"Ah," he said, "you have written here that you are a journalist. What kind of journalist are you?"

He was not amused when I told him my wife thought I was a very fine journalist. He seemed happier when I told him I was covering the New Zealanders' cricket tour, and departed.

So did we, some minutes later. As we moved toward the cars there came another tap on the shoulder and the same official said that I must report to the immigration authorities the next morning.

Next day—with the cricketers, in something like gallows-humour, promising to come and see me on visiting days—I reported, and eventually my permit to stay in Guyana was lengthened from one day to long enough to cover the two matches in Georgetown. My passport showed that I had first been given a 17-day permit. This had been amended to one day, and then extended. If it had not been extended I would have been on the first plane to Trinidad which, at the time, seemed like an interesting idea.

Some days later I found that the mix-up was caused by the fact that, at the time, journalists were not the most popular visitors to Guyana. A month or so before Duff Hart-Davis, of the *Sunday Telegraph*, London, had swung through the Caribbean and had written a series of penetrating articles on the various countries.

Hart-Davis' piece on Guyana had hardly been complimentary. He had taken some hearty swings at Forbes Burnham and his Government. There were allegations of graft and corruption in high places. Burnham, he said, was becoming a champion of Black Power. Unemployment was rife, Guyana was "in a sick state" and Hart-Davis was critical of Guyana's liaison with Communist China.

So I suppose it was natural for a journalist, even a cricket one, to be regarded with some suspicion. Being more concerned with the cricket, I had neither the time nor the wish to delve deeply into Hart-Davis' diagnosis of Guyana and its Government. However, it was possible to find that all was not well with Guyana. There is unemployment on a large scale. The Government's import policies are restrictive, even to a New Zealander. There is crime in the streets.

Before the New Zealanders arrived in Guyana they had been warned of "choke-and-rob" assaults and advised not to walk alone at night. Once there the warnings were repeated. Never walk alone. Even in a group, do not walk in certain parts of the city.

The choke-and-rob technique is to grab some lone walker by applying an arm-bar across his throat while the assailant, or his accomplice, frisks the victim's pockets. The local people told us it was better to have, say, $10 in your pocket if you were attacked. If you had money you lost it, and got some bruises. No money could mean a proper beating.

One night Bill Bates, the British High Commissioner, and his delightful wife Susie, had Jack Alabaster, Terry Jarvis and myself to supper. Their fine old house was only 400 yards from our hotel along one of the widest, best-lit streets in Georgetown. Bill's chauffeur drove us—there was never a suggestion that we should walk.

Burnham and his Negro government hold power. They have already taken over the Alcan bauxite complex, which pained the Canadians, and may have eyes on other foreign investment. While we were in Georgetown the Government announced with glee a $50 million interest-free loan from Red China, with the hint that more financial and technical aid might be forthcoming.

At the moment Cheddi Jagan, leader of the large East Indian community, is in Opposition. What would happen, I asked, if Jagan took over. Unlikely, was the reply, but the alternative was hardly better than the present Government.

The political and social unrest seems to provide an uneasy undercurrent to Guyanese life. Some people we talked with went so far as to say that nothing would be changed except by a massive, perhaps revolutionary, upheaval. Just how far below the surface are these revolutionary elements it is hard, and probably not wise, to find out.

I was given a small hint the evening before we left. Two young men approached me, identified themselves as members of the local Marxist-Leninist group, and asked if I would carry out of Guyana some material which they thought would be safer posted the next day in Jamaica. I would rather have carried an unexploded bomb.

There was a drab fascination about Georgetown itself. It is placed several feet below sea level and protected by a massive seawall, a legacy of its Dutch origins. Running along the broader streets are large, open drains. What happens when a high tide coincides with a downpour I shudder to think.

Apart from some of the newer office buildings almost all the construction is of timber. Some of this—in the massive St George's Cathedral, Stabroek Market and in the extravaganza in timber that is the City Hall—represents quite remarkable and eye-catching architecture.

But the rows and rows of wooden houses begin to pall after a while especially as most of them seemed unpainted and ghostly grey. The reason is simple. The salty sea air corrodes and disfigures the paint, so they are only painted once.

Yet all was not uneasiness and bleak wooden boards in Guyana. Time did not allow us to wander to the hills and savannahs of the inland country and so we could only hear second-hand of the majestic beauty of the hinterland.

Still, there was always Bourda, one of the neatest, best-kept cricket grounds it would be possible to see. Surrounding the superbly-smooth field were the grandstands, all sparkling and clean in their white and green paint. They play lawn tennis on the outfield, some indication of the smoothness of the surface. Bourda is not a big ground, but the appointments are first-rate. The Georgetown Cricket Club, which controls the ground, is the oldest in the West Indies, and justifiably proud of the fact. The players' facilities are first-rate and there is an airy spaciousness about the members' pavilion.

The pitch, regrettably, is another matter. Cunis maintained, after a shower of rain, that a sprig of grass had heaved itself through the hard-packed merciless clay. Poor Cunis, the sun must have got to him.

Amid the grey tints of Georgetown life there was another suprise. On Easter Monday the Georgetonians flocked to the seawall and soon hundreds of kites of all shapes and colours were zooming about in the sky. It was a fascinating sight, and just as intriguing to find the reason why it occurs only on Easter Monday, with the kites packed away that night to wait another year.

Why? Simply to greet the Resurrection. A perplexing place is Guyana.

Eleventh match. —— v. Guyana, Bourda, Georgetown, March 30, April 1, 2, 3. Drawn.

It was farewell to Barbados and its beaches by mid-day, greetings to Piarco airport for long enough for some fair "oil" on the Union Park races from Ossie Gonzales, and then to Georgetown that night, with the game on the morrow.

How dearly Congdon would have liked to win that toss. The New Zealanders had been in the field for two and a half days, and the day's travelling hardly revived them. But Congdon came back from the steaming heat with the usual sad news and the bowlers muttered away and prepared for another struggle.

It could only be thus. The pitch, famous—or infamous—the world over, looked as plumb as could be. The sun beat down and Guyana had assembled a strong team built round the batting of Lloyd (restored to health), Camacho, the durable Baichan, the dashing Kallicharran and Fredericks, way down at No. 5. They had Gibbs, if West Indies did not, Rex Collymore, a very tall slow left-armer and a new fast bowler, Robert Adonis, who was regarded as being the fastest in the West Indies.

Howarth, Cunis and Burgess were rested, Alabaster was given a chance to test his ankle and the manager, Chapple, was promoted to 13th man . . . and obviously liable for some exertion in the middle whenever the players could arrange it.

## FIRST DAY

Taylor's first ball to Camacho was a stunner, swinging in and moving away. Camacho afterward maintained he was not good enough to get an edge to it. Thereafter the batsmen had few worries. Camacho started briskly, but had to carry almost all the burden for Baichan seemed to think runs were out of fashion. Congdon had Camacho caught by Wadsworth standing up at 41. By lunch Guyana were 59 for one in two hours and somehow Baichan had acquired nine of them.

After lunch Campbell was given his first long bowl and had his usual dreadful luck, having Kallicharran dropped by Taylor and then Turner in his first over. Fortunately for everyone Baichan went at 65, taking 128 minutes for 10, when Alabaster stranded him and Wadsworth did the rest.

Perhaps the New Zealanders should have left Baichan there, for Lloyd was next and this tall, powerful man immediately began to distribute fours around the ground. Alabaster seemed in some trouble, for his bowling action was stiff, and Lloyd removed him with a towering six over long on. Campbell had 14 overs in a row, a wonderful effort in the strength-sapping heat, so Lloyd turned his attention elsewhere by hitting Morgan over the sight-screen.

By tea they were 199 for two, Lloyd 83 and Kallicharran, almost anonymous in Lloyd's shadow, 58. After tea came the massacre. Lloyd reached his 100 in 128 minutes, 13 fours and two sixes. Webb got the new ball and Lloyd hit him over long on for six from the back foot, an incredible stroke. By now Lloyd was hitting at anything, but Webb managed to get the edge and Turner held the catch. Lloyd took 167 minutes for his 133, and in that time added 213 with Kallicharran.

Just before stumps Kallicharran got his hundred (242 minutes) and Guyana were 301 for three at the close.

The New Zealanders had been told about Bourda. After this first day of Purgatory they believed what they had heard. Already they planned for a draw in the test there the following week. Any other decision was out of the question.

## SECOND DAY

More heat, more runs and the grim news that Alabaster's ankle injury had gone, but he now had a badly strained back. Fredericks and Kallicharran were quickly into business, 36 runs in the first half hour, and Kallicharran darted from 100 to 150 in an hour with a series of delightful strokes, especially through the covers.

Out of the blue Taylor bowled him at 406 for four. It was 448 for four at lunch and all that remained was the wait until Fredericks chimed in with his century in just over three hours, and the declaration. Webb was teased about his bowling "100" but he deserved better than that.

By 2.25 New Zealand were in, and by 2.26 Jarvis was out. Adonis, a very large young man, bowled a quickish first ball, but so lost his stride in the second that Jarvis was distracted. Adonis came on, the ball nipped from the bat to the stumps, the Georgetown crowd erupted—and some worthy gentleman in the press box insisted that Adonis must be in the fourth test.

Congdon had other plans. In his next over Adonis bowled three full tosses and Congdon happily put them to the fence. Adonis again, Congdon hit him 4, 4, 2, 4. Exit Adonis, three overs, 27 runs and one wicket, and Turner and Congdon settled down to enjoy the perfect batting pitch.

By tea they had 65, Congdon had eight fours in his 50 (80 minutes) while Turner, all massive concentration, took 155 minutes, with only two fours, for his 50. By stumps they had 139 for one and Guyana's score of 493 seemed within reach.

The news about Alabaster was worse. He had a recurrence of an old back injury, walking was awkward, running was painful. Still, the New Zealand bowlers put their feet up and wished the batsmen good hunting.

## THIRD DAY

Gibbs caused a stir at the start. He turned a ball, actually turned it, so much that it beat everyone and went for four byes. Turner became rather introspective about this astonishing feat, but Congdon went merrily on, reached his fourth century in four matches and hit a catch straight back to the angular Collymore. Hastings settled in, Turner reached his century in 261 minutes, dug in for his second and by lunch New Zealand were 241 for two.

Turner's rate increased, so much so that Hastings scored 26 of their century stand. At 132 Gibbs put down a return catch from Turner, who might have been his fourth New Zealand victim in about 160 overs. Hastings opened out, the 300 came in 349 minutes and by mid-afternoon Guyana seemed done. Gibbs called up Camacho, who seemed amused. His first ball skidded, Hastings was lbw after helping score 129 in 147 minutes. Camacho was even more amused, but the New Zealanders were not when Morgan also went lbw when given the chance for some valuable batting practice.

By tea New Zealand were 332 for four, Turner 170 and, apart from rest periods when the heat sapped his strength, utterly in command.

Vivian, who also needed the practice, nibbled at Collymore and Pydanna had the catch. Campbell brightened the day, and his test chances, with three powerful fours and Turner, in a rare moment of freedom, actually lofted a drive for four.

Collymore kept nagging away and, at 373, Campbell had an airy swing and was bowled. Wadsworth was as adhesive as ever, Turner went steadily through the 190s, and reached his 200 in 482 minutes, with 26 fours. By the close he was 205, New Zealand 397 for six.

So the bowlers put their feet up again, thinking that Turner was a champion—which he was.

## FOURTH DAY

Adonis—now unlovingly known as "Adenoids"—had the new ball but neither Turner nor Wadsworth was impressed. Turner hit a four to move past Dowling's New Zealand record of 239. Then he went past Bert Sutcliffe's 243 and looked for more worlds to conquer. However, just as he and Wadsworth reached a 100 stand (with Wadsworth getting 25 of them) Turner seemed to lapse. He pushed forward at Collymore, as he had done dozens of times, but only got the edge and Pydanna did the rest.

Turner had batted for 603 minutes, with 33 fours in his 259. The thin crowd, now sated with runs, applauded willingly enough, and then came alive as Pydanna stumped Wadsworth brilliantly. Taylor batted briskly until Lloyd took a fine catch and Alabaster quite needlessly came out to watch the Collymore-Pydannan trap snare Webb.

Collymore, with his high action and clever flight, had bowled superbly to take six for 115 from 55 overs. The New Zealanders were impressed, but they had already sung the praises of Howard, the Babados off-spinner, with a certain aim in view. They kept quiet about Collymore.

With less than four hours remaining Guyana filled in the rest of the day scoring 202 for five. Webb had a fine spell and two for 32 must have seemed like manna. Still, the afternoon belonged to Lloyd and his second wonderful century. No nervous nineties for Lloyd. At 87 he hit Morgan for one six, repeated the stroke and took only 124 minutes over his hundred.

The game, if you could call it that on such a pitch, had produced 1,183 runs for 19 wickets. If a territory game produced such a mathematical exercise, what would the coming test provide?

## GUYANA

| First Innings | | Second Innings | |
|---|---|---|---|
| S. Camacho c Wadsworth b Congdon | 32 | c Morgan b Webb | 17 |
| L. Baichan st Wadsworth b Alabaster | 10 | c Wadsworth b Taylor | 10 |
| A. Kallicharran lbw b Taylor | 154 | c Wadsworth b Vivian | 51 |
| C. Lloyd c Turner b Webb | 133 | not out | 104 |
| R. Fredericks not out | 100 | c Wadsworth b Webb | 5 |
| R. Ramnarace not out | 34 | c Campbell b Vivian | 11 |
| M. Pydanna did not bat | — | not out | 0 |
| Extras (b4 lb20 w1 nb5) | 30 | (nb4) | 4 |
| Total (for 4 wickets decl.) | 493 | (for five wickets) | 202 |
| Fall: 41, 65, 278, 406. | | 22, 32, 161, 191, 202. | |

*Bowling*

| | O. | M. | R. | W. | O. | M. | R. | W. |
|---|---|---|---|---|---|---|---|---|
| Webb | 30 | 6 | 115 | 1 | 9 | 0 | 32 | 2 |
| Taylor | 24 | 3 | 66 | 1 | 6 | 0 | 23 | 1 |
| Congdon | 19 | 2 | 66 | 1 | 9 | 1 | 16 | 0 |
| Alabaster | 22 | 5 | 84 | 1 | — | — | — | — |
| Morgan | 8 | 1 | 39 | 0 | 11 | 1 | 53 | 0 |
| Campbell | 18.2 | 3 | 70 | 0 | 8 | 1 | 39 | 0 |
| Vivian | 3 | 0 | 23 | 0 | 7 | 0 | 35 | 2 |

## NEW ZEALANDERS

*First Innings*

| | |
|---|---|
| T. Jarvis b Adonis | 0 |
| G. Turner c Pydanna b Collymore | 259 |
| B. Congdon c and b Collymore | 103 |
| B. Hastings lbw b Camacho | 37 |
| R. Morgan lbw b Matthews | 8 |
| G. Vivian c Pydanna b Collymore | 1 |
| K. Campbell b Collymore | 18 |
| K. Wadsworth st Pydanna b Collymore | 25 |
| B. Taylor c Lloyd b Gibbs | 15 |
| M. Webb st Pydanna b Collymore | 0 |
| J. Alabaster not out | 0 |
| Extras (b10 lb7 w3 nb2) | 22 |
| Total | 488 |

Fall: 0, 171, 300, 331, 336, 373, 473, 474, 488.

*Bowling*

| | O. | M. | R. | W. |
|---|---|---|---|---|
| Adonis | 20 | 1 | 80 | 1 |
| Matthews | 29 | 4 | 74 | 1 |
| Ramnarace | 27 | 0 | 87 | 0 |
| Gibbs | 43 | 17 | 66 | 1 |
| Collymore | 55.2 | 17 | 115 | 6 |
| Kallicharran | 4 | 0 | 14 | 0 |
| Fredericks | 1 | 0 | 4 | 0 |
| Camacho | 3 | 0 | 14 | 1 |
| Lloyd | 11 | 5 | 12 | 0 |

Twelfth match.—FOURTH TEST, Bourda, Georgetown, April 6, 7, 8, 9, 11. Drawn.

West Indies made the first move—Shillingford, Foster, Inshan Ali and Carew out, Lloyd, Kallicharran, Greenidge, Howard in. This placed Sobers probably at No. 7 in the batting order.

It could hardly be taken as a declaration of war, an unbalanced team such as this, rather a confession that the pitch at Bourda would reduce the test to a stalemate. The New Zealanders were pleased, once more, that Gibbs was left out, whether or not their praise of Howard after the Barbados game had anything to do with his promotion. The omission of Inshan Ali was a puzzle, which could only be explained that West Indies did not want to over-expose him on a pitch that wouldn't help his spinning and sleight-of-hand.

With Alabaster obviously not fit enough for a five-day ordeal on such a pitch New Zealand had less room to manoeuvre and held to their third test side, again with the accent on batting.

Sobers and Congdon went through the formality of going out to the pitch to toss—they could have done it in the dressing room for all the difference it would make—and Sobers' luck held. The crowd told the New Zealanders this long before Congdon came back talking dolefully how the coin had rolled for some feet looking as if it would come up "tails" and then with a final wiggle had flipped over to "heads".

The ground was packed and, if nothing else, the New Zealanders could not have asked for a better field on which to show their wonderful out-cricket.

## FIRST DAY

A bird sat on one of the stumps for five minutes before play started. It might have stayed there, without harm, for an hour or two. Greenidge made a gruesome prod, with the ball floating near Congdon at third slip, to get his first test run, but thereafter Greenidge and Fredericks went confidently through to lunch at 75 for no wicket.

There was a rain shower at lunch. The New Zealanders watched it with interest for they had been told that when it rains in Guyana the downpour can last for days. Faint hope. The shower was gone, and the game went on unchecked.

Strangely, it was not quite the same game. Greenidge and Fredericks, so accurate of stroke before lunch, were reduced to nudges and edges as Cunis and Taylor tied them down. Fredericks snicked Cunis short of Turner, Cunis worked on the flaw and the next time the catch carried. One for 79. Greenidge very nearly edged Cunis to Jarvis, Taylor made him chase one and Wadsworth held the catch.

So it was 103 for two, the New Zealanders came alive, the fielding was aggressively keen. Lloyd scrambled out at Howarth, fell as he came back but Wadsworth was off-balance and could not make the stumping. It was hard, engrossing cricket. Lloyd was no longer the charging cavalier, and Rowe seldom got through the tight field.

By tea West Indies were 151 for two after four hours of high-pressure cricket. Rowe managed one stroke worthy of him, a square drive for four, but straight away was bowled by Congdon as he played back. In a gamble Congdon tried Vivian, with no result.

Then came the drama. Lloyd, on the move, drove to Morgan at deepish mid-on and ran. If Davis had been quickly on the move there was a single there. Davis did not move, he held his ground and screamed "no" at the charging Lloyd. Morgan fielded cleanly, floated the return to Wadsworth and Lloyd was run out by a mile, with Davis hanging his head as if in despair.

This was too much for the crowd. The crowd booed Davis lustily, blaming him for the departure of their idol. They were still booing as Kallicharran began his first test innings, with Congdon crowding him with fieldsmen, the better to take advantage of the explosive situation.

Suddenly Taylor cantered in from the eastern boundary, exclaiming to the umpire Cortez Jordan, that the boos had turned to bottles in his sector. The crowd once again came to the boil and more bottles came from other parts of the crowd. Congdon tried to rally his troops, who were probably pleased at the unexpected rest, and also unwilling to go within throwing range of the fence even if the crowd's anger was directed at Davis.

In a brave move, Congdon went where the bottles were thickest, removed some and tried to reason with the crowd. A girl rushed toward Davis, was headed off by a mounted policeman, and returned unscathed. Plainly, there was no point in remaining, so the players went off.

Officials and police moved out, Lloyd broadcast an appeal for sanity over the radio (the crowd was thick with transistors) and gradually the crowd simmered down to a surly silence.

So the players came back, with Davis again in the firing line for jeers and catcalls. Howarth, fielding on the fence, was told to "bowl dat man Davis" which Howarth would have loved to do in any case. Somehow Davis and Kallicharran held on to stumps at 201 for four.

As Davis was being given a police escort to his hotel and a spectator was nursing a head cracked by a security guard, the New Zealanders thought of pleasanter things. Their bowling had been accurate, their fielding swift. To hold West Indies to 201 in a day was a fine achievement, the first step in the struggle to survival.

## SECOND DAY

The rains came, not in a downpour, but in niggling showers which had the covers crew busy and 162 minutes had been lost by the time of the 2.22 start. Cunis and Taylor soon had the new ball, Hastings put Davis down at 19 but Wadsworth repaired the damage when Davis went to Taylor at 28—237 for five.

Seven runs later Sobers was gone, hitting a simple catch to Burgess off Taylor. After tea Kallicharran struggled on, 22 minutes were lost to rain and just before stumps Congdon winkled out Holford. West Indies were 310 for seven, with Kallicharran 188 minutes over his 59 and if there was any doubt the match would be drawn it had disappeared with the rain.

## THIRD DAY

Kallicharran was a new man, full of rich strokes, for obviously Sobers' declaration, if there was to be one, would be held back to give the youngster a chance for a maiden test hundred. Kallicharran grasped the chance eagerly, a six off Howarth was a sumptuous shot and Kallicharran sprinted to his century, taking 59 minutes to add 41 runs. The crowd rejoiced, Sobers declared and Turner and Jarvis took 50 minutes before they reached the safety of lunch at 11 for no wicket.

Plainly, they were not in a hurry. Turner reached 50 in 160 minutes, the 100 stand came five minutes later. It was riskless, composed batting with Jarvis growing in stature minute by minute. They were slow, and they might have been quicker had they taken full advantage of some genial full tosses from Greenidge.

But they stayed together, 163 for no wicket at stumps, Turner 87, Jarvis 71. West Indies were hampered by Holder's attack of influenza, or some such complaint, which kept him off the field most of the day.

That night Turner and Jarvis were early to bed.

## FOURTH DAY

There was heat, and also Holder, and a tremor when Jarvis was almost run out at 85. Precisely at mid-day Turner reached his hundred, in 320 minutes, with eight fours and the small crowd gave little applause. Jarvis, on 92, played at Lloyd, the ball sped past Findlay and away for four. The runs were given to Jarvis and it was a technical chance, even if Jarvis claimed he had not hit the ball. He deserved some luck, and his century soon after in 363 minutes.

Lunch at 246 for none, and everybody searched through the record books. The scoring rate picked up a little, with Turner's third 50 taking 108 minutes. Then they passed 300 in 457 minutes. Jarvis had 150 in 486 minutes. After tea the records flicked by until only one remained—the world test opening record of 413 held by Roy and Mankad of India.

By this time Jarvis was plum-red with exertion and Turner was doing knee-bends between overs to keep limber. By now, too, Holford was bowling round the wicket and exceedingly well. Jarvis drove at him, not quite to the pitch, the shot was sliced and Greenidge darted in from cover to hold the catch. The stand was 387 and Jarvis 182 in 541 minutes with 19 fours and a five. Congdon saw Turner to his 200 in 553 minutes, with 18 fours—which did drag out some applause—and by stumps New Zealand were 410 and Turner 210, both in 590 minutes.

The critics got the acid out. Turner was slow, New Zealand was slow, a declaration might have had West Indies in trouble. The New Zealanders held their peace, wished Turner well on the last day and wondered how anyone had imagined that a result, contrived or not, could be achieved on such a pitch.

## FIFTH DAY

All that remained was to see just how far the incredible Turner could journey, perhaps near Sobers' world mark of 365. He hardly had time, for Holder was restored to health and bowled tidily with the new ball. Turner himself seemed slightly out of touch—little wonder considering his mental and physical output—and Congdon had a timeless air about him.

Just before lunch came the end, Turner trying to work Howard through the on side and going leg-before, a most undramatic way to end such a saga of 259 runs, 22 fours and 704 minutes.

Burgess had a brief flirt before lunch, Congdon accelerated a little and then declared at 543 for three, causing an upheaval in the New Zealand dressing room which had largely been given over to letter-writing and dart-throwing for two days.

There was less upheaval on the field. Greenidge and Fredericks filled in time pleasantly and, fittingly enough, Jarvis and Turner finished off the bowling.

Bourda had been a place of monumental innings, relieved only by the bottles and Lloyd's flashing blade. The critics cut at the New Zealanders again. They were slow, sometimes very slow. But by now they worried not about criticism. And with a pitch like that Bourda got just about what it deserved.

WEST INDIES

| *First Innings* | | *Second Innings* | |
|---|---|---|---|
| R. Fredericks c Turner b Cunis | 41 | not out | 42 |
| G. Greenidge c Wadsworth b Taylor | 50 | not out | 35 |
| L. Rowe b Congdon | 31 | | |
| C. Lloyd run out | 43 | | |
| C. Davis c Wadsworth b Taylor | 28 | | |
| A. Kallicharran not out | 100 | | |
| G. Sobers c Burgess b Taylor | 5 | | |
| D. Holford lbw b Congdon | 28 | | |
| M. Findlay not out | 15 | | |
| V. Holder did not bat | | | |
| A. Howard did not bat | | | |
| Extras (b10 lb5 w1 nb8) | 24 | (b4 lb2 w1 nb2) | 9 |
| Total (seven wickets decl.) | 365 | (for no wicket) | 86 |

Fall: 79, 103, 160, 178, 237, 244, 305.

*Bowling*

| | O. | M. | R. | W. | O. | M. | R. | W. |
|---|---|---|---|---|---|---|---|---|
| Cunis | 24 | 5 | 61 | 1 | 5 | 2 | 13 | 0 |
| Taylor | 37 | 7 | 105 | 3 | 6 | 3 | 9 | 0 |
| Congdon | 33 | 7 | 86 | 2 | — | — | — | — |
| Howarth | 38 | 10 | 79 | 0 | 9 | 3 | 12 | 0 |
| Vivian | 3 | 0 | 10 | 0 | 3 | 0 | 16 | 0 |
| Morgan | — | — | — | — | 9 | 3 | 10 | 0 |
| Burgess | — | — | — | — | 5 | 3 | 12 | 0 |
| Turner | — | — | — | — | 2 | 1 | 5 | 0 |
| Jarvis | — | — | — | — | 1 | 1 | 0 | 0 |

NEW ZEALAND

| *First Innings* | |
|---|---|
| G. Turner lbw b Howard | 259 |
| T. Jarvis c Greenidge b Holford | 182 |
| B. Congdon not out | 61 |
| M. Burgess b Howard | 8 |
| B. Hastings not out | 18 |
| Extras (lb11 nb4) | 15 |
| Total (for three wickets decl.) | 543 |

Fall: 387, 482, 496.

*Bowling*

| | O. | M. | R. | W. |
|---|---|---|---|---|
| Holder | 24 | 8 | 39 | 0 |
| Sobers | 42 | 15 | 76 | 0 |
| Lloyd | 36 | 11 | 74 | 0 |
| Howard | 62 | 16 | 140 | 2 |
| Holford | 54 | 24 | 78 | 1 |
| Greenidge | 14 | 4 | 34 | 0 |
| Davis | 25 | 8 | 42 | 0 |
| Kallicharran | 6 | 1 | 17 | 0 |
| Rowe | 5 | 0 | 28 | 0 |

# 10

# St Vincent: Welcome Interlude

The New Zealanders looked forward to St Vincent, if only because it was the home of Michael Findlay, the West Indian wicketkeeper, a thoroughly charming man they had cherished in New Zealand in 1969 and who they came to like even more on this tour.

Rum punch at the airport didn't hurt either. Then there was a hotel on the water's edge (with manager Chapple conveniently installed in a flat 400 yards distant) and a chance to unwind after the bottles and bother of Guyana.

A lovely, unspoiled place, St Vincent, with glamorously big charter yachts nodding in the anchorage off the hotel, with lush green bush pouring down from the hills, a main road that ran across the airstrip, and a Gilbertian political set-up.

There had just been an election. Cato, the sitting PM, had lost Mitchell, who ran as an independent. By the end of the counting Cato's party had six seats, Joshua's opposition had six seats, and Mitchell sat neatly in between.

So it happened that at the cocktail party put on by the Governor, Sir Rupert John, the New Zealanders could meet Cato, the Prime Minister. Two days later, at the match, the New Zealanders could meet Mitchell, the Prime Minister. In between times Mitchell had sided with Joshua, been granted the premiership, and that was that.

There were other curiously pleasant features of St Vincent. You don't, for example, usually have caged iguanas looking over your shoulder at mealtimes. And you don't very often strike a pitch such as that laid on St Vincent's handsome new ground at Arnos Vale.

The Vincentians had spent a lot of time and money on their new ground and within a year or two it will be outstandingly picturesque. The New Zealanders were the first team to use it and the appointments were excellent—the scoreboard would leave those at the test grounds, Kensington Oval and Bourda, for dead.

But the pitch had been hastily laid down, and it had not settled and it was a strange thing of ripples and ridges—to walk on it felt like rubber carpet underlay.

Still, it mattered little. The rains ruined the three-day game against the Windwards and the big memory of that game was the way the crowds sat stoically and quietly in the stands from 10 a.m. until play was possible about 3 p.m. on the first day.

As a mark of respect to the crowd, the New Zealanders happily agreed to a 45-over game on the last day, the crowd had their fun, joy was unconfined that night and there were genuine regrets when the team left next day.

Thirteenth match. —— v. Windward Islands. Abandoned.

With Taylor and Burgess required for the Sobers benefit double-wicket tournament and with Alabaster unfit, the New Zealanders needed reinforcement.

Fortunately Russell Vogtherr, the assistant Trade Commissioner in Trinidad had torn himself away from home and was on duty near St Vincent. Vogtherr, who had played for Wellington in the Rothmans under-23 tournament some years before and more recently with Queen's Park in Port of Spain, was posted to 12th man and there was great jollity when Chapple was moved into the playing eleven.

So, while most of the players lounged about the foreshore a short putt from their hotel, the Mariners' Inn, Chapple slipped away quietly for practice and came back bearing tales of a tremendously fast and bumpy outfield, and of massive blows from the Chapple bat.

Windwards, in the meantime, had assembled a useful side. Findlay and Grayson Shillingford were test players and Irving Shillingford, the skipper, had scored a fine century for the President's XI against the New Zealanders. Norbert Phillip was regarded as a most useful medium-fast man, while David Defoe was a promising medium-fast left-armer with a whippy action.

Unfortunately, the St Vincentians were less than efficient at organising the weather and the crowd of three or four thousand sat stoically in the stands as rain threatened to wash out all of the first day.

The New Zealanders played cards, wrote letters and devised a new game called "find the batting order". Congdon, impressed by the tales of Chapple's meaty hitting of the previous day, solemnly placed Chapple at No. 6 in the batting order, for with one look at the Chapple waistline it was obvious that if he was going to get runs he would have to get them quickly.

Chapple pulled rank and posted himself further down the order, but whenever his back was turned Congdon's order was put back and the list placed on the scoreboard.

The rain cleared, words were exchanged between the skippers and the upshot was that the game started just after 3 p.m. even though there were still puddles on the outfield and muddy parts near the pitch. Rather than disappoint the patient crowd a start was made, but was it coincidence that New Zealand batted first?

Batted was hardly the word. The pitch, recently laid, was full of bumps and hollows and Shillingford's first ball steepled up near Jarvis' nose. Campbell had to survive similar dangers. He fended down off the middle of the bat one ball that climbed sharply and somehow managed to break the handle of his bat.

In his gritty way Campbell extracted runs, but Jarvis soon holed out to Defoe and eight minutes later Morgan, who needed the practice if he was to hold his test place, was superbly stumped by Findlay. Campbell struggled on for 35 runs, wonderful batting on this pitch, before he swept at Joe Gibbs, the leg-spinner and was caught by Findlay. Hastings and Vivian rather gingerly held the fort until stumps at 70 for three wickets, while the New Zealand bowlers flexed their fingers in anticipation of the fun they would have on this pitch on the second day.

In the end no-one had much fun. The rain poured down and no matter how quietly the crowd sat and waited there was no chance at all of any play.

Rather than prolong the agony into the third day the teams decided to abandon the three-day match and to give the crowd some fun on the third day with a 45-over game.

There were plenty of showers, and Chapple did not come down in the last one. With the quickest side-step since Grahame Thorne, Chapple decided that rather than take part in the exertions of a one-day slog his return to first-class cricket should finish before he had either batted or bowled. What Chapple said went, no matter how the players protested and Vogtherr was promoted into Chapple's place.

Congdon won the toss and did a Sobers by inserting Windward Islands, a move that seemed to have misfired when Lockhart Sebastian, a doughty youngster, and Irving Shillingford took the score from four for one to 85 for two. By lunch Windwards were 120 for four from 32 overs and poised for a hearty and rather embarrassing slog in the early afternoon.

Fortunately for the New Zealanders Congdon got two quick wickets, Cunis performed an incredibly athletic run out, Webb hit the stumps twice in an over and Cunis finished the innings at 162 with another dashing run out.

Needing slightly fewer than four runs an over New Zealand started badly, with Jarvis out at 12 and Morgan, scoreless, at 13. Faithful Campbell stayed there, fashioning fine strokes no matter how the ball wriggled about. Hastings batted cleverly, too, and the New Zealanders were heading towards victory when Campbell and Hastings went at 107. Vivian and Wadsworth batted cannily and quietly for the winning runs, although they were remiss in not conspiring to give Vogtherr, who had fielded extremely well, a chance to bat at the tail end of the game. He had worked hard for them, and deserved the distinction of an innings, however brief.

NEW ZEALANDERS

| *First Innings* | |
|---|---|
| T. Jarvis c G. Shillingford b Defoe | 11 |
| K. Campbell c Findlay b Gibbs | 35 |
| R. Morgan st Findlay b Francis | 2 |
| B. Hastings not out | 11 |
| G. Vivian not out | 5 |
| Extras (b1 lb1 nb4) | 6 |
| Total (for three wickets) | 70 |

Fall: 42, 47, 59.

| *Windwards Bowling* | | | | |
|---|---|---|---|---|
| G. Shillingford | 6 | 1 | 18 | 0 |
| Phillip | 8 | 3 | 16 | 0 |
| Defoe | 7 | 3 | 8 | 1 |
| Francis | 8 | 2 | 16 | 1 |
| Gibbs | 4 | 1 | 6 | 1 |

MATCH ABANDONED

45-over match:

Windward Islands: (41.2 overs) 162 (L. Sebastian 58, I Shillingford 36; M. Webb three for 18, B. Congdon three for 29, H. Howarth two for 36).

New Zealanders: (42.3 overs) 163 for four wickets (B. Hastings 49, K. Campbell 46, K. Wadsworth 29 not out, G. Vivian 23 not out).

The New Zealanders won by six wickets.

# 11

# *The Fifth Test*

Rather like two boxers eyeing each other warily and waiting for the knockout blow that seemed sure to come in a six-day match, the New Zealanders and the West Indians manoeuvred gingerly in the days before the fifth test.

The New Zealanders' first achievement was the appointment of Douglas Sang Hue and Ralph Gosein as the umpires. On the surface these two seemed the obvious choices, but below the surface there had been some interesting ripples.

In fact the New Zealanders approached the appointment of these umpires in very much the same way the All Blacks secured Piet Robertse for the vital fourth test against South Africa in 1970. The All Blacks regarded Robertse as the best of the test referees. They had him for the first test, and by accepting other referees for the second and third, made sure that Robertse controlled the last vital test.

Similarly the New Zealanders regarded Sang Hue as the best umpire in the West Indies, and were not unpleased with Gosein's control in the second test. Sang Hue also stood in the first test and had Chapple and Congdon insisted he might have been called in for the fourth test at Guyana.

They did not, and accepted Cortez Jordan and Cecil Kippins —also fine umpires—for the fourth test knowing that all the omens pointed to a draw at Bourda, and that Sang Hue would be one of the leading candidates for the critical fifth test.

There were also ripples, and perhaps a wave or two, in the West Indies camp. All five selectors were summoned to Trinidad to pick the fifth test side, instead of using the normal three-man subcommittee. In the event this was less than satisfactory. Alan Rae, of Jamaica, did not arrive and this drew a public statement of disappointment from Joey Solomon.

Sobers, the sixth member of the panel in his capacity as captain, could not attend, either, for he was involved in the world double-wicket tournament being staged in Kingston as part of his benefit.

Then unfolded the curious case of Rowe, the incredible hero of the first test who had been reduced to the jitters by his own failures, and the crowds' hostile reaction, during the second and third tests.

Rowe had told some of the New Zealanders at the time of the fourth test that he hardly looked forward to another ordeal at Queen's Park, where he had been hooted and jeered unmercifully during the second test. The New Zealanders clucked in sympathy, for they had learned to like this essentially modest man who had become victim of the West Indian habit of idolising their heroes until they failed—and then of ridiculing them. The New Zealanders might also have preferred Rowe to play, rather than West Indies replace him with an in-form batsman.

Rowe suffered a leg injury during the double-wicket tournament at Kingston, but was still included in the West Indies 12 for the match. Ali came back for Howard, and Jumadeen was promoted. Even then it seemed certain that West Indies must drop a batsman and, on recent form, it could only be Rowe.

Further alarms, too, when Lloyd contracted some kind of mild influenza during the double-wicket event. The newspapers had a field day, estimating whether Lloyd or Rowe would be fit, and if not who would replace them. In the event the solution was simple. Lloyd went to Port of Spain, Rowe stayed at home nursing his leg and Maurice Foster was brought in to the 12 in case the call was for more batting strength at the expense of a spinner.

There was less conjecture in the New Zealand camp. Webb was hardly up to test form at that moment and Alabaster's back still made him a risk for a six-day game, even if the official view was that all 14 players were considered.

So it came down to the simple question: Morgan, who had not succeeded in the third and had not batted in the fourth test, or Campbell, whose 35 and 46 on the exotic pitch at St. Vincent had been gritty, extremely good innings. Morgan held his place, on the grounds of experience. Hard lines for Campbell, whose forbearance at the start of the tour and hard work thereafter deserved the reward of gaining his test cap.

Sensibly, the New Zealanders relaxed before the test and spent one day on a boat trip organised by Marge and Max Cunliffe, two New Zealanders living in Port of Spain where Max was attached to the United Nations and occupied with Trinidadian agriculture.

Twenty-four hours before the test Taylor went to net practice and then cried off. There must have been some germs lurking about Sabina, for Taylor seemed to have come down with the same affliction that was worrying Lloyd.

So the pasty-faced Taylor was packed off to bed by lunchtime in the hope that he would throw off his temperature and wobbly legs by the time of the test.

That night was very much like the night before Waterloo without the revelry. The theories flew round, but there was a quiet air of confidence among the New Zealanders. In the psychological battle that the test series had become they had given the West Indies a fright in the second test, a severe shaking in the third and had ground the West Indies bowlers down in the fourth. The West Indies were patently worried. If they had selected Gibbs, the New Zealanders might have been more concerned, but they had seen plenty of Ali in three games and Jumadeen in two and unless the pitch went crazy the gifted young Trinidad spinners could be handled.

And New Zealand must surely, after four failures, win the most important toss of the series.

## FIRST DAY

"Bourda did this," said a disappointed "Sonny" Murray, the secretary of the Queen's Park Cricket Club, organisers of the test, as he looked out over the half-full ground, in contrast to the first day of the second test when the ground had been crammed on the first morning.

Perhaps the Trinidadians had been put off by the slow draw at Bourda, or perhaps they had voted with their feet against a West Indies team that was not quite as triumphant as the fervent spectators hoped.

But Murray was hardly as disappointed as Congdon and the New Zealanders when Sobers again won the toss—and this time batted first. Five toss wins in a row, an incredible effort by Sobers and Congdon's face mirrored the team's sadness. The pitch was obviously easy and the side that batted first would have a tremendous advantage.

So, with Taylor looking as lively as a wrung-out dish-rag, the New Zealanders trudged out for the last battle—probably knowing even then that the odds were great against them winning it.

Taylor, gallant Taylor, mustered all his energy for his opening burst with the new ball. He made his first ball lift sharply, Fredericks almost played him on in the next over and then was hit painfully on the fingers. But after five overs Taylor's flame flickered low, he had to rest and from then until lunchtime Fredericks and Greenidge pick up 86 runs effortlessly and made the New Zealand fielding look patchy with their quick singles.

As at Bourda, however, Greenidge and Fredericks after lunch were strangely different. At 92 Greenidge drove at Howarth without getting near the pitch of the ball and the catch floated leisurely out to Hastings.

At 107 Kallicharran, promoted to No. 3, could not match Greenidge's skill at taking quick singles. He squeezed a shot towards point and stood there watching it while Fredericks hurtled down the pitch. Howarth fielded, Taylor had the ball at the bowler's end and with an extravagant swipe ran Fredericks out by 20 yards. No bottles, no crowd uproar this time—Fredericks was from Guyana so it did not matter all that much.

Davis started gingerly and when four snicked Howarth, but Turner could only get a fingertip to the ball as he lunged to his right. Thus fortified Davis and Kallicharran counter-attacked and Taylor was so weak at the knees that he had to go off the field for treatment. Kallicharran charged at Howarth—four to mid-wicket, four to long on, a superb straight drive for six. Fourteen from the over, Kallicharran 50 in 85 minutes, 36 in boundaries. The dashing little left-hander put Congdon twice through the covers, Davis whacked him to the mid-wicket fence. By tea they were 188 for two, the New Zealanders drooped off the field like beaten dogs, as if dreading the onslaught to come from these two, Lloyd and Sobers.

At tea Chapple and I talked about the possibility of Morgan having a bowl, if only for variety, for by then only Howarth seemed able to hold back the flood of runs.

Congdon seemed to have the same idea, for Morgan bowled and Davis hit a full-toss into the jubilant crowd at mid-wicket. West Indies were 200, the last 50 had taken only 44 minutes. Morgan bowled again, not quite so generous of length. Davis tried once more for the big hit, but the shot was not quite on and at mid-wicket Hastings leaped up for a splendid catch. Kallicharran and Davis had added 101 in 109 minutes for the third wicket and even Lloyd had to take a back seat while Kallicharran went explosively on.

Taylor, by now pumped full of drugs and lurching round the outfield like a punch-drunk boxer, managed one wobbly-kneed dive to stop a drive from Kallicharran, but it was a rare feat. Kallicharran pounded Morgan through the covers, cut him for another four, and then off-drove and lofted two more fours as he raced into the 90s.

Fifty runs in 43 minutes, the last 100 in 87, West Indies 250 for three and the impromptu steel-band down by third man belting out joyous music with every boundary.

Kallicharran drove again at Howarth, a full-blooded shot inches above the grass. At cover Vivian darted and then dived forward, shooting out his right hand and after a victory roll coming up with the ball held aloft.

Umpire Gosein said not out, Vivian froze in dismay and then booted the ball in disgust—a passable punt that Congdon had to scramble to stop at mid-on—which had the crowd hollering for Vivian's blood.

From the sideline it was impossible to judge whether it was or was not a catch, for the ball was hit so hard. Even some of the New Zealanders on the field could not be sure. Under the circumstances Gosein was quite right in his decision and Vivian was at fault with his outburst. But he deserved some sympathy for he had made fielding and catching an art and genuinely felt that he had made the catch.

So Kallicharran rather more soberly reached his 100, about 200 frenzied spectators rushed out on to the field, pounded and poked him in their ecstasy and caused a four-minute break in the play.

Three minutes later Cunis bowled a full-toss, Kallicharran—with his feet going the wrong way—made an ugly attempt to hook and the catch skied straight up and was a gift for Wadsworth.

No Sobers, Findlay instead as night-watchman. Taylor struggled back to the attack, tried to bounce his second ball at Lloyd, who made a hash of the hook and the catch lobbed gently to Howarth.

Still no Sobers, but Holford and Findlay to hold the fort until stumps at 278 for five.

Those two wickets, Kallicharran and Lloyd, at 265 had been like a life-saving drug for the New Zealanders. If they had not been out to such wild and woolly strokes West Indies would have been heading toward 500 or 600 and New Zealand would have been out of the game.

But there were words of warning afterwards from Davis, and from Russell Vogtherr who both knew Queen's Park. The pitch had played easily, they said, but it was hardly likely to get better, and almost certainly would get worse for batting.

## SECOND DAY

Sensation, sensation. Tony Cozier, writing in the *Express*, accused the New Zealanders of gamesmanship as the prelude to the dismissals of Davis, Kallicharran and Lloyd between tea and stumps yesterday. Cozier maintained that the New Zealanders had chipped the West Indies batsmen, had said words that broke their concentration and helped lead to their downfall.

This was hard criticism, for New Zealanders are seldom as gifted in the arts of gamesmanship in the middle as the hard-headed Australians or Englishmen. It might not have been completely accurate. If Davis was chipped for hitting Morgan for six he is hardly the kind of novice who could be teased into trying the shot again, and being caught.

Kallicharran may have been upset by the uproar surrounding Vivian's disallowed catch, and subsequent remarks from Cunis, but he was more likely to have been put off his stride by the pummelling he got from the charging spectators once he had reached his 100. Lloyd, no tyro, has been in cricket long enough not to be put off by gamesmanship—and long enough in cricket, too, not to play such a gruesome stroke a few minutes before stumps.

Still, Cozier's claims did provide something to talk about while the drizzle swept down from the hills, delayed play until 11.28 and then, eight balls and seven runs later, had the players scurrying off again until 12.30. Findlay flicked a ball from Taylor, almost restored to health, through Morgan's hands, Holford went for his shots and by lunch West Indies were 308 for five.

After lunch the mist disappeared, and so did Findlay, bowled by Congdon at 312. At last Sobers appeared, Howarth beat him utterly with a ball that skipped just over the middle stump, and so Sobers and Holford settled down to squeeze out what life remained in the New Zealand bowling. It was sound, sensible batting, but just when they seemed likely to stage a long partnership Holford pulled up lame after taking a quick single. Hamstring gone, Holford hobbled off and Congdon, after 13 overs for 16 runs, gave way so that Taylor could pursue his rabbit, Ali. It wasn't a chase. Taylor hinted at the bouncer that had disturbed Ali so often, Ali tried to slash and Wadsworth held the edge.

Sobers battled on in his private fight against Howarth. Enthralling cricket this, two champions pitted against each other and even Holder hitting a bouncer for six almost went unnoticed.

Sometimes Sobers middled the ball, just as often Howarth's curling flight into the rough outside the off stump beat Sobers' stroke. Thrust and counter-thrust, marvellous cricket. Then Sobers, chafing at the restraint, off-drove at murderous speed, the ball whizzing a yard or two above the ground. At deep mid-off Hastings got into line, but the ball curled away and, almost as an afterthought, he flung out his right hand and held the catch.

Holder had a swing or two, Taylor fed him with bouncers and Holder inevitably skied one, with Taylor loping across in front of Jarvis for the catch to end the innings.

West Indies 368, a good score but considering the state of the pitch and the collapse of second half of the innings—the last seven wickets, including the luckless Holford, fell for 103 runs—not a daunting one and when Jarvis opened the New Zealand innings with a graceful drive for four, the ball going "tock" plumb off the middle, the battle seemed reasonably even.

Turner looked as safe as ever, even against some very good bowling from Holder. All of a sudden the ground erupted. Holder produced a faster ball, beating Turner's stroke and as the middle and leg stumps keeled over the crowd let out a triumphant roar at the dismissal of their feared enemy—while Holder stood in mid-pitch, his eyes burning into Turner's back, not a smile flickering across his impassive face.

On came Lloyd, bowling medium-pace with almost an apologetic air, and away went Congdon, tickling the third ball for Findlay to pick up a fine catch on the leg side.

Burgess tried a light appeal that failed. Sobers, not slow to pick the uncertainty among the New Zealanders, brought on Jumadeen and Ali. Burgess was in trouble, prodding this way, padding that. Ali bowled, a shade outside off stump. Burgess, thinking it might go further away, tucked his bat away. Instead the ball nipped in and bowled him. The noise was incredible, and Cunis, the night-watchman, probably knew how the Christians used to feel in the Colosseum as he swaggered out and was surrounded by six fieldsmen, and by an incredible din from the crowd.

Cunis decided on bold measures, swung at Ali and the edge flipped over the close field and went away for two. Cunis should have realised the risk, but he still tried to blast away at Ali. Another sweep, this time a thin edge and Findlay did extremely well to hold the catch.

New Zealand 53 for four in 94 grisly minutes and Hastings dawdled out as slowly as possible to give Jarvis time to finish the day with a maiden.

Ali had taken two for three from three overs and in his generous way Sobers flung his arm round the little spinner's shoulders as the West Indians trooped triumphantly off the field.

New Zealand, 305 runs behind, six wickets and four days remaining—it seemed inevitable that the long, long trail would not come to a happy ending.

Chapple was distraught. That morning he had failed to light up, precisely at 10.40 a.m., the cigar which had become his pre-match good luck charm of the tour.

## THIRD DAY

Next morning, at 10.40 a.m., Chapple sucked away at his stogie with Churchillian gusto, but there were few other signs of joy. The rain seemed to have departed, the pitch was becoming hard and brittle (perfect for Ali?) and as Jarvis and Hastings went out to continue the struggle a bunch of buzzards circled menacingly overhead.

Jarvis and Hastings fought on, with one eye on the mist that was starting to gather in the hills. They batted sensibly and well, Jarvis especially so, but when Jumadeen drew him forward for the drive the ball spun away off the edge and Sobers took the low catch at first slip. Five for 86, Vivian arrived, so did the rain, and the New Zealanders had 50 minutes rest before play resumed at 1.25.

Hastings and Vivian, shot-makers both, held back their strokes and battled on, with Jumadeen rolling down maiden after maiden. The score had inched up to 106 when Jumadeen made the ball turn and jump, Hastings was not quick enough to cover the movement and Findlay had the catch.

Taylor, reinforced with pills and some of his old luck, poked hopefully at his first ball from Ali which zipped up, got the edge and looped just over Findlay's glove.

Thus restored Vivian and Taylor settled down, an hour brought 37 runs from 22 overs and Vivian broke Jumadeen's grip a little by sweeping him for four.

Down came the mist again, and at 2.28 Vivian happily led the race off the field. At 4.25 they were back, Vivian faced one ball, won an appeal against the light and, at 123 for six, New Zealand had gained some breathing space.

That evening all the talk was what Sobers might do if the New Zealanders did not reach the follow-on mark of 168. The optimists, fewer, in number, suggested that Vivian and Taylor, being left-handers, could bat on and on against Ali and Jumadeen, also left-handers and that the follow-on mark would easily be passed.

## FOURTH DAY

The New Zealanders looked keenly at the grey clouds, but they held off and at 11.02 Holder finished the over he had begun at 2.25 yesterday. Vivian greeted Jumadeen with a four, Taylor hooked Holder handsomely for another and even with Sobers taking the ball the follow-on crisis seemed past.

But Sobers' move paid off and with the sixth ball of his first over he bowled Vivian after his long and faithful fight for 24. Enter Morgan, and Sobers immediately recalled Ali. Morgan drove him straight for four, tried to pull the next for four but the catch went up and Holder at square leg held it. Taylor hit Ali for four, 162 for eight, but Sobers was not done and bowled him at that score. Wadsworth jumped out at Ali and, predictably, missed to give Findlay the stumping. The last four wickets had gone for 20, alas for the New Zealand optimists, and the New Zealanders went in probably dreading another assault from the confident Ali, who had the wonderful figures of five for 59 from 26.4 overs.

Sobers called a council of war, which decided that West Indies would bat again. Most of the New Zealanders were relieved, although one or two foresaw New Zealand scoring 350-plus in the second innings and having West Indies in trouble on the last afternoon.

Personally I had two views on the matter. The first was that Ali was bowling so well that he might have picked up three or four wickets in the remaining four hours of the day, placing West Indies in the dominant position. Against that, Sobers might not have wanted to risk either Ali or West Indies batting last on a pitch that would be worn and torn by the last day.

The West Indies decision to bat on, 206 ahead, might well have been the right one—provided they batted sensibly.

Instead they were incredibly erratic. Before lunch Fredericks put a catch through Morgan's hands at leg gully, very nearly French cut Cunis into his stumps and Turner dropped Greenidge off Taylor—all before the score passed 26. Just before lunch Fredericks had a hopeful swing at Taylor and Turner galloped back for the catch.

Soon after lunch West Indies were 48 for two when Greenidge snicked Taylor and Wadsworth dived in front of Turner for the catch. Kallicharran decided to cover-drive come what may. Taylor worked at the shot, Kallicharran got 18 and then the inevitable slice as he chased a wider one and Vivian held the catch. Three for 66; Lloyd all menacing power and Congdon moving himself into a short mid-on to Howarth's bowling.

The trap worked, Lloyd reared back, tried to pull-drive Howarth and Congdon jumped, knocked the catch up with one hand and recovered quickly to regain it a yard or two away.

Still the West Indians batted like sailors on the spree, and the New Zealanders swarmed on to the attack. Davis was dropped by Turner, but swatted at Howarth and 45 yards away Taylor juggled and then held the catch.

Five for 90, Taylor rammed a yorker through Sobers and knocked down his off stump. Six for 90. Howarth hustled one through at Findlay for an lbw, 97 for seven, with the hobbling Holford and Ali getting through to tea at 118 for seven.

In the two hours New Zealand had taken six prize wickets for 83 runs. West Indies led by 289, but the game had almost swung completely toward New Zealand.

After tea Taylor fired a yorker, instead of the usual bouncer, at Ali and had him lbw—123 for eight, with only the injured Holford, Holder and Jumadeen remaining. Two more quick blows and New Zealand would have a winning chance.

The blows, at least by the bowlers, never came. Holford batted nobly and Holder, with a mixture of luck and muscular strokes, did most of the attacking. A six off Howarth by Holder raised 50 in 44 minutes and they might have scored many more had not Holford tried his luck against Burgess' fielding and lost, being run out at 179. More swings from Holder, one dropping just clear of Hastings, and West Indies were 192 for nine at stumps.

Depending on your point of view Sobers was either a muggins or a magician in not enforcing the follow-on. Had not Holford and Holder rallied the troops at the end of the day New Zealand might have been chasing about 300 with a reasonable chance of success. The late rally lifted West Indies' lead to 398, and Sobers had two more days—after the rest day—to make his scheme work. All tradition pointed to a New Zealand defeat.

## FIFTH DAY

Chapple puffed at his cigar and the rain came down in sympathy, holding up play for 70 minutes and Cunis took only three balls to finish Holder and the innings at 194, giving West Indies a lead of 400 with approximately 600 minutes remaining.

By lunch Jarvis and Turner were 17 for no wicket. After lunch they batted superbly, picking the occasional four when Ali dropped short or over-pitched, defending doggedly against the accurate Jumadeen. Greenidge was bowled, a sign that Sobers was starting to look for miracles, but Turner and Jarvis went on so solidly that there were visions of New Zealand being about

150 for little loss by stumps. But by 2.30 the rain clouds mustered in the hills. By 2.43 the clouds marched down, the players raced off and New Zealand had 51 for no wicket.

Not all the New Zealanders were pleased with the rain. The pitch had played tolerably well, Ali was less hostile, Holford could not bowl. Under these circumstances, and given a strong start by Turner and Jarvis—which looked possible when they were in such command—New Zealand might have had time to get the runs on the last day. But the rain did come, New Zealand had little prospect of scoring a run-a-minute on the last day, and had only a draw to play for.

## SIXTH DAY

Jarvis and Turner soldiered on under a hot sun for another 45 valuable minutes before Ali made one bite and Jarvis, playing back, was lbw at 62 for one. Jarvis had struggled manfully for 158 minutes, no longer the tentative batsman of early in the tour.

Congdon was greeted by six men close-in, but was unperturbed and carried the fight back to the spinners. Turner hit Ali through the covers for four and Congdon hit out at Jumadeen 2, 4, 4 in eight balls.

A mild ripple of applause greeted Turner's 50 and then Holder pinned him down, forced Turner into a tickle down the leg-side and Findlay zoomed across for a superb catch—perhaps even the catch which would win the match.

So it was 105 for two at lunch, Congdon safe and solid with 26 and after lunch Burgess hit Ali for four. But the little Indian still had Burgess in trouble and when Burgess jabbed at one Greenidge at short leg dived across and back for a splendid catch. Three for 122.

Hastings settled in quickly, Congdon marched resolutely onward and the New Zealanders stepped down from their panic stations. By 2.30 Sobers called once more on the valiant Holder with the new ball, and took the other end himself.

The change worked immediately. With his second ball after drinks Sobers bowled a swinging full toss, Congdon quite simply hit down the wrong line and was bowled. Holder made a ball jump at Hastings, and the catch lobbed easily to Lloyd at gully.

Once more the New Zealanders were at panic stations. Holder twice bowled bumpers at Wadsworth who genially hit both for fours. Then came the drizzle, Vivian appealed unavailingly, Sobers appealed even more urgently for lbw against Vivian, but also without success—but umpire Sang Hue earned himself a round of boos at tea, with New Zealand 179 for five.

An hour and 20 overs to go, West Indies pressing jubilantly on to victory and even Wadsworth found it hard to raise his usual confident smile in the dressing room.

Sensing a West Indies triumph, the crowd seemed twice as large, and three times as noisy after tea, especially when Vivian, 38 minutes for four, was lbw to Holder. The steel band players abandoned their bottles for a victory dance, and they pranced even more violently when Morgan fashioned a crude hook at Holder and dragged the ball on to his stumps. Taylor joined Wadsworth, at 3.44 and 188 for seven, and almost left at 3.51 before he had scored. Fredericks was at silly mid-on, Taylor prodded a catch near him and Fredericks could only get one hand to it before the ball tumbled clear.

Back came the spinners, with Taylor stretching hopefully forward and Wadsworth, his blond long hair shining in the sun like a battle flag, playing the ball only when absolutely necessary.

Between every over, and sometimes in mid-over, Taylor and Wadsworth talked in mid-pitch. It seemed from afar that they were scheming some plot that would keep the rampant bowlers out. In effect they were, for Taylor, the left-hander, took as much of Ali as possible and Wadsworth took Jumadeen, who bowled rather too much of a width.

However, the plans were laced with swear-words as one remonstrated with the other about the bad shots of the previous over. Still, it seemed only a matter of time before the stand would be broken, especially when Wadsworth played one magical over from Ali. "Played" is not quite the word. Wadsworth survived as the ball cavorted this way and that, without getting the edge or the lbw.

Forty-five minutes gone, an hour or 20 overs to go. Six overs from Jumadeen and Ali, with Taylor and Wadsworth getting the middle of the bat to the balls they had to play. Sobers came on, and then Fredericks.

The New Zealanders breathed a little. If Sobers had to try Fredericks there was still hope, especially when Fredericks bowled a wide.

The overs were going by quickly, at about 25 to the hour. Curiously Sobers called back Holder for two overs, which used up precious minutes. Even Holder could not dent the New Zealanders' armour. Two empty bottles were pitched over the fence, and then several more, but they lay there undisturbed for this was no time for distractions from the crowd. Ali was back for the 17th over, Jumadeen with a maiden, Ali again, Jumadeen and more bottles. Finally it was Kallicharran with his wrist-spinners, and a vast sigh surging from the crowd when the end came.

Wadsworth, after battling for three hours, and Taylor, with him for 105 minutes, came off almost in triumph. The Queen's Park crowd, bless them, cheered the New Zealanders mightily and it said much for the West Indies players that they, so close to their first test win since 1969 and their first series win since 1965, should just as keenly applaud the New Zealand heroes.

Chapple lighted another cigar, the tops came off all kinds of bottles. For the New Zealanders it was quite a night.

WEST INDIES

| First Innings | | Second Innings | |
|---|---|---|---|
| R. Fredericks run out | 60 | c Turner b Taylor | 15 |
| G. Greenidge c Hastings b Howarth | 38 | c Wadsworth b Taylor | 21 |
| A. Kallicharran c Wadsworth b Cunis | 101 | c Vivian b Taylor | 18 |
| C. Davis c Hastings b Morgan | 40 | c Taylor b Howarth | 23 |
| C. Lloyd c Howarth b Taylor | 18 | c Congdon b Howarth | 5 |
| M. Findlay b Congdon | 9 | lbw b Howarth | 6 |
| D. Holford retired hurt | 46 | run out | 25 |
| G. Sobers c Hastings b Howarth | 28 | b Taylor | 2 |
| I. Ali c Wadsworth b Taylor | 0 | lbw b Taylor | 16 |
| V. Holder c and b Taylor | 12 | b Cunis | 42 |
| R. Jumadeen not out | 3 | not out | 2 |
| Extras (b2 lb6 nb5) | 13 | (b5 lb13 nb1) | 19 |
| Total | 368 | | 194 |
| Fall: 92, 107, 208, 265, 265, 312, 348, 360, 368. | | 35, 48, 66, 73, 90, 90, 97, 123, 179. | |

*Bowling*

| | O. | M. | R. | W. | O. | M. | R. | W. |
|---|---|---|---|---|---|---|---|---|
| Cunis | 20 | 5 | 61 | 1 | 4.3 | 0 | 21 | 1 |
| Taylor | 19.4 | 1 | 74 | 3 | 24 | 8 | 41 | 5 |
| Congdon | 31 | 6 | 73 | 1 | 15 | 2 | 39 | 0 |
| Howarth | 51 | 17 | 109 | 2 | 29 | 8 | 70 | 3 |
| Morgan | 7 | 0 | 38 | 1 | 2 | 1 | 4 | 0 |

NEW ZEALAND

| | First Innings | | Second Innings | |
|---|---|---|---|---|
| G. Turner | b Holder | 1 | c Findlay b Holder | 50 |
| T. Jarvis | c Sobers b Ali | 40 | lbw b Ali | 22 |
| B. Congdon | c Findlay b Lloyd | 11 | b Sobers | 58 |
| M. Burgess | b Ali | 5 | c Greenidge b Ali | 6 |
| R. Cunis | c Findlay b Ali | 2 | did not bat | |
| B. Hastings | c Findlay b Jumadeen | 27 | c Lloyd b Holder | 11 |
| G. Vivian | b Sobers | 24 | lbw b Holder | 4 |
| B. Taylor | b Sobers | 26 | not out | 42 |
| R. Morgan | c Holder b Ali | 4 | b Holder | 2 |
| K. Wadsworth | st Findlay b Ali | 1 | not out | 40 |
| H. Howarth | not out | 0 | did not bat | |
| Extras | (b3 lb6 nb12) | 21 | (b2 lb1 w1 nb14) | 18 |
| Total | | 162 | (for seven wickets) | 253 |

Fall: 18, 39, 51, 53, 86, 106, 142, 150, 162. — 62, 105, 122, 157, 157, 181, 188.

*Bowling*

| | O. | M. | R. | W. | O. | M. | R. | W. |
|---|---|---|---|---|---|---|---|---|
| Holder | 16 | 1 | 37 | 1 | 26 | 12 | 41 | 4 |
| Sobers | 11 | 5 | 17 | 2 | 29 | 12 | 45 | 1 |
| Lloyd | 3 | 0 | 10 | 1 | — | — | — | — |
| Ali | 26.4 | 8 | 59 | 5 | 51 | 16 | 99 | 2 |
| Jumadeen | 19 | 9 | 18 | 1 | 45 | 22 | 46 | 0 |
| Greenidge | — | — | — | — | 1 | 0 | 2 | 0 |
| Fredericks | — | — | — | — | 2 | 1 | 2 | 0 |
| Kallicharran | — | — | — | — | 1 | 1 | 0 | 0 |

# 12

# *Bermuda: Last and Loveliest*

After the heat and hustle-and-bustle of the West Indies Bermuda was like a cool, crisp oasis for the New Zealanders as they made tracks for home.

There was a nip in the air and from the hill on which the team's Sherwood Hotel sat there was a wonderful view of impossibly blue sea, golden beaches, sparklingly clean pastel-coloured houses, all with creamy-white coral-sand roofs, nestling among the thousands of trees.

Later there were leisurely drives through the spacious streets of Hamilton, rubber-necking round the tourist ships or sumptuous hotels, shopping in the tourist-traps or, best of all, twirling along the narrow roads on scooters, the basic form of transport.

Bermudans are immensely proud of their tax-free island, and rightly so. The roads, speed limit 20 miles per hour, amble through clumps of bush or shady parts cut out of the coral-limestone. The roads, the houses, the gardens are so impeccably kept it seems as if Bermudans dare a weed to grow or a blot to mark the paintwork.

The cricket officials, keen to push their outpost into the world cricket scene, were on the job, too. In each of the players' rooms were two gift bottles of Bacardi, as nice a piece of fifth-column work as a tired cricketer could wish to see.

Then there was the fine ground at the National Stadium, with a new and well-appointed pavilion built into one grass bank and another left untouched to provide lounging room for thousands. And it is not every day that you have salmon, followed by lemon meringue pie, as a cricket lunch.

Outside, regrettably, lurked the bogey. There was a large pitch area and most of it was solidly covered with grass. Turf pitches are comparatively new in Bermuda. The official view was that the New Zealanders should be presented with a pitch as similar as possible to those of the West Indies—perish the thought.

So the grass was shaved off and all that was left was bare, red-brown dirt. Instead of having what might have been a first-rate grassed strip that would have helped both batsmen and bowlers, the pitch from first ball to last was a devilish tricky thing that had the ball turning and jumping alarmingly.

The Bermudans were delighted, after conceding a 145-run opening stand to Glenn Turner and Terry Jarvis, that they wrapped up New Zealand for 249. The New Zealanders were delighted, in fact astounded, that anyone could score 150 on it. They were even more delighted when they spun out Bermuda twice, won the match and also a free day in which they could better enjoy this entrancing island.

In their eager way the Bermudans billed the three-day match as a "test" as part of their efforts to occupy a more prominent place in the cricket world.

Few of the players were known outside the island except for Clarence Parfitt, a tall medium-pace left-armer who picked up bags of wickets against minor visiting sides and was regarded, at least by the taxi-driver who took me to the lovely ground, as in world class.

If the New Zealanders did not know what to expect from the Bermudans, it took only a quick glance to know that the pitch would be paradise for the bowlers. It was a bare dry brown slab with a moist patch at one end. It would not get any better, and very likely would get worse for batting, so Jarvis and Turner blessed Congdon when he won the toss and set out on one of the most extraordinary partnerships of the tour.

Parfitt and his partner Winston Trott, also left-arm of medium pace, tried an over or two of inswingers and then switched to leg-cutters. As the ball lifted and whipped away, especially from Parfitt, Turner and Jarvis played and missed a good deal. Yet they survived and with the most adroit batsmanship possible kept up such a scoring rate that by lunch they had scored 111 together in two hours.

The astonishing stand went on to 145 until Jarvis succumbed to a full toss which flicked off his tummy and on to his stumps. Turner went eight runs later, Congdon seemed to be home but was given out run out when eight short of his tour 1,000 and Hastings went at 190. Burgess and Wadsworth rallied the innings with some exotic strokes, including a straight six by Burgess, but once they were separated at 229 for five Parfitt and Trott mopped up the tail and Bermuda were overjoyed at holding the New Zealanders to 249.

But for the incredible Turner-Jarvis stand the score might have been 100 fewer, and still a reasonable total on such a pitch.

Webb, making the ball fly high, was positively dangerous, Taylor was almost as vicious and by stumps Bermuda were tottering at 30 for three.

Next morning Howarth opened, bowled his normal warm-up ball of no special menace and it leaped up amazingly, giving an equally amazed Howarth a return catch. So Howarth sliced through the middle of the innings, turning the ball alarming distances and Bermuda seemed sure to fall far short of the follow-on mark of 99 when they were 50 for eight.

Suddenly the New Zealanders became alarmed. Eldon Raynor and Trott stuck fast and the score went to 87 before Congdon bowled Trott. The score inched into the 90s and the New Zealanders' hopes of forcing the follow-on, bowling Bermuda out cheaply and having a spare day on the morrow began to fade.

They cut it fine as could be, with Congdon catching Raynor at 99, leaving New Zealand precisely 150 ahead and just able to make Bermuda bat again.

Once again Webb and Taylor blasted the top off the innings, and Howarth spun through the middle. But still there was alarm among the New Zealanders. Alabaster, needing only two wickets for his 500 in first class cricket, had not been bowled by Congdon in the first innings. It was even more perplexing that Congdon held Alabaster back so long in the second.

Eventually, with three wickets left, Alabaster came on, immediately bowled Raynor and, with the most perfect ball imaginable—curling down about leg stump and nipping across to take the top of the off-stump—removed the obdurate Charles Daulphin for 50 and gained his 500. Howarth finished off the innings to give him ten wickets for the match and Chapple, on the grounds that the pitch was hardly suitable, politely declined a suggestion that the spare third day should be filled in with a one-day limited-over game.

It would be interesting if Chapple had accepted for he might well have had to scour the beautiful island to find his players the next morning.

So the long, hard trek finished with a short, easy game. In this strange tour of so many contrasts I suppose it was fitting that the greatest contrast of all should come in the final minutes.

## NEW ZEALANDERS

| *First Innings* | |
|---|---|
| G. Turner c S. Raynor b Parfitt | 70 |
| T. Jarvis b Trott | 63 |
| B. Congdon run out | 4 |
| M. Burgess st Wainwright b Parfitt | 39 |
| B. Hastings lbw b Trott | 17 |
| K. Wadsworth c Trott b Parfitt | 22 |
| K. Campbell c Parfitt b Trott | 0 |
| B. Taylor c Ali b Trott | 3 |
| H. Howarth not out | 5 |
| J. Alabaster c Gibbons b Parfitt | 0 |
| M. Webb st Wainwright b Parfitt | 0 |
| Extras (b20 lb6) | 26 |
| Total | 249 |

Fall: 145, 153, 156, 190, 229, 232, 240, 247, 247.

*Bowling*

| | O. | M. | R. | W. |
|---|---|---|---|---|
| Parfitt | 38 | 12 | 61 | 5 |
| Trott | 28 | 4 | 73 | 4 |
| Bailey | 12 | 2 | 45 | 0 |
| Ali | 13 | 1 | 25 | 0 |
| E. Raynor | 6 | 1 | 19 | 0 |

## BERMUDA

| *First Innings* | | *Second Innings* | |
|---|---|---|---|
| S. Raynor c Taylor b Webb | 10 | lbw b Howarth | 3 |
| D. Wainwright b Howarth | 4 | b Taylor | 7 |
| L. James b Taylor | 2 | c Jarvis b Howarth | 8 |
| N. Gibbons b Webb | 1 | c Congdon b Webb | 4 |
| C. Daulphin c and b Howarth | 9 | b Alabaster | 50 |
| J. Bailey c Hastings b Howarth | 2 | lbw b Webb | 0 |
| R. Scotland c Wadsworth b Webb | 13 | b Howarth | 11 |
| E. Raynor c Congdon b Howarth | 34 | b Alabaster | 0 |
| S. Ali c Turner b Howarth | 0 | c Congdon b Howarth | 5 |
| W. Trott b Congdon | 16 | b Howarth | 17 |
| C. Parfitt not out | 1 | not out | 1 |
| Extras (b2 lb2 nb3) | 7 | (b5 lb4 nb4) | 13 |
| Total | 99 | | 119 |

Fall: 11, 17, 18, 30, 33, 40, 46, 50, 87. 12, 12, 16, 26, 55, 72, 76, 89, 111.

*Bowling*

| | O. | M. | R. | W. | O. | M. | R. | W. |
|---|---|---|---|---|---|---|---|---|
| Webb | 11 | 4 | 26 | 3 | 7 | 2 | 13 | 2 |
| Taylor | 9 | 3 | 24 | 1 | 8 | 2 | 15 | 1 |
| Congdon | 7 | 4 | 10 | 1 | 2 | 0 | 11 | 0 |
| Howarth | 14.5 | 5 | 32 | 5 | 19.4 | 6 | 41 | 5 |
| Alabaster | — | — | — | — | 16 | 7 | 26 | 2 |

# For the Record Book

Records, records, records—they poured in day by day during the New Zealanders' tour.

In many of them Turner held pride of place, with Taylor challenging with his bowling, and with Congdon very often in the forefront.

Perhaps the most significant records were three new test partnerships for New Zealand for these were fashioned in the heat of the battle. Turner (259) and Jarvis (182) set the new first-wicket mark of 387 in the first test. Turner (223) and Wadsworth (78) more than doubled the old mark by scoring 220 for the sixth wicket in the first test, and the Congdon (166 not out) and Cunis (51) stand of 136 for the eighth wicket in the second test was of the stuff from which true records are made.

Turner's four double centuries were another record, and only once before produced in West Indies—by Patsy Hendren in the 1930s. Turner, with his 259 in the fourth test, also moved past Dowling's test mark of 239 and Bert Sutcliffe's New Zealand mark of 243.

The 13 centuries were also a record for New Zealand on tour.

On the bowling side Taylor had two great records. He became the first New Zealander to take seven wickets in a test innings with his seven for 74 in the third test. His 27 wickets in the series surpassed the old mark of 22 shared by Alabaster and Tony MacGibbon and, in fact, Taylor needed only one more wicket to pass Alf Valentine's record of the most wickets in a test series in West Indies.

There were other records. This was the first New Zealand team to remain undefeated in a major tour. On the reverse side New Zealand was also the first tour side to trail each of the four main countries in the first innings.

When the New Zealanders returned to Port of Spain for the fifth test they found their stockpile of New Zealand beer had grown to 61 dozen cans. This challenge, remarked Wadsworth, had the makings of being the best record of the tour. The New

Zealanders tried hard, as they did in other directions during the tour.

The record escaped them—there were many dozens of cans left at the end.

In an area where records seem to grow on trees, the West Indians set fewer new marks during the test series. Kallicharran's average of 109.5 from two completed innings in his first series seems sure to be some kind of record. However, the West Indies did manage to develop the odd situation—owing as much to the selectors' changes as to Sobers' generosity—that they produced more bowlers than batsmen in the series. The West Indies used 18 players and, apart from Findlay, they all bowled at some time or another. In contrast, West Indies used 16 batsmen with Dowe and Howard not batting.

TOUR BATTING

| | Inns. | N.O. | H.S. | Agg. | Avge. | 50s | 100s |
|---|---|---|---|---|---|---|---|
| G. M. Turner | 17 | 2 | 259 | 1284 | 85.6 | 3 | 4 |
| B. E. Congdon | 16 | 4 | 166 | 992 | 82.6 | 5 | 4 |
| K. J. Wadsworth | 12 | 4 | 78 | 334 | 41.7 | 2 | — |
| M. G. Burgess | 17 | 2 | 101 | 575 | 38.3 | 4 | 1 |
| B. F. Hastings | 18 | 4 | 105 | 503 | 35.9 | 1 | 2 |
| T. W. Jarvis | 15 | — | 182 | 521 | 34.7 | 3 | 1 |
| G. T. Dowling | 7 | — | 124 | 212 | 30.2 | — | 1 |
| B. R. Taylor | 11 | 2 | 47 | 216 | 24.0 | — | — |
| G. E. Vivian | 12 | 3 | 61 | 200 | 22.2 | 1 | — |
| R. S. Cunis | 9 | 2 | 51 | 143 | 20.4 | 1 | — |
| K. O. Campbell | 9 | 1 | 42 | 146 | 18.2 | — | — |
| R. W. Morgan | 7 | — | 75 | 114 | 16.2 | 1 | — |
| J. C. Alabaster | 9 | 2 | 48 | 82 | 11.7 | — | — |
| H. J. Howarth | 7 | 3 | 16 | 37 | 9.2 | — | — |
| M. G. Webb | 6 | 2 | 8 | 19 | 4.7 | — | — |
| R. O. Collinge | 2 | — | 4 | 4 | 2.0 | — | — |

TOUR BOWLING

| | O. | M. | R. | W. | Avge. |
|---|---|---|---|---|---|
| B. R. Taylor ... ... ... | 352 | 68 | 974 | 46 | 21.1 |
| B. E. Congdon ... ... ... | 305 | 71 | 712 | 21 | 33.9 |
| H. J. Howarth ... ... ... | 495.4 | 140 | 1102 | 32 | 34.4 |
| J. C. Alabaster ... ... ... | 211 | 56 | 604 | 15 | 40.2 |
| M. G. Webb ... ... ... | 169 | 36 | 535 | 13 | 41.1 |
| G. E. Vivian ... ... ... | 44 | 5 | 173 | 4 | 43.2 |
| R. S. Cunis ... ... ... | 296.1 | 53 | 970 | 16 | 60.6 |
| M. G. Burgess ... ... ... | 16 | 4 | 70 | 1 | 70.0 |
| R. O. Collinge ... ... ... | 59 | 17 | 189 | 2 | 94.0 |
| R. W. Morgan ... ... ... | 88 | 19 | 293 | 2 | 146.5 |
| K. O. Campbell ... ... | 32.2 | 5 | 135 | 0 | — |
| T. W. Jarvis ... ... ... | 3 | 1 | 7 | 0 | — |
| G. M. Turner ... ... ... | 2 | 1 | 5 | 0 | — |

## NEW ZEALAND TEST BATTING

| | Inns. | N.O. | H.S. | Agg. | Avge. | 50s | 100s |
|---|---|---|---|---|---|---|---|
| G. M. Turner | 8 | 1 | 259 | 672 | 96.0 | 2 | 2 |
| B. E. Congdon | 8 | 2 | 166 | 531 | 88.5 | 3 | 2 |
| K. J. Wadsworth | 6 | 3 | 78 | 177 | 59.0 | 1 | — |
| T. W. Jarvis | 6 | — | 182 | 277 | 46.1 | — | 1 |
| B. R. Taylor | 4 | 1 | 46 | 114 | 38.0 | — | — |
| B. F. Hastings | 8 | 2 | 105 | 222 | 37.0 | — | 1 |
| M. G. Burgess | 8 | 1 | 101 | 248 | 35.4 | 1 | 1 |
| R. S. Cunis | 5 | 1 | 51 | 93 | 23.2 | 1 | — |
| G. E. Vivian | 4 | — | 38 | 66 | 16.5 | — | — |
| G. T. Dowling | 4 | — | 23 | 45 | 11.2 | — | — |
| J. C. Alabaster | 2 | — | 18 | 20 | 10.0 | — | — |
| H. J. Howarth | 4 | 1 | 16 | 24 | 8.0 | — | — |
| R. W. Morgan | 3 | — | 4 | 8 | 2.6 | — | — |
| M. G. Webb | 1 | — | 0 | 0 | — | — | — |

## NEW ZEALAND TEST BOWLING

| | O. | M. | R. | W. | Avge. |
|---|---|---|---|---|---|
| B. R. Taylor | 172.2 | 39 | 478 | 27 | 17.7 |
| B. E. Congdon | 200 | 49 | 446 | 13 | 34.3 |
| H. J. Howarth | 338 | 100 | 703 | 14 | 50.2 |
| R. S. Cunis | 183.1 | 33 | 617 | 6 | 102.8 |
| R. W. Morgan | 48 | 12 | 130 | 1 | 130.0 |
| J. C. Alabaster | 50 | 13 | 164 | 1 | 164.0 |
| M. G. Webb | 30 | 5 | 120 | 0 | — |
| G. E. Vivian | 18 | 4 | 56 | 0 | — |
| M. G. Burgess | 7 | 3 | 27 | 0 | — |
| G. M. Turner | 2 | 1 | 5 | 0 | — |
| T. W. Jarvis | 1 | 1 | 0 | 0 | — |

## WEST INDIES BATTING

| | Inns. | N.O. | H.S. | Agg. | Avge. | 50s | 100s |
|---|---|---|---|---|---|---|---|
| A. I. Kallicharran | 3 | 1 | 101 | 219 | 109.5 | — | 2 |
| L. G. Rowe | 7 | 1 | 214 | 419 | 69.8 | 1 | 2 |
| C. A. Davis | 9 | 1 | 183 | 466 | 58.2 | 1 | 1 |
| R. C. Fredericks | 10 | 1 | 163 | 487 | 54.1 | 2 | 1 |
| G. A. Greenidge | 4 | 1 | 50 | 144 | 48.0 | 1 | — |
| G. S. Sobers | 8 | 1 | 142 | 253 | 36.1 | — | 1 |
| D. A. Holford | 7 | 1 | 50 | 175 | 29.1 | 1 | — |
| V. P. Holder | 5 | 1 | 42 | 103 | 25.7 | — | — |
| M. C. Carew | 6 | — | 45 | 153 | 25.5 | — | — |
| T. M. Findlay | 6 | 2 | 44 | 99 | 24.7 | — | — |
| M. Foster | 6 | 2 | 28 | 93 | 23.2 | — | — |
| C. H. Lloyd | 3 | — | 43 | 66 | 22.0 | — | — |
| G. Shillingford | 1 | — | 15 | 15 | 15.0 | — | — |
| I. Ali | 5 | — | 25 | 56 | 11.2 | — | — |
| R. Jumadeen | 2 | 2 | 3 | 5 | — | — | — |
| L. R. Gibbs | 1 | 1 | 3 | 3 | — | — | — |

U. Dowe and A. A. Howard did not bat.

## WEST INDIES BOWLING

| | O. | M. | R. | W. | Avge. |
|---|---|---|---|---|---|
| V. P. Holder | 153 | 55 | 285 | 12 | 23.7 |
| U. Dowe | 42 | 8 | 121 | 4 | 30.2 |
| G. Shillingford | 62.1 | 17 | 160 | 5 | 32.0 |
| G. S. Sobers | 181 | 55 | 332 | 10 | 33.2 |
| I. Ali | 193.3 | 53 | 391 | 11 | 35.5 |
| D. A. Holford | 179 | 61 | 312 | 8 | 39.0 |
| R. Jumadeen | 64 | 31 | 64 | 1 | 64.0 |
| A. A. Howard | 62 | 17 | 140 | 2 | 70.0 |
| C. H. Lloyd | 39 | 10 | 84 | 1 | 84.0 |
| L. R. Gibbs | 130 | 37 | 267 | 3 | 89.0 |
| M. Foster | 53 | 21 | 93 | 1 | 93.0 |
| C. A. Davis | 47 | 17 | 78 | 0 | — |
| R. C. Fredericks | 21 | 7 | 37 | 0 | — |
| M. C. Carew | 21 | 1 | 53 | 0 | — |
| G. A. Greenidge | 15 | 4 | 36 | 0 | — |
| A. I. Kallicharran | 7 | 2 | 17 | 0 | — |
| L. G. Rowe | 5 | 0 | 28 | 0 | — |

## FIELDING

WICKETKEEPING:

21: K. J. Wadsworth (19 catches, 2 stumpings).
6: K. O. Campbell (5 catches, 1 stumping).

CATCHES IN THE FIELD:

14: G. M. Turner
9: B. E. Congdon
8: B. F. Hastings
5: H. J. Howarth
4: R. W. Morgan, G. E. Vivian, T. W. Jarvis, B. R. Taylor
3: M. G. Burgess
2: G. T. Dowling
1: J. C. Alabaster, K. O. Campbell, R. O. Collinge, R. S. Cunis, K. J. Wadsworth
0: M. G. Webb.

## CENTURIES

FOR: (13)

*G. M. Turner* (4)

259 v. West Indies, Fourth Test
259 v. Guyana
223* v. West Indies, First Test
202 v. President's XI

*B. E. Congdon* (4)
166* v. West Indies, Second Test
126 v. West Indies, Third Test
119 v. Trinidad
103 v. Guyana
*B. F. Hastings* (2)
105 v. West Indies, Third Test
100* v. Jamaica
*T. W. Jarvis* (1)
182 v. West Indies, Fourth Test
*G. T. Dowling* (1)
124 v. President's XI
*M. G. Burgess* (1)
101 v. West Indies, First Test

AGAINST: (17)
*L. G. Rowe* (3)
227 for Jamaica
214 for West Indies, First Test
104*
*A. I. Kallicharran* (3)
154 for Guyana
101 for West Indies, Fifth Test
100* for West Indies, Fourth Test
*R. C. Fredericks* (2)
163 for West Indies, First Test
100* for Guyana
*C. A. Davis* (2)
183 for West Indies, Third Test
156 for Trinidad
*C. H. Lloyd* (2)
133 for Guyana
100*
*G. S. Sobers* (1)
142 for West Indies, Third Test
*G. A. Greenidge* (1)
126 for Barbados
*I. Shillingford* (1)
124 for President's XI
*M. C. Carew* (1)
100 for Trinidad
*R. de Souza* (1)
100 for Trinidad

## FIVE OR MORE WICKETS IN AN INNINGS

FOR: (5)

*B. R. Taylor* (2)
7 for 74 v. West Indies, Third Test
5 for 41 v. West Indies, Fifth Test
*H. J. Howarth* (2)
5 for 32 v. Bermuda
5 for 41
*J. C. Alabaster* (1)
5 for 130 v. Jamaica

AGAINST: (5)

*I. Ali* (2)
6 for 79, for Trinidad
5 for 59, for West Indies, Fifth Test
*R. Collymore* (1)
6 for 115 for Guyana
*E. Willet* (1)
5 for 65 for Leeward Islands
*C. Parfitt* (1)
5 for 61, for Bermuda

## BEST PARTNERSHIPS AND OTHER CENTURY PARTNERSHIPS

*First Wicket*

387: G. M. Turner (259) and T. W. Jarvis (182), v. West Indies, Fourth Test.
268: G. M. Turner (202) and G. T. Dowling (124) v. President's XI.
145: G. M. Turner (70) and T. W. Jarvis (63), v. Bermuda.
101*: M. G. Burgess (51*) and B. E. Congdon (39*), v. President's XI.

*Second Wicket*

171: G. M. Turner (259) and B. E. Congdon (103), v. Guyana.
139: G. M. Turner (95) and B. E. Congdon (82), v. West Indies, Second Test.
119: G. T. Dowling (43) and B. E. Congdon (73), v. Jamaica.
119: G. M. Turner (202) and T. W. Jarvis (51), v. President's XI.

*Third Wicket*

129: G. M. Turner (259) and B. F. Hastings (37), v. Guyana.

*Fourth Wicket*

175: B. E. Congdon (126) and B. F. Hastings (105), v. West Indies, Third Test.

110: B. E. Congdon (119) and G. E. Vivian (46), v. Trinidad.

*Fifth Wicket*

63: B. F. Hastings (103) and G. E. Vivian (38), v. West Indies, Third Test.

*Sixth Wicket*

220: G. M. Turner (223*) and K. J. Wadsworth (78), v. West Indies, First Test.

*Seventh Wicket*

100: G. M. Turner (259) and K. J. Wadsworth (25), v. Guyana.

*Eighth Wicket*

136: B. E. Congdon (166*) and R. S. Cunis (51), v. West Indies, Second Test.

*Ninth Wicket*

43: K. J. Wadsworth (15*) and R. S. Cunis (27), v. West Indies, Third Test.

*Tenth Wicket*

50: K. J. Wadsworth (67) and M. G. Webb (8*), v. Leeward Islands.

FIRST BALL BOWLED FROM South END — Third Test — First INNINGS OF West Indies

Kensington Oval, Bridgetown, Barbados. on March 23rd, 1972.

HOURS OF PLAY from 11.34 to 3.44 } 210 minutes
LUNCH 1.00 – 1.40 TEA –

| ON Over | ON Score | OFF Over | OFF Score | BOWLERS | O | M | R | Wkts | NO B | W |
|---|---|---|---|---|---|---|---|---|---|---|
| 1, 31 | 0, 69 | 15, 33 | 34, 83 | Cunis R.S. | 10 | 3 | 26 | 1 | - | - |
| 2, 20, 40 | 1, 48, 95 | 18, 30, 49³ | 44, 69, 133 | Taylor B.R. | 20³ | 6 | 74 | 7 | 1 | - |
| 17, 19, 32, 35 | 42, 44, 74, 83 | 17, 29, 32, 49 | 42, 66, 76, 133 | Congdon B.E. | 16 | 3 | 26 | 2 | - | - |
| 34 | 83 | 38 | 90 | Howarth H.J. | 3 | 1 | 6 | - | - | - |

| BOWLERS | 1 | 2 | 3 | 4 | 5 | 6 | 7 | 8 | 9 | 10 | 11 | 12 | 13 | 14 | 15 | 16 | 17 | 18 | 19 | 20 |
|---|---|---|---|---|---|---|---|---|---|---|---|---|---|---|---|---|---|---|---|---|
| Cunis R.S. | 1·11.34 1 1·1 | 3·11.44 1 2·6 | 5·11.56 W M1 | 7·12.07 M2 | 9·12.19 4 1 7·17 | 11·12.28 1 1 1 10·20 | 13·12.37 M3 | 15·12.45 4 14·34 | 31·2.29 4 1 19·74 | 33·2.37 2 4 1 26·83 | | | | | | | | | | |
| Taylor B.R. | 2·11.39 4 4 5; 50·3.43 W 74·133 | 4·11.49 W W M1 | 6·12.02 1 4 1 10·12 | 8·12.13 W M2 | 10·12.24 M3 | 12·12.33 M4 | 14·12.41 2 4 4 20·30 | 16·12.50 4 4 28·42 | 18·12.56 2 W 30·44 | 20·1.43 M5 | 22·1.50 M6 | 24·1.56 2 W 32·52 | 26·2.05 2 1 2 0 37·61 | 28·2.13 1 1 39·64 | 30·2.25 1 2 42·69 | 40·3.04 1 3 W 3 49·102 | 42·3.15 2 3 54·107 | 44·3.22 1 1 4 60·114 | 46·3.29 1 1 1 4 67·122 | 48·3.35 4 2 1 74·132 |
| Congdon B.E. | 17·12.54 M1 | 19·1.40 4 4·48 | 21·1.47 1 5·49 | 23·1.53 1 6·50 | 25·2.01 2 1 9·55 | 27·2.10 1 10·62 | 29·2.19 2 12·66 | 32·2.34 1 1 14·76 | 35·2.45 W M2 | 37·2.52 1 15·85 | 39·2.58 1 2 1 1 20·95 | 41·3.11 W M3 | 43·3.19 1 21·108 | 45·3.26 1 22·115 | 47·3.33 3 25·125 | 49·3.39 1 26·133 | | | | |
| Howarth H.J. | 34·2.42 M1 | 36·2.49 1 1·84 | 38·2.55 4 6·90 | | | | | | | | | | | | | | | | | |

| Batsmen | How Out | Bowlers | Scores | Out in over no. | Fall of wickets |
|---|---|---|---|---|---|
| Fredericks R.C. | c. Hastings | Cunis | 5 | 5 | 3 - 6 |
| Carew M.C. | c. Morgan | Taylor | 1 | 4 | 1 - 6 |
| Rowe L. | c. Wadsworth | Taylor | 0 | 4 | 2 - 6 |
| Davis C.A. | c. Jarvis | Taylor | 1 | 8 | 4 - 12 |
| Sobers G.S. | c. Wadsworth | Congdon | 35 | 35 | 7 - 83 |
| Foster M.L.C. | c. Wadsworth | Taylor | 22 | 18 | 5 - 44 |
| Holford D.A.J. | c. Wadsworth | Taylor | 3 | 24 | 6 - 52 |
| Findlay T.M. | not out | | 44 | | |
| Ali Inshan | bowled | Taylor | 3 | 40 | 8 - 99 |
| Holder V.A. | bowled | Congdon | 3 | 41 | 9 - 102 |
| Shillingford G.C. | c. Morgan | Taylor | 15 | 50 | 10 - 133 |
| No ball 1. | | Total | 133 | | |

B. R. Taylor is the first bowler to take more than six wickets for New Zealand in an innings of a Test match.

| | |
|---|---|
| Time for innings - minutes | 210 |
| Runs per hour | 38·0 |
| Overs bowled | 49³ |
| Overs per hour | 14¹ |
| Runs per over | 2·68 |

A facsimile of the New Zealand bowling in the West Indies' first innings of the third test, showing Bruce Taylor's record shattering